Achiel Van Walleghem

1917 – The Passchendaele Year. The British Army in Flanders: The Diary of Achiel Van Walleghem

EER
Edward Everett Root, Publishers, Co. Ltd.,
30 New Road, Brighton, Sussex, BN1 1BN, England.

www.eerpublishing.com
edwardeverettroot@yahoo.co.uk

First published in Great Britain in 2017.

Achiel Van Walleghem
1917 – The Passchendaele Year.
The British Army in Flanders:
The Diary of Achiel Van Walleghem

The original diary text, the English translation, and the Introduction by
Dominiek Dendooven © In Flanders Fields Museum, 2017.

This edition © Edward Everett Root Publishers Limited, 2017.

ISBN 9781911454403 Paperback.
ISBN 9781911454410 Hardback.
ISBN 9781911454427 ebook.

Cover design and typesetting by Head & Heart.

Printed in Great Britain by TJInternational Ltd., Padstow, Cornwall.

Achiel Van Walleghem

1917 – The Passchendaele Year. The British Army in Flanders: The Diary of Achiel Van Walleghem

Edited, with Introduction, by Dominiek Dendooven.

Translated from the original Dutch by Guido Latré, Professor of English Literature and Culture (Louvain and Ghent), and Susan Reed, researcher in English Linguistics .

EER

EER Edward Everett Root, Publishers, Brighton, 2017

Contents

List of illustrations   vi

Publisher's Note   ix

Acknowledgements   xi

Introduction: Achiel Van Walleghem and his Diary
Dominiek Dendooven   1

Translators' Note
Guido Latré and Susan Reed   25

A note on the spelling of Flemish place names   39

The Diary of Achiel Van Walleghem: 1917   45

Illustrations

1 Achiel Van Walleghem as a young priest, photographed in Ypres, 1905. In Flanders Fields Museum, Ypres   135

2 Van Walleghem's daily notes for February 1918, written on official British Army stationery. Archives of the Bishopric of Bruges   136

3 The edited 'neat' version of the diary for the same period. In Flanders Fields Museum, Ypres   137

4 Achiel Van Walleghem with those members of his family living in unoccupied Belgium. In Flanders Fields Museum, Ypres   137

5 Assisted by Germain Forceville, Achiel Van Walleghem celebrates mass in his temporary church in the barn of Cyriel Lamerant, 1916. Germaine Forceville, Ypres   138

6 A map of the parish of Dickebusch and immediate surroundings, hand drawn by Achiel Van Walleghem, and indicating the farms and their owners. Archives of the Bishopric of Bruges   138

7 A German aerial photograph of Dickebusch on 30 March 1916. In Flanders Fields Museum, Ypres   139

8 Dickebusch in June 1917: a YMCA canteen has been organised in the houses along the road from Ypres to Bailleul. Imperial War Museum, London   139

9 The impact of the war on the landscape: a historical aerial photograph superimposed on today's landscape shows us the military installations, north of Dickebusch. In Flanders Fields Museum, Ypres   140

10 A French officer in the remains of the church of Dickebusch, 1918. Archives of the Bishopric of Bruges   140

11 Members of the Chinese Labour Corps marching through Vlamertinghe. In Flanders Fields Museum, Ypres   141

12 Reninghelst church seen from the ruins of the brewery, July 1919. In Flanders Fields Museum, Ypres   141

13 A British military laundry employing local women. Australian War Memorial, Canberra   142

14 In the neighbourhood of Dickebusch, September 1918. Imperial War Museum, London   142

Publisher's Note

Third Ypres,' also known as 'Passchendaele,' is the battle that epitomized the western front of the First World War: trenches full of mud, total annihilation of the landscape and major attacks achieving minor results while leaving hundreds of thousands dead. Yet it was also an operation of unprecedented logistics which required months of preparation.

This book, the diary of Achiel Van Walleghem, recounts the untold story of life immediately behind the front line during the tragic year 1917.

Living in Reninghelst, just west of Ypres, village priest Achiel Van Walleghem kept an extensive day-to-day account. Well informed by the officers lodging in the parsonage, and driven by his innate curiosity, he witnessed the arrival of tanks and the increasing importance of the artillery. He visited the camps of the Chinese Labour Corps and the British West Indies Regiment. On 7 June 1917 Van Walleghem wakes early to see the mines of the Battle of Messines going up and he is present when a deserter is shot at dawn.

As a bystander living amidst the troops, Van Walleghem often had a unique perspective on the events that unfolded before his eyes, gauging the morale of troops and civilians, and even noting the influence of bad weather on the mood of both. His comments on the different attitudes of English, Irish, Australian or other Empire troops are often priceless. But Van Walleghem also recorded the misery of the local Flemish population and their relationship with the British rank and file and their officers: in bad times such as when a local farmer is accused of spying, but also in good times, for instance when a village girl gets married to a British soldier.

This diary is not just a forgotten source for our understanding of the Western Front, it is one that will forever change our views on the conflict.

The publisher wishes to record his debts to Dominiek Dendooven and to the fluent translators Professor Guido Latré and Susan Reed. Their work reads as if the diary had first been written in English, which is the highest praise due. Without Dominiek's historical knowledge, his enthusiasm and commitment to the project – first introducing it to the publisher – this book could not have been produced in such a handsome and timely way. His expert, informed, historical and contemporary editorial guidance – together with the support of his colleagues in Ypres – has been invaluable.

JS, Brighton, 6 March 2017

Acknowledgements

The editor and translators wish to express their gratitude to

The Van Walleghem family (Pittem) for their permission to have the manuscript translated and published, and for their enduring support

The colleagues at In Flanders Fields Museum, in particular Piet Chielens and Dries Chaerle

Professor John Spiers of Edward Everett Root Publishers for believing in this project

Elke Brems, Professor of Translation and Intercultural Transfer (University of Louvain at Brussels), for her financial and moral support

The Research Project Memex WWI – Experiences and Memories of the Great War in Belgium (financed by BELSPO)

Paul-Johan Desegher (Reningelst), Danny Suffys (Dikkebus) and other inhabitants of Dikkebus and Reningelst who provided us with vital background information to assess Van Walleghem's descriptions of their villages

André Latré for his clarifications on all things agricultural and Dr Paul Arblaster for his assistance in translating ecclesiastic terms.

Introduction: Achiel Van Walleghem and his diary

Dominiek Dendooven

A very Catholic background

Achiel Van Walleghem was born on 18 December 1879 in Pitthem, a rural village in the east of the Belgian province of West Flanders. Catholicism permeates Pitthem. Beside the Romanesque tower of the church of Our Lady there has stood since 1913 a statue of the Jesuit Ferdinand Verbiest (1623-1688), a missionary who entered the service of the Chinese emperor as astronomer, founder of Peking's observatory and reformer of the Chinese calendar. The village is still home to the thriving mother convent of the 'Sisters of Mary of Pitthem' and from time immemorial the municipality has been governed by the Catholic and later the Christian-Democratic party. In the heart of this village lived the family of farmer August Van Walleghem (1843-1920) and Sylvia Lauwers (1851-1925). August was a long-standing member of the local church council and was for many years its chairman. From 1884 he was part of the local municipal council, from 1901 to his death even sitting as an alderman. Founder of a local fire insurance fund which still exists today, and president of the Guild of Saint Eloi, he surely belonged to the great and the good of Pitthem. He and his wife were blessed with eight children, of whom Achiel was the eldest. And truly blessed they must have felt, as none of the children died in childhood, certainly an exception in those days. The second son, Modest, (1881-1948) remained unmarried and spent most of his life on the farm. He, too, sat on the Pitthem church council. During the First World War Modest resided as a refugee in unoccupied Belgium or France and thus he is occasionally mentioned in the diary of his elder brother. The eldest sister, Marie (1883-1959), became a nun and was known as Mother Angélique of the Sisters of Mary in Pitthem. Hélène (1884-1960) did not marry either: she devoted most of her life to her elder brother Achiel, being his resident housekeeper. Her role in his life must have been more important than her presence in the diary would indicate. She makes an appearance now and then, but much less frequently than would be expected of a resident and close family member with whom one shares joys and sorrows. This is another indication of her subservient role in the service of her elder brother, the priest. Jules (1886-1905) is the only family member who died before reaching full adulthood. The two youngest sons, Joseph (1888-1965) and Remi (1891-1963), also appear briefly in the diary: during the First World War both served in the Belgian army, with the Grenadiers and the 13th *régiment de ligne* respectively, which enabled them to keep in touch with their brother Achiel and sister Hélène and even to meet each other during exceptional periods of leave. Both later farmed: Joseph on the family farm in Pitthem where, following in the family tradition, he became a member of the church council. Despite marrying at an older age – a consequence of the war – he fathered seven children, including an Achilles who in his turn entered the priesthood. The youngest in the family of father August and mother Sylvia was Rachel (1893-1966), the only one who remained at home in German-occupied Pitthem. With her sister Marie in the convent and her other sister, Hélène, and all her brothers beyond reach or even contact on the other side of the front line, she took on the care of her ageing parents.

It will be clear that the Van Walleghems were a quintessential farmer's family, strongly embedded in the local community. The father, August, and several of his children can be regarded as leading members of the village community. That several family members entered the clergy will have enhanced the family's local prestige. Not without importance is the impact the Great War had on this Flemish family: five family members resided on the other side of the front line, where it was virtually impossible to keep in touch with their parents in occupied Belgium. The parents were entrusted to the care of the youngest daughter Rachel, who as a consequence sacrificed her youth and eventually remained unmarried. The war years were also to blame for the belated marriage of Joseph, who served in the Belgian Army.

The diarist: Achiel Van Walleghem

Achiel Van Walleghem enjoyed an excellent education for someone from a rural background: elementary school in his native village and a secondary education in St Joseph's College in nearby Thielt were followed by enrolment in 1899 in the episcopal seminary in Bruges. The first decade of his priesthood was characterised by a series of temporary duties as curate in villages all over the bishopric of Bruges, interrupted by a long period of illness between 1908 and 1911. In September 1913 he was appointed curate of Dickebusch, a small village west of Ypres where he had previously served for a year and a half at the beginning of his career. Less than a year later, war broke out and he took up the pen to record the extraordinary events happening in his parish. While he wrote very little about himself – Van Walleghem is more a chronicler than a diarist – the war clearly had an impact on his personality. His portrait photos from the end of the war speak volumes: despite being not even forty, the priest looks many years older. He was visibly marked by the war. Besides the misery which he daily witnessed within his 'flock,' he was also personally affected by the contingencies of war. Thus he was forced to move several times: on 19 July 1915 he left the parsonage in the centre of the village, taking up a room at the farm of a parishioner less than half a kilometre to the west. Eleven months later, on 14 June 1916, he was forced to leave Dickebusch and to move in with his colleague in Reninghelst, a village five kilometres further west. From Reninghelst he continued to visit his parishioners in Dickebusch daily. After all, since the flight of his anxious superior, pastor Dassonville, on 3 November 1914, he bore full responsibility for the salvation of those residing in Dickebusch, both villagers and refugees. As acting pastor in a besieged and occupied village, he frequently acted as a middleman between the different military and civilian authorities and the local population, for whom he was an important adviser. Finally, the onslaught of the German Spring Offensive forced him into exile on 18 April 1918. The remainder of the war he spent in Normandy, serving the community of Belgian refugees in Cagny (near Caen). Only in mid-1919 did Van Walleghem settle in Dickebusch once more, becoming one of the main advocates of the reconstruction of the totally destroyed village. It was his responsibility to supervise the rebuilding of the schools, the convent, the parsonage and the church. A major setback was the fire which destroyed his temporary wooden church in January 1924, also destroying the church treasures which he had managed to save during the war. Throughout this equally trying period of reconstruction he continued to act as middleman between his parishioners and the authorities and he was a much respected village notable when in 1928 he was appointed to a different parish. Van Walleghem would eventually end his active career in 1947, by then no longer capable of celebrating mass due to increasing deafness and forgetfulness. He was taken care of by his family in Pitthem where, suffering from severe dementia, he died on 21 November 1955, a sad fate for a diarist who had given proof of his remarkable powers of observation.

For indeed, his diary shows us Achiel Van Walleghem as someone with a great gift for detail and a strongly inquisitive nature. On a number of occasions he paid visits to the camps of non-European soldiers and auxiliaries such as the British West Indies Regiment or the Chinese Labour Corps, commenting on their food and other habits. In the 1915 pages of his diary he accused the Indian soldiers of being too nosy, and this while he himself had enquired into their customs and had even tasted Indian food. This double standard is a recurrent feature throughout his writings: without much distinction he generally looked at Christians of other denominations (Protestants, Presbyterians etc.) negatively. As a Catholic clergyman he naturally held fast to the truths of his religion. Yet, the inherent prejudices and even xenophobic traits he displayed in his descriptions and judgments of the French, and even more so of the British, as well as the troops from the British colonies and the Chinese labourers, were mainly due to ignorance: no one in the rural west of Flanders in 1914 had encountered southern French or kilted Scots, not to mention Africans, Indians or Chinese. The quiet back of beyond in which he performed his clerical duties was all of a sudden submerged by thousands of people speaking very different languages and displaying very different cultural habits. The local population had become a minority, small and powerless, in its own country. It was a situation which encouraged a retreat into an inward-looking mentality. And yet we also note a certain openness, probably reinforced by his curiosity: Van Walleghem was always keen to find out more about who was present in the rear of the Ypres Salient. He differentiated between the various ethnic groups and army units and tried to fathom them. While they are only very seldom mentioned, he must have had numerous conversations, especially with officers. This explains why he is so well informed on military matters, even on issues which others might consider of a secret nature. In addition, his duties entailed travelling large distances within his parish and within an ever-increasing adjacent area (which at one time reached all the way to the outskirts of Ypres and Voormezeele) to minister to the handful of remaining inhabitants. And his actions certainly speak for his sense of responsibility and duty towards those under his care. Without being uncritical – after all he was their religious leader – he again and again stood up for those he considered 'his people.' Despite his usually prosaic, even matter-of-fact narrative style, his sincere sympathy with the population of the front zone is obvious. His no-nonsense Flemish common sense often clashed with what he sometimes considered as absurd military logic. Finally we should stress that Van Walleghem was not devoid of *joie de vivre* and humour. His way of writing often testifies to a mild (and sometimes less mild) sense of irony and at times he actually makes fun of someone or something.

All in all Father Van Walleghem was a child of his time and a product of his social environment: strongly connected with the peasantry of rural West Flanders and very conscientious in his role as a Catholic priest.

Dickebusch and Reninghelst

Before focusing on the restricted area of the front where Achiel Van Walleghem was living, we must stress the exceptional nature of the situation which confronted the local population in the Flemish front zone. In Belgium the front line ran for a mere 50 kilometres, from Nieuport on the coast to Ploegsteert on the French-Belgian border. The deadlock here began in October 1914, and ended on 28 September 1918, when the war of movement finally resumed. The war-stricken zone was the southern part of the province of West Flanders, a rural backwater, less densely populated than the rest of the country, better known under its unofficial name Westhoek (the 'West Corner'). The front line ran through or near the towns of Nieuport, Dixmude and Ypres, while Furnes and Poperinghe formed the backbone of the rear area. These five towns were all small in size – none had more than 17,000 inhabitants. The language spoken in this region was and is a local dialect, one of the many Flemish versions of Dutch. The local Flemings who did not flee or who stayed on as long as possible found themselves in the position of a minority not only due to the arrival of refugees from other parts of Belgium, but also due to the influx of hundreds of thousands of military. In the Yser area (Nieuport-Dixmude) the majority of these military belonged to the Belgian Army, but near Ypres and Poperinghe, it was a highly multinational (and multicultural) force that occupied the territory. For the locals, most of whom had never come into contact with foreigners (except for French people), it was a most extraordinary situation, a fact which, indeed, is reflected in other diaries, memoirs and interviews. Due to the lack of any census or later research we do not have a precise number for the population of the Westhoek at this time. We therefore do not know what percentage of the total population the local inhabitants represented as against the temporary population (including both refugees and military). However, it seems that at no point could the local inhabitants have made up more than 10-15% of the total population, making them a very small minority indeed.

While Achiel Van Walleghem was curate of Dickebusch and continued to visit the remaining inhabitants during 1917, from June 1916 he was living in the neighbouring village of Reninghelst. Dickebusch is about three kilometres from Ypres in a south-westerly direction. It was, and still is, mainly a street village characterised by ribbon development along the main road from Ypres to Bailleul. Only in the neighbourhood of the church, in the middle of the village, was there a small, more densely-built centre. The wide 88 acre Dickebusch Lake, once dug to provide the mediaeval population with drinking water, was the only place of interest which attracted visitors from beyond the village.

Both Dickebusch and Reninghelst were quintessential rural municipalities. Neither in physical size nor in number of residents could they be considered important: Dickebusch had just under 1,400 inhabitants in 1914 while Reninghelst, including the parish of La Clytte, had a total population of about 2,500. Nowhere in either place was more than an hour's walk from the municipal boundaries. Unlike nearby Vlamertinghe, neither Dickebusch nor Reninghelst had a resident doctor or solicitor. The most notable persons were the burgomaster (as a mayor in the Flemish part of Belgium is called), the pastor and the curate. Yet, as was usual in Flanders, each village had its own brewery and a large number of inns, both in the village centre and in the rural part of the municipality. It was customary to use the names of inns to indicate particular locations. 'At *De Hert'* (i.e. The

Hart) thus means 'in the neighbourhood of the De Hert inn'.
If we suppose the level of education in Dickebusch and Reninghelst to have been the same as that in the rest of Flanders, this would mean that on the eve of the Great War about 29% were unable to read or write. Many children, especially in a rural community, only attended school in winter. As a result, during the rest of the year they all too easily forgot, in an environment that boasted few books, what they had learnt in the winter. Taking into account the nature of their population – with very few belonging to the upper classes – few if any inhabitants had French as their mother tongue, a notable contrast with towns such as Ypres or Poperinghe. On the contrary, Achiel Van Walleghem provides evidence of a certain sensitivity to the status of Dutch, or better, of its Flemish variants. He remarks, for instance, on 3 November 1917: 'Le Vingtième [Siècle] increasingly seems to us to be a hateful paper because of its sly propaganda against the Flemish cause.'

As was the case for all villages near the front, the war meant a radical caesura for Dickebusch and Reninghelst. Not only did thousands of military from different armies flood into the region, but the perils of war also brought refugees looking for shelter. In mid-1915 Van Walleghem estimated that Dickebusch had five times as many residents as before the war. While the farmers tried to maintain their traditional lifestyle working the fields, this was increasingly difficult: servicemen were billeted in barns and other farm buildings, camps were built in pastures, batteries were positioned and many other military installations were established. Civilian life was totally subordinated to the necessities of warfare.

Due to its short distance from the front line – it was barely three kilometres from the village church to the trenches of Saint-Eloi or Wytschaete – and the many military establishments there, Dickebusch was throughout the war a target for the German artillery. By 1917 it was the nearest village to the front line that was still in part inhabited by its civilian population. The large majority, however, had by then fled or had been evacuated. In Reninghelst on the other hand, barely a handful of inhabitants had left by 1917. While the village increasingly became the target of German guns and airplanes, it was only in 1918, during the onslaught of the German Spring Offensive, that the entire local population here was forced into exile. Eventually both villages would share the same fate: total obliteration.

The diary

What we today call the diary of Achiel Van Walleghem is a collection of twelve handwritten notebooks with the overarching title *The War in Dickebusch and Its Surroundings*, a total of 1,180 pages describing events between July 1914 and 1929. A thirteenth notebook contains various lists of names, including those of children evacuated from Dickebusch to Belgian refugee schools in France, the local inhabitants who were serving in the Belgian army, and the deceased parishioners. Van Walleghem also drew up a list of all military casualties buried in war cemeteries within the municipality of Dickebusch.

The manuscripts, still today in the possession of the Van Walleghem family, have been held since 1999 in the In Flanders Fields Museum in Ypres as a permanent loan. The thirteen notebooks are in fact an edited, 'neat,' version drawn up shortly after the events described. During the war, Van Walleghem made day-to-day notes on loose pieces of paper, not infrequently official British Army stationery. Just a few of these original notes have been preserved and are kept in the archives of the bishopric of Bruges. The priest later checked and corrected his notes, sometimes adding to them, and in the end produced a fluently readable continuous text.

This method, whereby the record of events is checked as to its accuracy, is one explanation for why factual mistakes are relatively rare in the priest's diary. Another explanation is the fact that he often got his information first-hand: he shared the parsonage with a number of well-informed officers who were billeted there and they often told their housemate more than they were officially allowed to. On 6 June 1917, for instance, he is warned by a British officer that the attack will take place the next day at 3 a.m. The officer asked the priest to keep this to himself, but Van Walleghem writes that that same afternoon many more people informed him about zero hour. In many cases, Van Walleghem's information is very detailed and turns out to be correct when checked against other sources – a rare thing for a diary. Hence, on the 23rd and 24th of July 1917 he wrote that at that very moment, the 8th, 18th, 23rd, 24th, 25th, 30th, 41st and 47th Divisions are in his neighbourhood, that the 47th Division had carried out a raid towards Hollebeke taking 30 prisoners, and that the Brigadier-General of the 123rd Brigade of the 41st Division and his adjutant were killed by a shell. All in all, compared to many other personal accounts from the First World War the writings of Van Walleghem contain fewer myths and many more concrete facts.

While his English must have improved considerably in the course of the war, his initial knowledge of the language was limited, if not non-existent. And every language contains too many subtle shades of meaning to be perfectly understood by non-native speakers. Lyn MacDonald touches on this subject when she includes a quote from Van Walleghem in her bestseller *Passchendaele*. On 16 September 1916, he wrote:

'Last night there was a fight at *the Canada* between English and Belgian soldiers. One of the Belgians was stabbed in the arm. There are trouble-makers in both armies. The most common complaint made by the English against the Belgians is "fake Belgium".' It might be clear to the contemporary reader that the British soldiers' most common insult was not 'Fake' but rather another four letter word beginning with F and ending with K, perhaps luckily unknown to our Belgian Catholic priest. From the diary it is also clear that the interpreters played a vital role in the communication between the local inhabitants and the armies. As mentioned above, since officers were often billeted in the parsonage, they are very frequently mentioned by Van Walleghem, both in a positive and in a negative sense. They were certainly among his prime informants.

That the definitive version of the manuscript was only edited at a later stage is also shown by certain short passages written in the past tense: they are clearly later comments on the recorded events, or signposts to similar, related events which would occur later. Considered in the light of this, *The War in Dickebusch and Its Surroundings* is not a diary in the strictest sense of the word. Perhaps the term 'war chronicles' is more accurate. For, besides the above-mentioned reflections in hindsight, some episodes, especially at the beginning and towards the end of the war, are not recounted day-to-day but considered in their entirety over a longer period. Nor was Van Walleghem concerned to talk about himself and those near to him. His resident sister is not even once mentioned by name. Similarly, it is remarkable that he does not mention the frostbite that, by 8 March 1917, he has had for two months, until it prevents him from carrying out his duties (and equally importantly, one suspects, from getting out and about in general). He was, rather, primarily concerned with communicating factual events, another characteristic of a chronicle. Nevertheless, he did not fail to add personal comments and particular remarks, and this makes his writings somewhat more hybrid than one would expect from a chronicle. It is important to stress that he did not wait too long to edit his notes into a final form – most probably this was done within weeks, at a maximum some months after the events related had occurred.

Despite its mixed character – halfway between a chronicle and a diary – we chose to publish the manuscript under the title 'The Diary of...,' since in the end, day-to-day notes were at the root of this work. Moreover, it was as 'the diary of Father Van Walleghem' that this document was known not only to local inhabitants with an interest in history but also to First World War buffs on both sides of the English Channel. Even if until now only excerpts have been translated, Achiel Van Walleghem is an old acquaintance to many: quotations from the diary have been cited in museums, documentaries and books such as Lyn MacDonald's *Passchendaele* (Joseph, 1978; Penguin, 2013) or David Olusoga's *The World's War* (Head of Zeus, 2014). Yet there has not so far been a translation into English apart from those short excerpts. For some decades, it was hard to get hold of the text even in Dutch: issues of the three volumes which contained the diaries and which were published in 1964, 1965 and 1967 respectively, were increasingly hard to find. It was not until 2014 that an integral edition in modern Dutch spelling was eventually published.[1]

---

1 Achiel Van Walleghem: *Oorlogsdagboeken 1914-1918. Hertaald door Willy Spillebeen*. Tielt, Lannoo, 2014, 693 pp.

A historiographical assessment of Achiel Van Walleghem's diary

The main motive for publishing and translating Achiel Van Walleghem's diary is its exceptional quality. Without any doubt, it is not only the most elaborate but arguably also the most important diary from a civilian on the Western Front: as a historical source it has the potential to provide an invaluable complement to the existing historiography of the Great War. Local sources are generally neglected, not least in traditional military history writing, for all too often the positioning of a unit or the unfolding of a military operation is described as if it happened in a place where no one lived. The voices of the local population living on or near the front are seldom or never heard in First World War history writing. And yet it is of the utmost importance to have them included as they are often complementary to the existing historiography of battles and warfare: they allow us a glimpse of life in the hinterland of the front, arguably the most forgotten area, being neither the 'proper front' nor the 'home front.'

Those local sources have the potential to inform us about facts mentioned nowhere else. Van Walleghem, for instance, is alone in mentioning the presence of Portuguese troops near Locre. On 29 July 1917 he describes a mustard gas attack on Armentières, stating that 'over 1,000 civilians were poisoned and suffered horribly in their lungs and their eyes, and more than 300 died.' As I knew little about this gas attack, and as the number of civilian casualties seemed somewhat exaggerated to me, I contacted the town archivist of Armentières. According to his calculations, 500 civilians living in Armentières died in or shortly after the 29 July mustard gas attack. Despite the enormity of this event, it is virtually unmentioned in the history writing on the war in this area.

Obviously, information in local diaries can also complement or substantiate other factual data. For example, gathering information on how a cemetery or a set of cemeteries came into being is not always easy: the cemeteries were created by units and when these left, they were taken over by others. On 6 November 1914 Van Walleghem describes how his churchyard is now full and how a new cemetery (now Dickebusch Churchyard Extension) has been laid out in a field on the other side of the road. On 3 February 1915 he reports that the British intend to use as a cemetery another field further up the road towards Kemmel: Dickebusch New British Military Cemetery. And finally, on 10 June 1917, this cemetery was also full and now a new cemetery was made 'on the triangular field used by Jules Philippe, along the other side of the gravel road': today's Dickebusch New Military Cemetery Extension. Van Walleghem also offers interesting observations on the ever highly controversial subject of executions. When 20-year-old Private W. Smith from the 3/5 Lancashire Fusiliers was executed on 14 November 1917, Van Walleghem describes how remorseful some of the soldier's pals were.

Evidently this diary, like other local sources, can teach us a lot about the living conditions of the civilian population. Hence, on 3 July 1917 Van Walleghem draws up an overview of the destruction in Dickebusch: how many houses had been completely destroyed, how many were beyond repair, how many could still be repaired and how many had been hardly damaged until then. Yet, more than material possessions, it was the personal fate of his parishioners that was close to Van Walleghem's heart. He was, after all, a shepherd concerned with the welfare of his flock. In the months before the 1917 Flanders offensive, Van Walleghem describes the daily bombardments

15

and how these eventually force locals who had hitherto remained in their houses or on their farms to flee after all.

In cruel detail he registered how certain families suffered. The story of the Tahon family, for example, referred to in the translators' note, is particularly poignant. Another example is to be found on 6 July, where he relates the story of a family whose house is demolished by a bombardment, but who survive because they had fled the house in time and had been in the stable, which was only partly destroyed. The woman of the house, who has just returned from hospital with half-healed wounds, is injured again in this bombardment: 'But still these good people are happy that everything has worked out so well and consider themselves lucky, even though they have had their share of misfortune. They have twice lost all their furniture, first through fire, then through this bombardment, 2 daughters dead from typhus and the other daughter, Reine, injured in 1915, and now the mother injured twice in 7 weeks.'

In mid-July 1917, he reports on the general feeling of depression and indignation among the local population, due to the evacuation that had just been ordered. Only those farming or working for the army were allowed to stay. Those who had to leave were only allowed to carry one bundle and were given only a few hours to pack. Father Van Walleghem found it the most hateful and cruel measure taken so far since he was unable to find any reason for the evacuation. In addition, he reports that violence was needed in some cases to evict the inhabitants. The newly evacuated zone not only comprised the villages of Dickebusch, Vlamertinghe, Woesten and Elverdinghe in the Ypres rear area, but also most villages in the Yser area. The priest no doubt expressed the general opinion of most of the Belgian population when he described the evacuation as a deportation. 'This is how the Germans behave in the occupied part of the country,' he exclaimed in his diary. Van Walleghem complained bitterly that the local population in the war zone was completely abandoned and ignored by all the authorities.

Local sources such as this diary also have the potential to offer us insights into the often difficult cohabitation of the Belgians with the many foreign troops. The destruction by allied soldiers of local people's property, including buildings and crops, whether due to carelessness or some other reason, is a recurring theme. He also comments on the employment by the British Army of local inhabitants. More than once Van Walleghem refers to the suspiciousness of, in particular British, military personnel towards the Belgian civilians, who were very readily treated as spies. This 'spymania' was a general complaint of the Belgian citizens regarding the British, even from the beginning of the war, but it significantly intensified in the spring and summer of 1917. On 9 July, having described how and via which route a column of tanks had moved towards the front, Van Walleghem wrote at length about the preparations for the coming offensive, how new batteries were being installed, railroads being laid and new ammunition dumps being created. Yet, when a farmer requested permission from the military government to take his animals away to safety, given the danger that was posed by the imminent offensive, the man 'received a visit from the local policemen: "What's this? An imminent offensive? How do you know that? How dare you betray the details of the military preparations?".' Father Van Walleghem added ironically that 'the spy has not been shot.'

But it wasn't all negative: on 9 October 1917 he reported on the marriage of an English soldier and a local girl. And one month earlier, at the beginning of September 1917, he noted how intelligence officers visited all civilians originating from villages on the other side of the front line and how they collected postcards and wrote down all useful information. Some of the intelligence reports of 1917 on the Ypres area, today in the National Archives, with among other things a very detailed map of Passchendaele village centre with information on nearly every house, indeed explicitly mention that the information was gathered from refugees from the village then living in the Ypres rear area.[2]

Van Walleghem even pondered on the cohabitation of different military forces, as when he voiced the opinions of French Canadians or Irishmen on their British 'overlords.' He listened carefully when his informants assessed particular units or troops: 'I hear that the 30th division are rather weak fighters' (11 August 1917). The priest is probably at his best when describing overseas troops from the dominions and colonies such as the Australians, Indians, West Indians or the Chinese Labour Corps. Almost as a contemporary anthropologist he observed them in their camps, even reading their letters or trying their food. In his descriptions and opinions he is seldom harsh. However, his diary displays both the general feeling of white superiority that prevailed at the time, and the prejudice that helped to stereotype individual races.

In this volume, with the translation of Van Walleghem's diary for the year 1917, the Third Battle of Ypres takes centre stage: The prelude is the Battle of Messines on 7 June 1917. After this come the allied preparations in July, during which the Germans with their Operation Strandfest wrecked the allies' initial plan to attack simultaneously along the Flanders coast, and in the course of which the Germans also shelled the British with mustard gas for the first time. Then the first day of the battle on 31 July 1917, followed eventually by the change of strategy to 'bite and hold' in September, up to the

---

2 WO 157/424 & WO 157/425

final stage with the capture of what was left of the village of Passchendaele in early November 1917. While all these events and developments, well known to British scholars, are certainly reflected in the diary, so too are less familiar features of the Third Battle of Ypres.

For instance, the French participation in that iconic battle is conspicuously absent from nearly all British studies, despite the fact that it involved the entire French *1ère Armée* and that these troops were, relatively speaking, more successful than the British to the south of them even though they were fighting in exactly the same circumstances. Not so in Van Walleghem's diary. When on 3 October 1917 he travelled by car to visit some of the Dickebusch refugees in the French sector north-west of Poperinghe, he mentioned the many different kinds of French troops he encountered: some of them were Flemish-speaking from just across the border, but there were also *chasseurs* from the Alps, 'Turcos' from North Africa and Annamites (from Vietnam).

Besides numerous facts, a local source such as the diary of Achiel Van Walleghem can also offer us an analysis of events from a different point of view, that of a Belgian citizen. Van Walleghem lived among the troops and attentively observed what was going on, without really being an involved party. He was a bystander, a spectator offering the contemporary reader an often more neutral view of events, or just another, new and unusual look. Thus he observed the different groups involved in the war, whether civilians or military, and reported on their morale and mentality. A case in point is indeed his account of the preparations for and the course and close of the Third Battle of Ypres in the summer and autumn of 1917.

In July, while the preparations for the coming offensive are continuing apace, Father Van Walleghem expresses the impatience that was widespread among the local population, at the same time often commenting that most people were less hopeful of a happy outcome than they had been before the Battle of Messines Ridge. Strangely enough, on the days following 12 July, no mention whatsoever is made of the first use of mustard gas. Only on 26 July does Van Walleghem mention the use of a new type of gas, describing the agony of the gassed soldiers. On the 12th all his attention is on the loss of the allied positions on the east side of the Yser estuary: Van Walleghem was angry with the English newspapers who only stressed the limited size of the territory lost during the German attack near Nieuport, but said not a word about its strategic importance.

The practice of sounding out people's states of mind is inherent to the task of being a priest and Van Walleghem performed it conscientiously, not forgetting his own emotional state. Apparent from his dairy is the influence the weather had on the morale of both troops and civilians, and weather reports are frequent in his diary, often combined with thoughts on morale. On 30 July at noon, a day after Van Walleghem explicitly noted the abundance of rain, he learned that zero hour was settled for the next morning. He witnessed the excellent spirit among the troops, confident that the last weeks of the war had started. The next day, not only the first day of the offensive, but also the third anniversary of the mobilisation of the Belgian troops, the parish priest was somewhat more sceptical towards the many contradictory and over-optimistic rumours. Already at noon, when lorries loaded with wounded were constantly passing by, he concluded that the British had 'not had it as easy as they had in their victory at Wytschaete.' That same evening, an officer gave him an accurate report of the events and the progress of the day, information he saw confirmed in the official statements the next day. His worries about the bad weather were increasing daily and on

Wednesday 1 August, he recorded a rare personal remark: 'In all my life I've rarely been as sad about the bad weather as I am now.' On the other hand, a clear sky, especially in combination with a full moon, was not to his liking either, as this meant a greater chance of German air bombardments.

In the third week of the new offensive, our priest complained that no news was to be had on the fighting of the previous days, concluding that this meant that things had not gone too well. The change of strategy and the introduction of Plumer's bite and hold tactics is also reflected in the diary, albeit indirectly. On 20 September, for instance, he was amazed that he at first had not noticed that a major attack was going on. It is also striking that his entries on dates of important attacks in September and October are usually not longer than the entries of other 'ordinary' days, while in July and August, several pages were needed to describe his impressions on the days of major attacks.

After the Battle of the Menin Road he reported on morale in the 41st Division: 'The men are not happy because they have had to fight so long here on the Ypres front. It has been almost a year' (26 September 1917). More than a month later, when it became clear that the Third Battle had been another failure, Van Walleghem noticed resignation and defeatism, certainly when the news was broken that the Italian ally had been suffering heavy losses: 'The soldiers here are very much affected by this setback and are saying that the enemy is impossible to beat. People long more and more for peace' (3 November 1917). The 'official' end of the Offensive is not reported on 11 November as such, when the priest was particularly impressed by the 30 hour barrage over the 10th and the 11th. Finally, a couple of days after the close of the battle, on 13 November 1917, he concluded: 'Lloyd George says: "We have been fighting this war for 3 years and for 3 years we have been making stupid mistakes because of a lack of unity in action." This is precisely what the farmers of Dickebusch have been saying from the beginning, and now they are adding: "Next year, people will be saying: 4 years of stupid mistakes".'

Conclusion

The voice of the locals is truly a forgotten voice in the historiography of the First World War and it is needed if we wish to make a proper assessment of what really happened. Most First World War historians offer us great insights 'from within.' They write and rewrite, again and again, the history of armies, army units and battles. However, far too often we are given the impression that 'their' men are fighting in a void, against no one, with no one on their left or on their right. If we wish to arrive at a fuller understanding of events, it is surely a good idea to check what the other side, the enemy, is doing and thinking, and to describe what is happening on the flanks and further on along the front line and in the rear areas. It seems unlikely that errors and successes can be adequately described and analysed exclusively from within the organisation that is the subject of the research. One forgotten source of 'external' information that can help us in rounding out our account of the Great War in Flanders is provided by the records of inhabitants in the rear area. Without any doubt, Van Walleghem's diaries are prime among these.

Last but not least: the importance of the diary of Father Van Walleghem has recently also been officially recognized. At the time of its new integral publication in Dutch, in the summer of 2014, the Flemish government put the diary on its new First World War related list of heritage of national importance.

This means that the works are under government protection and cannot be exported or even loaned to institutions abroad without official sanction. Van Walleghem's diary is one of only two diaries on this list. This represents official confirmation of its extraordinary historical importance.

Dominiek Dendooven,

In Flanders Fields Museum

Translators' note

The source text as a mix of languages

This book presents itself as a translation, from the Dutch text, of one year from Achiel Van Walleghem's First World War diary. That it is not purely a diary, and in various respects more like a chronicle, has already been indicated in Dominiek Dendooven's introduction. When one looks more closely at the language in which this diary or chronicle was written, the phrase 'translated from the Dutch' likewise appears to be a simplification. When Van Walleghem filled his thirteen notebooks with his journal about the four years of the Great War and its aftermath, there were no Flemish authors or journalists in Belgium writing in what would have been regarded in the Netherlands as standard Dutch. In Flanders, an astonishing variety of dialects were spoken, with a degree of diversity that made it hard for someone from Van Walleghem's parish of Dickebusch to be understood in Ghent, less than 80 kilometres away. For inhabitants of the provinces of Antwerp or Limburg, understanding a West-Fleming would have been well-nigh impossible. Van Walleghem may never have heard standard Dutch as it was spoken in the Netherlands in his whole life up to then. Standard Dutch had not yet been adopted at that time as a common language for all Flemings, even though since then, many attempts have been made to give it that kind of status, with varying degrees of success. The language of Van Walleghem's diary was therefore not so much a particular Flemish adaptation of the standard language spoken in the Netherlands, as an adapted version of his native dialect and that of the Ypres area, which both belong to the Belgian province of West Flanders, and are fairly close to each other from both a geographical and a linguistic perspective. His language is essentially a combination of these two West-Flemish dialects, from which he has clearly filtered out some of the more idiosyncratic features in order to make his writing more generally accessible, combined with occasional attempts to use what he sees as 'standardised' (and which is in fact usually Brabant) Flemish.

The result, while considerably more accessible than Van Walleghem's usual spoken dialect would have been, is a language not easily understood today by Flemings 50 kilometres or more east of Ypres, and Dutch speakers from the Netherlands find it even more difficult to read his original text. The language Van Walleghem used in the journal is in fact so remote from standard Dutch that the In Flanders Fields Museum in Ypres asked Willy Spillebeen, a well-known West Flemish writer familiar with Van Walleghem's idiom, to translate the four years of the diary into 'proper' Dutch, as has already been mentioned in Dominiek Dendooven's introduction. Spillebeen's translation still preserves some of the local colour of the West Flemish text, but for the most part uses standard Dutch, and is much more readable to Dutch speakers outside West Flanders than the original. It appeared in 2014, and we have sometimes used it to inform our interpretation of Van Walleghem's writing.

To complicate matters even further, from a linguistic point of view, the language used in the diary has more ingredients than just two West-Flemish dialects and standard Dutch. French also exerted a strong influence on its author, even when he wrote in his particular brand of Dutch. At the time that he was writing, although Flemish was the mother tongue of most Flemings, and indeed of most Belgians, French was the only language of instruction in secondary schools and in higher education in Flanders. If there was a language of which Van Walleghem felt confident about there being a *norm*, it was French rather than Dutch. This explains why his syntax often follows a French word order rather than the order one would expect in the speech of Dutch people or Flemings. On 25 January, for instance, he writes 'Nogthans geen enkel soldaat is gevlucht' ('And yet not a single soldier has fled'). Here the verb follows the subject, whereas in standard Dutch or in Flemish dialects the order would be 'Nochtans is geen enkel soldaat gevlucht' ('And yet has not a single soldier fled'). Also in his vocabulary, the French influence is strong, as is still the case today among West-Flemings (an assault, for instance, is often called not an 'aanval' but an 'attaque'). And being the avid collector of knowledge that he is, he even picks up some military English to describe the action on the battlefield. He talks, for instance, about a 'raid,' spelt variously in the English manner ('raid') and in his own 'Dutch' way ('rit,' which the historical Dutch dictionary WNT mentions nowhere as having this meaning). That he sometimes misunderstood idiomatic English has already been demonstrated in Dominiek Dendooven's example of 'fake Belgium,' where he gets the four-letter word wrong. His English spelling left something to be desired as well. Where it seemed of interest, and not misleading, to quote literally, we have kept his spelling errors in our text. In other cases, we have adapted the spelling.

Place names

The toponymy in the diaries constitutes its own interesting linguistic cat's cradle. As a superb chronicler, Van Walleghem is very precise in his linking of events with places. However, the place names that he uses would often not have been recognised by the allied soldiers who had arrived in his area. As is indicated in the note on the spelling of place names, maps at this time bore French place names where such were available, even in Flemish-speaking areas, and these tended to be the names used by the military. Van Walleghem, however, usually uses the local West-Flemish place names in his diaries, but not always. Occasionally, he uses what he sees as a standardised Dutch place-name, for example ''t Vogelken' (which is in fact a Brabant diminutive), and sometimes a name conferred by English-speaking troops, for example 'Glenscore bosch' (his rendering of 'Glencorse Wood').

We may add to this that today many Flemish place names have changed to some extent, especially in their official spelling (see the note on the spelling of place names). Thus what for Van Walleghem was 'Rooberg' (literally, 'red mountain', though in fact 'red hill' would be more accurate), was for French-speakers and for the British during WW1 'Mont Rouge,' and is today officially 'Rodeberg.' In the translation of the diary, we use as far as possible the place-names that would have been used by British soldiers at the time, which in many cases means that we are using the French name.

Van Walleghem sometimes distinguishes place names from names of pubs and farms by using quotation marks for the latter category, and sometimes he does not. If he wrote his diary for others than himself, he probably assumed that they would be reading his manuscript and not a published book, and that they would be sufficiently familiar with the West-Flemish topography to distinguish pubs and farms from geographical areas, towns or villages. In order to give the readers of the English some help, we have put the names of pubs and farms in italics, whereas ordinary place names are not in italics.

Facts and figures, times and tenses

Van Walleghem loves facts and figures, as Dominiek Dendooven amply demonstrates, and is usually very precise about distances. In the diaries, local distances are measured in terms of the time taken to walk from one place to another, as was the custom in West Flanders in those days. Thus Van Walleghem will say 'a shell landed 5 minutes to the north of the village,' meaning '5 minutes' *walking* distance north of the village.' We have often added mention of 'walking distance' in order to avoid confusion, but at times have left it to the reader to fill this in, to allow a flavour of the original text to come through. We might also note in passing that Van Walleghem almost never uses words for figures, preferring to use Hindu-Arabic numerals (as in '5 minutes' instead of 'five minutes'). We have preserved this characteristic feature of his reporting style.

As mentioned in the historical introduction to this publication, a preparatory form of the diary entries in this book was usually written down at the end of a day in the shape of little notes on loose sheets, and a few days or weeks later Van Walleghem looks back at the events and transforms the notes into the entries as they appear in their final shape. When he thus revised the notes at a slightly later stage, he often added information that was not yet known on the day of the original notes. On 13 July 1917, for instance, he mentions that Cyriel

Jacob's daughter 'is hit by a motor car and seriously injured' that day, and goes on to say: 'However, she recovered after a few weeks.' The 'narrative' or 'historic' present tense which he so often uses, as here, in his lively narration of events, gives way to the simple past tense to add a factual footnote. At other times, however, there is a mixture of 'historic' present and simple past tense within the same narrative. This more arbitrary alternation of present and past tenses may result from his method of working, perhaps taking present tenses directly from his notes but mixing them more or less indiscriminately with past tenses reflecting the standpoint of the time when he is writing up his notes. We have mostly kept this feature of the text, in part because it seems to us to reflect the nature of what Dominiek Dendooven has defined as a hybrid work, mixing diary and chronicle. In some cases, however, where the preservation of the alternation between tenses would have led to confusion or would have become particularly awkward in English, we have made the use of tenses more uniform.

Finally, we should note that Van Walleghem does not often distinguish between the English, the Welsh and the Scots. For him, these are all 'English.' We have not corrected this in the translation. A distinction he does make very clearly is that between those he calls 'English' and those that come from Ireland. He has a lot of praise for the Irish, which is not surprising, because among them he finds far more Catholics than Protestants. Although Van Walleghem is not immune to the xenophobia of his age, as noted in the historical introduction to this volume, his views on Protestantism constitute one of the rare instances where his judgment is very largely subordinated to prejudice. Although he directs some scathing comments at certain English and even Irish Catholic priests, it is clear that for him, Protestant chaplains are, to say the least, rarely as hard-working, brave and dignified as their Catholic peers.

Resources

In 1967, Jozef Geldhof published the manuscript of Van Walleghem's entire journal under the title *De oorlog te Dickebusch en omstreken* (*The War in Dickebusch and Its Surroundings*), with an introduction and editorial comments, in a series of contributions to the history of West Flanders. This is a very reliable edition, and we have used it as the basis of our translation. In some rare cases, the original manuscript had to be consulted.

Guido Latré's parents came from very close to the area in which Van Walleghem was born and grew up, and they determined his 'mother tongue,' although he himself grew up further to the south of West-Flanders and went to a primary school in a hamlet of Langemarck – just north Ypres, and a place that is mentioned several times in the diary. This background gives him considerable access to both the dialects that are combined in Van Walleghem's diary. However, there remained many occasions on which outside help was required, either because the meaning of a word remained obscure or because our understanding of Van Walleghem's world was incomplete or because we lacked sufficient knowledge of the history of the area, and, especially, of the Great War in this area. If the meaning of an individual word was obscure, and where Spillebeen's translation did not help (often where he decided not to translate the colourful West-Flemish into standard Dutch), we could rely on other sources, such as L.L. de Bo's dictionary, *Westvlaamsch Idioticon*, or the Ghent University website of Flemish dialects ('dialektloket'), which is the result of decades of work by Ghent linguists who specialise in the vocabulary of rural Flanders.

These resources, however, solved only a certain number of

problems. For an understanding of Van Walleghem's world we were able to call on André Latré's vast knowledge of old farming techniques and of the agricultural vocabulary used by older generations of the farming community. Of the chemical fertilizer called 'zout' ('salt'), for instance, which today is no longer in use, he knew not only the name and the effect but also the chemical composition (see the entry for 24 April 1917). André Latré was also able to advise on the nature of certain church artefacts and on folk traditions, such as that of predicting the future at the time of the first quarter of the moon. For the translation of ecclesiastic terms, so much a part of the world of the priest Van Walleghem, precious assistance was offered by Dr Paul Arblaster of the Louvain School of Translation and Interpreting (Marie Haps). Paul helped us find the *mot juste* in other instances as well.

Above all, we relied upon the encyclopaedic knowledge about the Great War in Flanders of Dominiek Dendooven, who saved us from numerous *faux pas* and educated us in countless aspects of this topic. He corrected and elucidated place names and the names of inns and other landmarks, both local and military, as well as using his knowledge of local geography to solve puzzles in Van Walleghem's text. He also corrected and informed us about all sorts of military matters, such as which army units were in which locations during which periods, what types of shelters the soldiers used, the type and size of armaments and much more. We benefitted, too, from his knowledge about many of the individuals mentioned in the diary, whether politicians, war-heroes, locally-famous priests or simply local inhabitants.

Literary ambitions, or their absence

If in spite of some rare inaccuracies the diary offers us a goldmine of historical facts and their interpretation, this is due to its writer's insatiable curiosity, and his unwavering determination to find out the truth. There is, however, a deeper truth that he uncovers on almost every page. He conveys the fragility and suffering of the local population in passages imbued with a strong empathy, which not only have historical importance, but also, as will be demonstrated below, show considerable literary talent. When it comes to other nationalities, his empathy is of course less in evidence, though his humanity remains, but we should perhaps note his treatment of one category of the wartime population in particular. Notwithstanding the racial stereotyping and prejudice which seep into his views, reflecting perhaps surprisingly mildly the age in which he lived, his matter-of-fact descriptions of the small and large cruelties of life and death for Chinese labourers behind the front provide a rare glimpse of the conditions in which these men lived. His comments are often all the more effective for their simplicity.

Indeed, Van Walleghem eschews high rhetoric and deliberately remains prosaic in most of his descriptions. Although he knew his Latin and would have known about the rhetorical devices used by classical authors, his prose remains considerably more sober than that of the journalists of his day. A clear demonstration of this is to be found in his translation of an article written in English by Philip Gibbs on 8 June in the British newspaper *The Daily Chronicle*. Van Walleghem adds it to his report on 7 June, but he leaves out some of the more rhetorical paragraphs of the original, and tones down the high rhetoric of the paragraphs he translates whilst otherwise remaining faithful to Gibbs's text. As it did not make much sense to translate Van Walleghem's translation back into English, we copied the original text, which now serves as a superb example of how much more rhetorical the pathos of contemporary British journalists sounded. In the end, Van Walleghem's lack of literary ambition further enhances the value of his diary-cum-chronicle as a historical source.

In general, Van Walleghem speaks the language of ordinary civilians like himself much more often than that of the intellectual which he also was. His prose is simple, with a paucity of punctuation that often evokes spoken language, but many a paragraph of his demonstrates exceptional literary skill, and makes him a good deal more readable than the bulk of Flemish writers of his day.

In the following passage, the horrendous suffering is encapsulated in a paragraph that takes stock, as it were, of the material damage done by a shell that bursts through a house and kills a mother and child (12 July 1917):

The shell went in turn through the roof, a trunk full of clothes and then the ceiling, went through the child that sat on his mother's lap, blasted off the right thigh of the mother, went through the floor and bored almost 1 metre deep into the ground. Little Albert Tahon, 18 months old, died instantly. His mother (Maria Van Elstlande from Dickebusch, 32 years old) was taken to Couthof and died early in the morning. Never have I seen anything so sweetly cruel as the poor little child. He was laughing with delight when his little body was pierced through, and death was so instantaneous that the lamb never changed his expression. He laughed still on his little deathbed and now he laughs just the same way in heaven.

The combination of the clinical description, almost like an inventory drafted in typical Van Walleghem fashion, of the stages of the damage done by the shell, with the pain the writer feels at the death of the child whose laughter is cruelly fixed for eternity by the murder weapon, is heart-rending. The mentioning of the exact age of mother and child, in the same breath as he mentions the exact distance the shell bores through the floor ('almost 1 metre deep'), likewise fits into the typical Van Walleghem register that combines objective fact with a deep sense of pity and anger at the senseless destruction of a young child and his mother. In its ending the paragraph provides a rare instance of something like sentimentality creeping into Van Walleghem's writing. The angelic image of the laughing child may have connected to the more emotive type of religious literature that the Catholic priest will certainly have been familiar with. At the same time, the matter-of-fact tone of the paragraph as a whole prevents the sentimentality from getting the upper hand.

Van Walleghem is also a master in the use of irony – which often serves as an outlet for his indignation at the stupidity or callousness of military or civilian authorities, or the thoughtless behaviour of the ordinary soldiers. A typical comment combining humour and (somewhat resigned) exasperation can be found in the diary entry for the early morning of 25 December, following widespread drunken revelries among the soldiers: 'It was pitch dark going to Dickebusch, but the soldiers had the happy thought of setting fire to one of their huts along my road and so they lit me on my way.'

In spite of its lack of literary ambition, Van Walleghem's text thus seems to us to acquire literary status. There was no shortage of literary models in his West Flanders. It is perhaps no coincidence that the poet and priest Guido Gezelle and the novelist Stijn Streuvels, two West-Flemish writers of the period between 1850 and the beginning of World War 1, are undoubtedly the Flemish authors of that time with the most enduring legacy in the history of Dutch-language literature. Both understood and identified with the predicament of the common man or woman. Streuvels in particular, whose masterpiece *De Vlaschaard* appeared in 1907, wrote a masterly prose that is evidence of as much talent to describe a rural society as Thomas Hardy's.[3] The seeming simplicity of Van Walleghem's style is often not very remote from that of either Stijn Streuvels or of Thomas Hardy, whom Paul Fussell in his seminal *The Great War and Modern Memory* (1975) praises as a writer with a profound sense of the 'Satire of Circumstance' in the build-up towards World War 1. Sadly, Van Walleghem does not show the empathy with the plight of women that is such a strong feature of Hardy's novels, but at his best he does manifest a literary talent in his expression of indignation towards the authorities, and compassion towards the common man, that reminds one of the most powerful passages in Hardy's novels.

Van Walleghem's critical, often ironic description of the mentality of the authorities makes one think of another great literary talent in the English-speaking world, viz. Siegfried Sassoon, who in his famous *Declaration* and other texts (especially poems) of 1917 launched a public attack against the authorities. These, however, were written by a military

---

3 Stijn Streuvels was also the first West-Flemish writer of fame to publish a war diary. It dealt with the year 1914 under the title *In Oorlogstijd* ('In War Time'), and appeared in six parts in Amsterdam in 1915-16. We do not know whether Van Walleghem had read any of this, but it is unlikely that the fierce controversies around Streuvels' report on the early war months remained unnoticed to the Dickebusch priest. However, whereas Streuvels stated explicitly that he wanted to render the *atmosphere* rather than the facts, Van Walleghem deliberately chose to remain more factual.

man, whereas Van Walleghem's diary gives voice to the hopes and frustrations of a civilian. Moreover, Van Walleghem's text was kept private rather than being made public, and did not jeopardize his position as a respected mediator between the local population and both the Belgian and the British authorities. In spite of these differences, they share a similar ironic tone. For the translators, the awareness of an ironic register among Van Walleghem's British contemporaries directly involved in the war undoubtedly contributed towards the preservation of the tone of the original in the target language.

Rendering the combination of objectivity and strong empathy, doing justice to the delicate balance between the prosaic and the literary, and preserving the irony in Van Walleghem's prose, was not an easy task for the translators. It is for the reader to decide whether they have succeeded.

Guido Latré and Susan Reed

A note on the spelling of Flemish place names

Most towns, villages and hamlets in Flanders have names for which more than one spelling exists. While the vernacular language in this part of Belgium was, and is, one or more of the varieties of Dutch that are usually called 'Flemish,' throughout most of the 19th century and the beginning of the 20th century, French was used as the main language of higher administration and jurisdiction. Hence maps from that period – including those used by the British during the First World War – mention the French names of locations. Thus we find 'Ypres' instead of 'Yper.' To complicate matters, in the 20th century Dutch underwent a series of spelling reforms which further affected the spelling of the names of towns and villages. As a consequence, several decades ago 'Yper' became 'Ieper' (with a capital i – not an L !). Throughout this book we have opted to use the historical names as they would have appeared on official documents, such as maps or government documents, during the Great War.

The following list gives the names of towns and villages as mentioned in the diary and in their contemporary spelling:

Diary	Today
Abeele	Abele
Becelaere	Beselare
Bixschoote	Bikschote
Boesinghe	Boezinge

Courtrai	Kortrijk
Crombeke	Krombeke
Dadizeele	Dadizele
Dickebusch	Dikkebus
Dixmude	Diksmuide
Dranoutre	Dranouter
Elverdinghe	Elverdinge
Furnes	Veurne
Gheluvelt	Geluveld
Ghistel	Gistel
Iseghem	Izegem
La Clytte	De Klijte
La Panne	De Panne
Langemarck	Langemark
Locre	Loker
Louvain	Leuven
Luighem	Luigem
Menin	Menen
Merckem	Merkem
Messines	Mesen
Mont Rouge	Rodeberg
Moorsleede	Moorslede
Neuve-Eglise	Nieuwkerke
Nieuport	Nieuwpoort
Oost-Roosebeke	Oostrozebeke
Oost-Vleeteren	Oostvleteren
Ostend	Oostende
Passchendaele	Passendale
Pilckem	Pilkem
Pitthem	Pittem
Poelcapelle	Poelkapelle
Poperinghe	Poperinge
Reninghelst	Reningelst

Roulers	Roeselare
Rousbrugge	Roesbrugge
St. Eloi	Sint-Elooi
St. Jean	Sint-Jan
St. Julian	Sint-Juliaan
Thielt	Tielt
Vinckem	Vinkem
Vlamertinghe	Vlamertinge
Voormezeele	Voormezele
Wervicq	Wervik
West-Roosebeke	Westrozebeke
Wevelghem	Wevelgem
Westoutre	Westouter
West-Vleeteren	Westvleteren
Wulverghem	Wulvergem
Wulveringhem	Wulveringem
Wytschaete	Wijtschate
Ypres	Ieper
Zantvoorde	Zandvoorde

For the locations of hamlets, farms and other places of interest in the municipalities of Dickebusch and Reninghelst, go to the website www.achielvanwalleghem.be, where a historical map of the area is available.

The Diary of Achiel
Van Walleghem

1917

1 January, Monday. New Year's day. 4th year of the war. We start in good hope that peace will come in the course of this year, but live in some doubt as to whether it will be the peace we desire. May God grant it to us! Courage and faith!

45 people attend mass. 15 holy communions. It's uncommonly warm and I walk to Dickebusch with my overcoat over my arm.

Last night there was a great deal of noise in the streets, and, sadly, much heavy drinking. In the morning I encounter 2 Belgian soldiers, a civilian between them, weaving down the street as if pacing out its width, who must have suffered very little thirst in the course of the night. In this period of Christmas and New Year, the Belgians are on very good terms with the English. It is sweet indeed to drink the Englishman's health at a time when the English are so generous, and the Belgians know how to make the most of this.

But on the whole the relations between Belgians and Englishmen have been good for quite a while and at the batteries[4] even excellent. The Belgians each receive a parcel from the Queen that is worth 1.20 francs.

---

4 i.e. the 7th (later 13th) Belgian Field Artillery, an artillery regiment from the Belgian Army which was detached to the British 2nd Army near Ypres from February 1915 to May 1917. Its name lives on in the British military cemetery Belgian Battery Corner in Ypres.

2 January, Tuesday. In the morning I give Julie Gombeir the last rites at *De Hert*. Then I go to the village. I notice that even more wood has been removed from the houses. Sister Placide's girls' school has collapsed. At first sight I thought the building had been bombarded. But once I got nearer, I saw that there were very few broken tiles, which would have been impossible if it had been shelled. I was able to ascertain beyond doubt that the building had been torn apart by the pressure of the bags of earth inside the building squeezed between the walls and the corrugated iron sheets which formed the shelter. I had already noticed several times how the walls were giving way under the pressure and were threatening to collapse. I see new shell holes in the meadow in front of the presbytery. I go to the English cemetery and find out that even more funerals are taking place. I also notice that the 2-family home of Doise-Capoen, the 3-family home of Swingedauw and *De Cavete* have collapsed and have been partially carted off already. First all the woodwork was removed and then the rest collapsed.

Of the whole of Hemelrijk all that is left to see is Het Kasteelhof and Tahon's inn, which, however, are both on the brink of collapsing as well. The *Café Belge* has likewise disappeared.

The mayor's wife still remains on her farm. In August just about all her animals were killed or wounded, and now she has bought new ones and already has 17 cattle large and small, as well as a few pigs. The English officers forbade her to live in her house any longer, but she's living in her cowshed. The mayor himself now sleeps at Marcel Coene's place, but goes back to the farm for the daytime. The danger remains considerable, and few people think she's right. Once a fortnight the Belgian chaplain celebrates mass in the attic there for his batteries. Some neighbours attend. The Belgian soldiers are on very good terms with Lucie, the mayor's wife, and are truly grateful to her for her compassion and goodness. At Dalle's quay a lot of wood and other materials have been stacked for the trenches, fortifications and roads. 60 wagons would not be able to carry it all.

The guns of the Heugebaert and Comyn farms are firing ceaselessly.

In the chicory oast house of Widow Delanotte of Dickebusch, and in that of Henri Kestelyn of Westoutre, a drying room has been installed for the washing from the English laundry in Reninghelst. Every morning about 20 young women are taken to the laundry by motor car together with soldiers. One can see at a glance how wild and unrestrained these girls look. Such a pity!

3 January, Wednesday. The 2nd Belgian artillery group is bombarded.

4 January, Thursday. The princes Xavier and Sixtus of Bourbon-Parma, brothers to the current Empress of Austria,[5] have been back in Westoutre for some days. They are part of the general staff of the 7th regiment of Belgian artillery stationed at Den Ondank, on the farm of Rouseré-Coene, under the command of Colonel Moraine (it used to be Colonel De Grendel). Since last summer already the staff has been staying with the supply column. It used to be in Poperinghe, but moved from there because of the bombardment. The princes have taken up lodgings with brewer De Keuwer. They are very respectable and earnest, but seem to be in

---

5 Whilst Sixtus and Xavier Bourbon-Parma served in the Belgian army, three other brothers of this large family were in the Austro-Hungarian army. Their sister Zita was empress of the Austro-Hungarian double monarchy, which would come to an end in 1918.

47

somewhat poor health and rather melancholy. They are very devout and go to mass and Holy Communion almost daily.

Today the princes are attending the inspection of troops by the second English general and the Belgian colonel, for the second group at Cyriel Lamerant's farm.

The gunners of the batteries and the headquarters have a black strip of cloth on their collar, and those of the supply column and aid post a blue one.

5 January, Friday. Clear weather, a lot of firing at aeroplanes. In front of the tavern *De Koevoet* the case of a shell which had been fired at the aeroplanes comes down and goes right through a Red Cross vehicle that happened to be passing by there at that very moment.

The chicory oast house of Widow Delanotte, where soldiers' laundry was dried, burns down. The usual causes.

6 January, Saturday. Epiphany. The princes of Bourbon dine with the major of the 1st group at Lemahieu's farm.

7 January, Sunday. In the course of the night, intensive bombardment around the farms of Theophiel Huyghe, Amand Heughebaert and Comyn. From my bed I can very clearly hear the German gun firing and the shell landing and exploding. After high mass I see a German aeroplane shoot down an English one that crashes in Locre.

There are still Australian and Canadian engineers here. They say that there have been mines under Wytschaete for a year.

8 January, Monday. A lot of firing in the afternoon and evening. For the last month there has been much more violence here.

9 January, Tuesday. Heavy shelling on Ypres and on the woods beyond Leroye's farm. They call these *Ridge Wood*, and those nearer the lake *Scots Wood*.[6] Madame Mahieu's country house is called *The Bluff*,[7] and Thevelin's warehouses *The Brewery*. In the evening, a German attack around Kemmel.

10 January, Wednesday. In the afternoon 15 shells fall on Poperinghe. German aeroplanes set fire to the captive balloon at Locre. There are rumours that the Germans carried this out using an English aeroplane they captured a while ago, and with which they have crossed the line unnoticed several times.

In the evening a very heavy German attack stretching from St. Eloi to Boesinghe.

The Belgians stationed at the edge of Boesinghe say that these days they are shelled almost constantly.

I receive news from my brother Joseph who has been in the army since October, has left the training camp and joined the Grenadiers. He is now with the 6th Division at the Mailly camp for the big manoeuvres.

11 January, Thursday. The princes of Bourbon pay a visit to the presbytery of Reninghelst. They've also been to the presbytery of La Clytte.

12 January, Friday. An NCO of the 2nd Belgian battery is shot dead in his observation post, and the 2 telephone operators standing next to him, two brothers, were wounded.

13 January, Saturday. Rain. Nothing special.

---

6 Actually Scottish Wood.
7 This sector of the front was called *The Bluff*, the country house itself was referred to as *White Château*.

14 January, Sunday. Frost, icy cold in the barn, and only 150 people in all the masses together. A boy of 14 dressed like an English soldier has moved in here in the curate's house along with the orderlies. He's from Nancy and goes along with the English artillery as a messenger and a musician.

They say that there are again 2 German prisoners of war that have escaped.

15 January, Monday. A lot of firing in the afternoon and evening.

16 January, Tuesday. More or less continuous firing. The soldiers are given much less beef than they used to get, just 30%, and for the rest tinned meat most of the time.

17 January, Wednesday. The 7th artillery regiment has now become the 13th. This because so many regiments have been split in two.

18 January, Thursday. Nothing special.

19 January, Friday. Around noon the village of Dickebusch is shelled. Two shells are dropped on Arthur Minne's house. Shells also around the mayor's farm and in the afternoon, shells around Achiel Vandermarliere's right up to Oscar Ghesquiere's. The last time shells were dropped there was 4 months ago. In the evening, shells at Amand Heugebaert's farm.

An English raid in the night, heavy shelling from 11 to 12 along Wytschaete and St. Eloi. The 3rd Belgian battery has the sector from Wytschaete to the Bluff (Madame Mahieu's chateau) and did a lot of firing last night.

Again more guns are posted near Theophiel Huyghe's farm.

20 January, Saturday. Yesterday the frost set in and this morning temperatures are already well below freezing. No one foresaw that the frost would be so severe and certainly not that it would last for another 4 weeks.[8]

I conduct Julie Gombeir's funeral in our war cemetery.

21 January, Sunday. A lot of firing.

22 January, Monday. Terrible firing in the afternoon around Wytschaete and Messines. The coldest day so far.

23 January, Tuesday. A lot of shell-fire all day around Wytschaete and Messines. At 11 a.m. shells on the village and alongside the dairy and at 1.30 p.m. very many shells between Dalle's farm, *De Hert* and Florent Dauchy's place. One of them drops just in front of Camiel Capoen's house. The Germans are probably aiming at the English who have their machine gun posts in the abandoned fields over there. They say that no fewer than 500 shells were fired that day.

24 January, Wednesday. The Vandenpeereboom chateau is heavily shelled. So far this mansion had been preserved in a reasonably good state, but now several shells have been dropped on it, and the tower has been gunned down. It's there that the staff of the 2nd Belgian group is billeted. The English call it *Belgian Chateau*. The ice is thick enough to walk on. On August Verdonck's moat the soldiers are sliding round with the girls from the laundry.

25 January, Thursday. At 11 a.m. the 3rd Belgian battery located in the dam of Dickebusch lake, to the left of the

---

8 This sentence was clearly added at a later date. This sort of addition occurs several times in the diary.

mayor's farm, is pounded terribly. More than 350 shells are dropped on one hectare of ground. 2 guns are blown to pieces. An ammunition dump of more than 400 shells is blown up. A shelter is smashed, 1 soldier heavily wounded and two lightly, and *sous-lieutenant* Claes likewise lightly. And yet not a single soldier took flight, and the authorities congratulate them on this. This battery has been active there for 9 months but has only just been discovered. It is thought that this has happened because of the carelessness of the soldiers. Yesterday afternoon Belgians and Englishmen were skating, and today there they were on the ice again, hunting guinea fowl.

26 January, Friday. 3 German aeroplanes fly to Poperinghe and drop 5 bombs. Near the fuel depot 10 horses are killed. At Het Hooge a civilian who was riding a bike is wounded, seemingly by a shrapnel shell that was fired at the aeroplanes and exploded on the way.

Few civilians are allowed to ride a bike. Just doctors and some workers employed by the army.

27 January, Saturday. Freezing cold all week. Shells are dropped on Dickebusch. Also near Jules Lamote's farm, between Dickebusch and La Clytte.

28 January, Sunday. Between the two masses I go and have a look at the village. Soldiers go there all the time to get wood to warm themselves with, so that nothing remains of most houses but the roof and the walls. In about 10 houses soldiers are still billeted. As a result, these houses are spared somewhat, but those in the neighbourhood are the worse for it. Soldiers have been in the houses of Thevelin, Delanotte, Deleu, Maurits Devos, Leeuwerck, Noyelle, Ollivier, Francis Goethals and in some houses around the school: Nollet,

Devos, Grimmonprez, Van Wonterghem, and Opsomer. In the church, as well, all the woodwork has vanished. The only remaining piece I see is the canopy above the pulpit. Chaplains are housed in Delanotte's house. Protestant services are held in Thevelin's. The houses of Jules Devos and Maurits Devos serve as canteen.

At long last, after having written several letters, Charles Maes has received a reply confirming that the queen has agreed to be godmother to his 7th daughter in a row.[9] After high mass I perform the baptism ceremony of the already baptized child. This is done in the room above the cellar[10] of Cyriel Lamerant's house. Jules Maerten, treasurer of the church wardens, is the godfather and Lucie Derycke, the mayor's wife, stands in for the godmother Queen. Godfather and godmother offer a very decent lunch in the village constable's room and a good glass is drunk to the health of the little Elisabeth. The Belgian officers of Lamerant's farm also offer a bottle for good measure and reproach Charles for not being a good patriot, by having only girls. 'Not to worry,' says Charles, 'who knows, perhaps the king will have to be godfather one day.' The 3rd Belgian battery is keeping its 2 good guns in the same place and gets a 3rd from the 2nd battery. As a result, these 2 batteries now consist of only 3 guns. The cold in the barn church was unbearable.

29 January, Monday. In the afternoon the farms of Henri

---

9 According to tradition, when a family has seven daughters in a row, the queen becomes the seventh daughter's godmother. In the case of seven sons, the king becomes godfather.

10 Van Walleghem refers to the 'vaute.' This West-Flemish term is the name for the room above the cellar vault, which (because the floor is higher) has a lower ceiling than the adjacent rooms. This space was often used for storage or sleeping (see diary entry for 20 June) but in larger houses the ceiling was high enough for the space to be used as best room or parlour.

Vandecasteele and Jules Spenninck are shelled at the same time, as well as the areas around Lemahieu's and Doom's farms.

Two days ago, guns were installed at Doom's farm and discovered as soon as they fired their first shots. Guns have been placed there for the 3rd time and each time they were discovered straightaway. It seems to be the case that this farm can be observed from Madame Mahieu's chateau, and I can well believe this, since from Lemahieu's farm, or right next to it, one can see white glimmers of the chateau in the distance. This, however, would not be a good enough reason for the guns to move out, and soon another 2 would be added.

30 January, Tuesday. I go to La Clytte and see that in front of De Rozenhil a very neat German camp has been erected. Such beautiful, warm huts, surely no Englishmen have such good huts. I encounter a group of Germans who are on their way back from work. How much their health has improved since they arrived here. They have a healthy complexion and are dressed warmly. Their wages are 3 francs a week and they get good food. One really has to acknowledge that the English treat their prisoners of war well.

Heavy shelling on the Belgian front. At night Edmond Derycke's farm near the village catches fire because of the carelessness of the soldiers.

31 January, Wednesday. Big guns are positioned on the farms of Theophiel Huyghe and Celeste Planckeel, and on the meadows between Planckeel and Florent Dauchy.

Shrapnel shells explode above Dickebusch. The following inhabitants of Dickebusch join the army: Vercruysse Remi: class 11 (married), Depriester Klaas: class 06 (married), Goethals Camiel 04, De Baene Hector 03, Buseyne Cyriel 01,

Claerebout Jerome 05, Van Eeckhoutte Camiel 02, Adriaen Gustaaf 01, Van Elstlande Isidoor 02, and Coene Arseen 06. On 20 February Parrein Camiel 03 joins as well. Their enthusiasm was not great, but a few days later most of them write that they dislike their new lives less than they expected.

1 February, Thursday. In the morning, from 4.30 to 6 a.m., a heavy German attack around Wytschaete. It fails. In the course of the morning, shrapnel shells explode above the farms of Lemahieu and Doom. In the evening shells are dropped along the road in front of the Verschoore chateau. Several English soldiers are killed.

New guns are added constantly in the entire Ypres sector. Their number is very large. The question is, to what end. To attack or to defend? Later on we are informed that there were fears of a large-scale German offensive here because the Germans had taken a horrifying amount of extra artillery to this front. But preparations had been made for this. From Planckeel's farm to Ypres there are guns everywhere.

2 February, Friday. Candlemas. Consecration of candles in the barn, 2 church wardens and 30 others attend. It has already happened more than once that the water that was to be used for mass was frozen, and also that after the ablutions the rim of my chalice was covered with ice. This time, however, the frost was so severe that at the moment of Holy Communion my chalice was frozen and had to be thawed by my breath.

A lot of firing throughout the day.

3 February, Saturday. At least 200 shells are dropped around the guns of Comyn's farm. They burst into hundreds of fragments on the frozen ground and some pieces are flung 500 metres out. In addition, two shells also fall on Celeste

Planckeel's farm. The bombardment lasts for almost the entire day.

The civilians who do the soldiers' laundry now need special permission for this. Some English officers are now having their torn shirts mended. How different this is from the days when clean clothes and perfectly good and untouched food were just thrown into the fire. If they had thought ahead then, they wouldn't have to be so frugal now. There's a great shortage of bread. There used to be one large loaf for 3 men, now it's a small one for 4. As a result, there are a lot of soldiers who are buying bread at the baker's and that's why so many civilians are also finding it very hard to find bread. Now the English are happy to have a few tins of meat. And to think that in 1915 they buried or burnt cartloads of the stuff, even when it was still in perfectly good condition.

4 February, Sunday. A calm day.

An order is issued for the farmers by the military governor re the sowing of their fields. 3/8 of their fields are to be used for corn, 3/8 for fodder crops, 1/8 for potatoes and only 1/8 is to be used for industrial crops.

Police officers come and requisition tools for the Belgian army, which intends to plant potatoes on the abandoned fields.

The chicory beans[11] are sold at 90 francs per 100 kilos. Their high price is a result of so many of them being smuggled into France, which is a very easy thing to do.

5 February, Monday. A calm day.

6 February, Tuesday. More firing. The fear of a large-scale

---

11 The chopped, dried roots of chicory, used in making coffee or to make an ersatz coffee, were called 'chicory beans.'

German offensive has diminished since there are rumours that the enemy is withdrawing his artillery from the Ypres area. A good many aeroplanes pass overhead each day, the weather being so clear. The frost is unrelenting.

7 February, Wednesday. We hear that the United States has broken off diplomatic relations with Germany.

In the evening shells are dropped around Celeste Planckeel's farm.

8 February, Thursday. Some shells fall on Hallebast. At 10 p.m. an English raid around Wytschaete. They take 15 prisoners of war. The shelling lasts all night.

9 February, Friday. At 8 a.m. Achiel Jacob's farm and Henry Verdonck's coach house, both in Reninghelst, are on fire. Yesterday the stables of Westoutre's law court were alight. The same causes for all three of them.

Widow Delanotte's oast house has been repaired with iron sheets and the soldiers' laundry is being dried in it again. As everything has been frozen here for 3 weeks, many streams no longer have running water, nor is there any in wells with pumps, which causes a lot of trouble for the army.

10 February, Saturday. More or less constant shelling day and night.

11 February, Sunday. In the afternoon shells were dropped between the farms of Alouis Adriaen and Achiel Vandermarliere. Last week there were more or less daily bombardments around the farms of Comyn, Planckeel and Huyghe. Just about all the potatoes that are left are being requisitioned by the Belgian army at 11 and 11.5 francs. In spite of the frost, the farmers are expected to deliver constantly. No wonder therefore that a lot of the potatoes get frozen. It is hard to imagine how stupidly an army does things. Just when the heavy rains of early winter were falling, the farmers had to deliver straw nearly all the time, and now, when everything is frozen, it's potatoes. The farmers are very unhappy about the price. The yield was low, fertilizers and wages very expensive, and now, after all the worry they've had with them over the last 5 months, and having suffered substantial losses because of the frost, they have to deliver them at ordinary peacetime prices. What is more, many farmers do not receive any sort of proof that they have delivered the potatoes, and so it has happened that when payday arrived, there were farmers who got the reply: 'Your name isn't on the list.' It's hard to believe. What is likewise unbelievable is the low price that is paid for the requisitioned wheat, just 33 francs for a hundred kilos of the best quality grain. And this when the farmers have to buy back the bran for their animals at about the same price, and pay more or less double for the same ingredients in fodder cakes. There isn't the slightest balance between the prices farmers are paid for requisitioned supplies and the prices they pay for their own purchases. There is a lot of dissatisfaction among them, and with good reason.

The billeting of higher ranks (a general, a colonel, a major) is paid at a rate of 1 franc per person, of an NCO at 0.50, of an ordinary soldier at 0.08. That's the way it has been since last summer. It used to be double. They pay rent by the square metre for the places they use, and by the acre for the land.

Today, after 22 days of deep frost, there has been a slight thaw. News reaches me that my brother Joseph, of the 2nd Regiment of Grenadiers, has arrived in Woesten.

Heavy shelling in the morning. Nearly every day about 10 ships are sunk by German submarines.

12 February, Monday and 13 February, Tuesday. Quite a lot of shelling. Not much news in the newspapers. The food rations of soldiers are constantly being reduced. We are wondering whether by any chance the time has arrived that even the well-mannered English can now empty their plates, for English good manners are exactly the opposite of ours in this matter. Leaving a bit of everything is seen as refined in England, and leaving half one's plate uneaten is the height of refinement.

14 February, Wednesday. A lot of shelling all day. Shells fall around Dalle's farm. In the morning 3 shells are dropped on Poperinghe and in the afternoon 9. News reaches us that Private Camiel De Crock from Dickebusch is lying wounded in La Panne, a rifle bullet right through his belly. He was in a critical state at first, but seems to be on the mend already. The freeze has set in again but isn't quite as severe.

15 February, Thursday. Heavy shelling at night. I have a bad cold, mainly in the head.

The chicory beans are being sold at 105 francs for a 100 kilos. In spite of the prohibition a lot of them are smuggled into France and it seems that this isn't difficult at all. A lot of men along the border have become chicory salesmen. Coffee is likewise getting scarce.

News arrives that Henri Scheldeman, who is from here, has died in La Panne. All 3-month deferrals[12] for our Dickebusch men are renewed except Marcel Coene's. He's appealing against this. What is the reason for this refusal? There are those who think that he has been too much engaged in horse-trading and too little in farming. There is a lot of jealousy among folk

---

12 Farmers could have the date on which they had to join the army postponed.

and people are prepared to lodge complaints against others and likewise to spread nasty rumours about others, whether there is any truth in them or not. However, it's a fact that some farmers busy themselves solely with trade, and the authorities no longer turn a blind eye. On the other hand, the area is teeming with policemen, and they prick up their ears when anyone utters the slightest sound. God knows why there are so many policemen here. From being governed by police, deliver us oh Lord!

The Reninghelst sexton is going to the court of appeal in La Panne. His application for the 7th group has been rejected.

16 February, Friday. After 4 weeks of frost, thaw begins. A calm day.

17 February, Saturday. At 4.30 a.m. shells on Charles Hoflack's farm. Funeral of Widow Declercq, who died here.

18 February, Sunday. A calm day.

19 February, Monday. The chaplain Father Bull O.P. leaves for Calais, where he can take a rest from the exhaustion of his cumbersome and dangerous life at the front! In the 5 full months of his stay here he has been closer to the front than Ouderdom on no more than 2 occasions. A true Englishman he is: 'Only in England is perfection to be found, elsewhere nothing half-decent.' He had enjoyed the hospitality of the curate for 5 months. Not the slightest word of thanks after his departure.

In the afternoon I go to Poperinghe. At Widow Van Cayseele's and Verdonck's farms the construction of new railways still continues.

20 February, Tuesday. In the morning I go with the chaplain to the soldiers' day of recollection. A couple of months ago an order was given by Mgr. Marinis, main chaplain, for priests, members of religious orders and seminarists in the army to gather on a monthly basis for a spiritual recollection. Last month the clergy of the 7th Artillerly gathered in the Vandenpeereboom chateau. This time it's the chapel of La Clytte. Present were the chaplains Peeters and Ratie, the seminarists Coveliers and Cos, the Jesuit novice Daneels as well as the parish priests of Kemmel and La Clytte and the curates of Reninghelst and Dickebusch. It was very comforting for us to take part again in this kind of exercise and Rev. Ratie's sermon was very beautiful. A hearty lunch was waiting for us at the chaplain's house. Unfortunately, Rev. Ratie and Rev. Daneels had to leave at once because the English had planned an attack on Zillebeke at 2 o'clock in which the 1st group were to be involved. And indeed at 2.30 p.m. the guns were roaring full blast. In the afternoon shells fell on Theophiel Huyghe's farm.

21 February, Ash Wednesday. I celebrate mass on Cyriel Lamerant's farm. 32 present, 14 communions. After mass I take communion to Alderman Henri Doom. The man still lives on his terribly dangerous farm right in the middle of the guns, 4 of which are in the farmyard itself. He has been poorly for the last few weeks, but will not hear a word about moving out. He's more attached to his farm than to life itself. He's in no mind to leave it, even after death. 'Isn't it a sad thing, Reverend,' he says to me, 'to be buried in Désiré Lamerant's meadow? If I should die, surely 'twould be better for me to be buried in one or other corner of my own land?' After my visit to Doom I go and smoke a cigar with Rev. Peeters at Lemahieu's farm. He shows me his little chapel that he has cobbled together with sand bags. In the centre of the village I notice that the *Café De Commerce* has been demolished and also the gate of the court house and the next house as well. Where the houses were, there's now a painted canvas creating the illusion of a wall. Just a handful of houses are still inhabitable. The best houses are those of Thevelin (where the services of the chaplains take place), Delanotte, Leeuwerck, Devos, Deleu, De Baene, Noyelle and further on Henri Dumortier, Jules Devos, Van Wonterghem, Delforche, Grimmonprez, Dumortier and Opsomer. I return via Razelput and Hallebast. Colonel Morel of the 23rd artillery catches up with me in a motor car and invites me to get in, which I gladly agree to do. The colonel is very friendly. He tells me that the English took 115 prisoners of war at yesterday's attack. Later I was told that the prisoners passed by Hooggraaf.

In recent days the gun has been thundering around Boesinghe as well. At Hector Coene's and Widow Delanotte's farms there is a large military encampment called *Micmac camp*.

22 February, Thursday. 23 February, Friday. Thaw and everything quiet in the Ypres area.

24 February, Saturday. In the afternoon an English attack around Wytschaete. Very heavy. 50 prisoners of war, among whom 2 officers, came through La Clytte.

25 Febuary, Sunday. Nothing special.

26 February, Monday. Nice weather. Not fully thawed yet. There are rumours that a lot of German artillery has moved away from the front and therefore there's less fear of a German offensive.

In the evening from 6 to 7.30 p.m. heavy bombardment on Doom's farm and further towards Cafmeyer's. A few of the soldiers' horses are killed. A shell is dropped a couple of metres in front of Doom's house and the furniture is blown to pieces, but fortunately no one is wounded. Daughter and granddaughter flee. Doom gets up from next to the shattered stove and lies on his bed right in front of the window on the most dangerous side of the house, saying 'If I'm struck dead here, at least I'll die in my own bed.'

As it happens, one of the common sayings of our parishioners who don't want to recognise the danger is: 'If you're in debt to Death, he'll come for the cash wherever you are.' That's also how the mayor's wife speaks. But they prefer not to think too hard about the meaning of the saying.

8,500 francs have been paid to the inhabitants of Dickebusch as a compensation for their occupied lands. The authorities are prepared to pay for the rent but not for the damage.

27 February, Tuesday. A calm day. The men of the artillery that stayed at Hector Dalle's farm have left, but not without behaving scandalously towards refugee Jan Gotenaere (called Jan Plak) from Voormezeele, who, with his wife Stephanie, lives in Dalle's oven shed. They invite Jan and his wife into the house and have a drink with them, and in the meantime they load up all his furniture and off they go. Why this Jan and his Stephanie, both of them in their 60s and living very simply, as people here used to do, want to carry on living there in the most dangerous spot in Dickebusch, is beyond comprehension. They cannot make a better living there than elsewhere, and what's more, for a year now they've had their hut ready in Reninghelst, at Kasteelmolen. They've used it to protect their wood, but they seem less protective of their lives. In the meantime, Jan goes to Reninghelst to work every day. Good people, but not very clever. This is the 3rd time that Jan has fled, and now he has arrived at Dalle's farm. Until April 1915 he remained in his house near Ridge Wood

(Voormezeele). Until 15 October he lived with Petrus Leroye across the lake. Then he came to Door Capoen at Dalle's farm. In May 1916 he was evacuated and moved a few yards away, still on Dalle's farm. There he lives in an oven shed half destroyed by shells. Whilst he was living with Door Capoen a heavy bombardment took place one day. Door's family fled after the first few shells, but Jan and Stephanie remained. Jan at the stove and Stephanie in the parlour. Suddenly a large shell drops in front of the door. The door and furniture are blown to pieces, a hell of smoke and dust. Then after a couple of minutes: 'Stephanie, are you alive?,' Jan asked. 'I am, and you?' 'So am I.'

28 February, Wednesday. Shells land on Poperinghe, first in the town, then soon enough on De Leene (Lijssenthoek), even right up to the big Boonaert hospital (Lijssenthoek). It's the first time that the shelling has reached that far.

In the evening the new chaplain, Father Hurley, arrives, Mr Bull's successor. He will stay at the curate's house. The chaplains of the 46th Division are the Fathers Bickford, Bleasdale and Hurley. Of the 41st Division, Fathers O'Brien,[13] MacHavy and Sheridan.

1 March, Thursday. Nice weather today. 4 German observation balloons spy on the Ypres front. In the afternoon 2 shells fall at Millekruisse in the meadow of *De Koekuit*. Shells also fall on the farms of Comyn and Dauchy, where the English are playing football. My brother Joseph, off-duty grenadier, chances his luck and comes and pays me a visit in the afternoon. On his way back he walks straight into the last police post, but they let him pass. Unfortunately, there was an unexpected

---

13 Van Walleghem spells the name 'O'Bryen.'

inspection of troops while he was absent, and in this way he was caught out after all. It's difficult to cross from the Belgian to the English front, and permission is only given for leaves of absence.

2 March, Friday. Funeral in our war cemetery of Jules De Bruyne's wife, who had fled from Kemmel. Mother Superior of La Clytte leaves for the school colonies[14] in France (Montluçon). She had been of good service there in the course of the war, and her presence was welcome there. It's a pity that she couldn't stay.

3 March, Saturday. A lot of shelling during the night.

4 March, Sunday. By special permission of Monsignor De Brouwer we can hold the day of prayer today instead of tomorrow because given our current circumstances, a prayer day in the course of the working week is very difficult. The Blessed Sacrament is displayed from 6 a.m. until after high mass. For this occasion we decorated our chapel as best as we could. This morning I administered Holy Communion to 105 people. The weather was very bad. In the afternoon shells are dropped at the police station. A shrapnel shell fired at an aeroplane explodes in Oscar Ghesquiere's cowshed and kills 3 yearlings. The ground has only now finally thawed completely.

5 March, Monday. Once again I go to Dickebusch to say mass in order to allow people who haven't yet had the opportunity to do so to observe the day of prayer. Another 45 come to confession, and I reckon that 150 have respected their day of

---

14 School colonies were boarding schools for evacuated children.

prayer. In view of the circumstances I'm very pleased with this, taking into account that one third of the population go to other churches.

An order is issued stating that bread can be sold only at 50 cents a kilo rather than 70 as has been the case so far. The bakers must have made a good profit considering the fact that wheat has been requisitioned at 33 francs. This measure has been taken much too late. The price of chicory beans rises to 115 francs. Piglets have become very cheap because of the lack of potatoes and because scraps from the soldiers' food have likewise become scarce. By contrast, the fattening pigs have again reached the steep price of 2 francs. The added tax has been abolished because it became clear that with that added to the price the pig-breeding trade would be destroyed.

Shells fall on the farms of Doom and Indevuyst. 1 is dropped on Indevuyst's cowshed, killing one cow.

6 March, Tuesday. One brigade of the 43rd Division has left and has been replaced by the 39th.

7 March, Wednesday. It snows and the frost is so hard that it has covered the windowpanes of my bedroom completely. On the farm of Oscar Ghesquiere in Dickebusch (Millekruisse) they were threshing using the big machine when they were rudely interrupted by Fritz, who must have seen the smoke coming from the engine. 1 hour before nightfall a bomb suddenly lands 6 metres from the thresher. The men flew out in every direction like sparrows, mercifully only one was lightly wounded. Another 6 or 7 shells followed but without causing any injuries.

On the Poperinghe road a painful accident befell René Vandelanotte, 60 years old, nicknamed 'Netje Fikke,' beadle at the Reninghelst church. The man, already a little feeble-minded, was on his way to Poperinghe to do some errands. At about 15 minutes from the town he wants to get out of the way of a motor car but is caught unexpectedly by another coming from the opposite direction. The poor fellow's chest was crushed and he died an hour later in Couthove hospital.

The trade in lace has collapsed almost completely. The main reason is probably that officers and soldiers have less money to spare for this than before, and that many have enough 'souvenirs' already. Butter is now 7 francs a kilo.

8 March, Thursday. For some days it has been quieter at the front. For 2 months now I have had frostbite in two places in my right foot. But a fortnight ago the wound opened. At first I didn't pay much attention and thought it would heal with the usual treatment. But alas, this has proved wrong and the wound has got so much worse that I'm forced to keep still. For this reason, the Reninghelst curate is celebrating mass today in my stead in Dickebusch.

The officers of the 39th Division are much more decent than those of the 43rd. The 16th Division of the Irish have been in Locre since the beginning of October. Some Catholic chaplains have the rank of major, whilst others are only captains. These ranks are attributed on the basis of their length of service.

Shells fall on the farms of Arthur Deraedt and Gustaaf Desmarets.

9 March, Friday. The Grim Reaper seems to bear a grudge against the churchgoers in Reninghelst. Netje Fikke has barely been laid out and the days of one of our altar boys are ended in the same manner. Nestor Lahaye, an 11-year old orphan, came back from school, and right opposite the sexton's house, whilst crossing the road, he too is caught by a motor car and killed instantly. Yesterday also a boy was killed in Locre and a policeman in Watou. A week full of disasters, and yet it is astonishing that more accidents don't happen, for in the wide streets of Brussels there isn't more traffic and commotion in peacetime than you now see constantly in the streets of our once so empty village. Add to this that those who are in charge of motor cars or horses are not infrequently drunk, the civilians as well as the soldiers. Wealth is a monster and some cannot keep it under control. Rare are those civilians that haven't tasted champagne yet. Some drink it almost daily. At the baptism of a child of small innkeepers 15 bottles of champagne were drunk. 17-year old youngsters are not averse to the stuff either. Chocolate and sweets have less than a tenth of the value for children that they had before the war. Both priests and lay people of Reninghelst find it hard to get a bit of fresh meat. Everyone has got money and everyone wants to buy the best with it, in spite of the high prices.

10 March, Saturday. Funeral of the beadle René Vandelanotte. The men of the 2nd group of the Belgian batteries go and rest in Godewaertsvelde. The staff officers continue to take their rest on the farms themselves, partly in order to keep their billets, partly because they cannot find space for their horses elsewhere. The staff officers are very pleased that they can stay on the farms where they have all set up home.

11 March, Sunday. On Cyriel's farm there's no mass with the chaplain, since he's joined the batteries that are gone to Godewaertsvelde.

An order has been issued by Minister Berryer telling parents who still want to send their children to school colonies that henceforth they'll have to pay for board and lodging. Nevertheless, those that want to send their children to

Switzerland through the good services of Miss Fyfe[15] can do so very easily and some children have recently left Reninghelst this way. Wulveringhem likewise remains free of charge, but is full.

12 March, Monday. These days milk has become very scarce. There aren't many cows left in the area, and most of them are dried off. The milk is sold at 15 cents a pint, but only after it has been baptised with a good splash of water.[16] We find ourselves obliged to have it delivered by Cyriel Lamerant of Dickebusch.

13 March, Tuesday. At 10 p.m., a ferocious German artillery attack.

14 March, Wednesday. Shells fall into the lake.

15 March, Thursday. More shells fall into the lake. The Reninghelst curate, who goes to Dickebusch to say mass in my stead, gives the last rites to Widow Braem on evacuated territory, accompanied by the local policeman.

16 March, Friday. Nothing special.

---

15 Glasgow-born Georgiana 'Georgie' Sutherland Fyfe (d. 1966) had initially joined Dr Hector Munro's Flying Ambulance Corps in Flanders in October 1914 but soon ran her own relief organisation for aid to the civilian population in war-torn Flanders. Besides running several hospices, one of her main concerns was the evacuation of Belgian children from the war area into France and Switzerland through 'Le Foyer Ecossais.' Largely forgotten today, she was a much respected figure during the First World War, receiving honours from the King and Queen of the Belgians.
16 Van Walleghem uses the Flemish word 'gedoopt' (literally 'baptised'), which was commonly applied to milk that had been diluted.

17 March, Saturday. News reaches us of the revolution in Russia, and the deposition of the tsar. This is something the newspapers had scarcely prepared us for.

18 March, Sunday. Rev. Lamerant, who lives in Reninghelst, goes to Dickebusch to say mass in my stead. We've been reading for some days that the Germans are beginning to withdraw from the Somme. Today news reaches us that Bapaume has been taken.

19 March, Feast of Saint Joseph.

Mr Dermaut, as obliging as ever, goes to Dickebusch to replace me.

In the morning, departure of the entire 2nd group of the Belgian artillery that has been stationed here. They go to train in Eu in order to learn to fire the 105 mm guns.[17] They don't know whether they'll have to return to the English front or whether they will be transferred to the Belgian front. Most of them would prefer to return here. Admittedly, there's more danger here than at the Belgian front, but they are much more independent here, and get some perks that aren't to be found on the Belgian front. The 1st group will stay here a bit longer.

Capture of Péronne.

A little while ago an order arrived from the Belgian military governor Andringa[18] stipulating that all those who want to offer coffee or food to the soldiers need to make a special application. Are they trying to annoy people? One would truly think so. Once the application has been made, a few weeks

---

17 Van Walleghem mistakenly wrote '115 [mm] guns,' whereas it was the French *Canon 105 mm L mle 1913 Schneider* which they had to learn to fire.

18 As military governor of the province of West-Flanders General Andringa (1855-1919) was responsible for a lot of decrees in the unoccupied part of Belgium.

later a doctor from the Health Inspection Service arrives to take a look at the house or hut. One of the requirements is that there must be no cooking at the place where the soldiers eat or drink, which means that more than half the huts don't meet the conditions, and precisely those that belong to the poorest. In addition, several other things need to be checked. If the inspection is satisfactory, one shouldn't expect permission to be granted in under a month. If all goes well, they will receive permission after 2 or 3 months. I know people who haven't received anything after 5 months. In all these administrative matters there probably aren't enough people to cope with the work, just as one finds in the police station!

In the afternoon shells fall on Poperinghe.

20 March, Tuesday. Again shells on Poperinghe, around the Elisabeth hospital and on the unloading quay, in the direction of De Leene (Lijssenthoek).

21 March, Wednesday. Shells fall at the mayor's farm. At 3 p.m. shells fall around Hallebast. 1 next to Braem's little chapel and several in the meadow. Locre is also shelled. 1 on the garden of the village priest and another one beyond the village.

22 March, Thursday. Very severe frost again. Such a hard winter! Funeral of Jules De Bruyne, refugee from Kemmel, in our war cemetery, Rev. Dermaut in charge of the service. 2 shells fall on Millekruisse and several on Poperinghe.

23 March, Friday. A German aeroplane drops 4 bombs north-northwest of Reninghelst near the clogmaker's house. No casualties. Also bombs on Dranoutre, near the village square.

24 March, Saturday. At 5 a.m. German attack near St. Eloi, Hill 60. The attack is repelled and 1 German officer and 7 soldiers are taken prisoner. The shelling continues more or less all day. A lot of shells fall around the farms of Doom and Indevuyst. 2 soldiers are killed. In the evening fierce shelling around Boesinghe.

25 March, Sunday. At midnight the clocks are set back by an hour. Solemn communion of the Reninghelst children. Rev. Lamerant remains as ready to help as always and replaces me in Dickebusch whilst I celebrate high mass at Reninghelst. In the afternoon the Germans fire no fewer than 500 shells at an English battery at *Lake House*.[19] It's a real miracle that neither guns nor men were hit.

They plan to construct a railway next to the church of Reninghelst, beyond the moat belonging to the Verdonck farm. Soldiers are busy pumping the moat dry, in order to fill up a part of it for the track. In this manner the war destroys yet another part of the parish heritage, a relic of the Middle Ages, the last remnant of the castle of the Lords of Reninghelst.

26 March, Monday. The cold weather persists. I notice that the English horses and mules have grown much thinner lately. A lot of them are really in a pitiable state. The cold weather is probably the main cause, and though the stables are in relatively good repair, it must be very cold in there. The other important reason is the shortage of food, the rations of oats and hay having been substantially reduced.

The bakers are no longer allowed to use pure white flour.

---

19 The inn referred to here is called *Het Vijverhuis*, which means 'lake house.' For purposes of clarity, we make an exception in this case by not keeping the name in Dutch.

No more sweet loaves[20] then, except on the sly and hidden from sight. Every farmer has had to declare the quantity of his wheat, a part of which he's allowed to keep for his own consumption. All the rest he has to deliver to the Supply Committee (alas at the price of only 33 francs). Each farmer in his turn must cart his wheat to the gas-powered mill at Poperinghe. There it is ground, mixed with flour, and transported to the bakers in the area. Each baker gets his portion and is allowed to sell his bread only to civilians and only at a fixed price: 50 cents a kilo and later on 55 cents. The person put in charge of the requisitionings and the provisioning of the area is Mr Nevejan, the mayor of Poelcapelle.

Guns have been positioned in the hedge of Dalle's meadow, and 3 big ones on Claeys's farm.

27 March, Tuesday. Nothing special.

28 March, Wednesday. Our little Marie-Thérèse Dalle, 5 and a half years old, who lives in this house, received her First Holy Communion. To celebrate the occasion, a meal for friends at the house of the curate. At noon 2 shrapnel shells explode above Cyriel Lamerant's farm, followed by 3 shells in or around Dalle's farm, one of which goes through a wall of the house, and smashes to pieces the room where I lived for 10 months.

New guns are constantly being added here. For 3 weeks no fresh malt has reached the area. Six's brewery has stopped producing.

We receive a visit from Father Norcott, chaplain of the 39th Division. The good man has lost an eye, at the Somme, and now often stays in Ypres.

---

20 'Koekebrood,' or a loaf of sweet white milk bread, was as much a part of the Sunday ritual in Flanders as going to mass.

29 March, Thursday. Father Hurley, who lives in the parlour here but is outside his sector, has to go and live in Ouderdom. A protestant chaplain takes his place. He looks like a good, hard-working man but is very shy with us.

30 March, Friday. Shells fall on the mayor's land.

31 March, Saturday. Percussion shrapnel shells on the village, and one on Désiré Delanotte's laundry.

1 April, Sunday. A lot of shells on the farms of Doom and Indevuyst.

2 April, Monday. The 3rd Belgian battery at the lake dam is shelled heavily. At least 300 shells fall into the lake, where they also explode. 'What a magnificent spectacle, the water splashing up wildly, sometimes 20 metres into the air, and falling down in a thick mist,' subdeacon and witness Jan Coveliers tells me. Two shells also fall on *De Koevoet*, where the officers live. At least another 300 fall on the fields around the guns. People were still getting water from there. Although neither men nor guns were hit, the English are by no means happy about a bombardment of the lake, for it appears that the water works have been damaged. The water remained turbid for several days, and what's more, it appears that since the bombardment, the water has been poisoned, and that as a consequence several horses may have been killed by poisoning. In any case, no new batteries are being installed at the lake any more, and those that are already there are forbidden to shoot except in extreme necessity, all of this in the hope of avoiding a new bombardment of the lake. Today shells also fall on Poperinghe.

Yesterday all the parish priests were told by Monsignor

De Brouwer, following a request from General Andringa, to launch an appeal to their parishioners for them to deliver all the potatoes they could possibly spare, in order that the Belgian army might have a sufficient supply of potatoes for planting and thus cultivate the abandoned fields that are suitable for this kind of use. In Dickebusch, where last year under the very eyes of 14 Belgian policemen a quarter of the potatoes were stolen by soldiers, the call meets with little success. It's not much better in other parishes. Everyone is disgruntled about the way in which the potatoes have been requisitioned and about their price. It's hard to feel much sympathy if one knows that the army deliberately let hundreds of thousands of kilos of potatoes get frozen by having them delivered continuously during the period of deep frost. Add to this that very few people can still spare potatoes. That's why I haven't insisted much among my flock. For the last few days neither the Belgian nor the English soldiers have been getting any potatoes. The civilians have been forbidden to sell any more large potatoes for chips to the soldiers. A good measure. Among the civilians the selling price is 18 francs.

3 April, Tuesday. A hard frost and 12 hours of snow on top of it. Probably the worst day of the year.

There are a great many guns now in Dickebusch and many more positions have been prepared for fresh artillery. Also heavy shelling every day.

4 April, Wednesday. My brother has arrived to spend a few days of his holiday here with me.

5 April, Thursday. Maundy Thursday. The curate of Reninghelst provides the services in Dickebusch whilst I replace him in Reninghelst.

6 April, Good Friday. Last night the English made a raid on Wytschaete, and took 31 prisoners of war. The farms of Doom and Indevuyst are shelled almost daily.

At noon, at 12.30, Mr Gustaaf Six, who has been mayor of Reninghelst for 13 years, died a Christian death here.

7 April, Saturday. In the evening the English make a raid on Saint Eloi and Verbrande Molen. It's a total failure. They took 18 prisoners of war but they themselves lost more than 250 men. Apparently the Germans had smelt a rat. They had evacuated the nearest trenches and responded with massive machine gun fire. I myself and several other civilians knew about it several hours beforehand.

8 April, Sunday. Easter Day. I, too, rise again at Easter. My foot is getting better and I can allow myself to be taken to Dickebusch. The weather is pleasant but a bit chilly. I administered 65 Easter communions. Last night there was a lot of shelling. We have noticed a great deal of ammunition being transported into this area recently. It seems to us certain that the English are planning a large-scale offensive here in the next few weeks.

9 April, Monday. 48 people take the Easter Sacrament in midwinter weather. At least 40 shells fall around the farm of Isidoor Kestelyn and Drie Goen. At Vrambout's 2 soldiers are struck dead and 16 horses and 12 men are wounded of whom 4 die the next day.

Nothing contradicts some of the proverbs of the English more than the way they actually live. Take 'Time is money,' for example. An Englishman always has time and never seems in a hurry, but is wonderfully patient. 'Early to bed, early to rise, makes a man healthy, wealthy and wise,' but an Englishman goes to bed late and gets up late in the morning.

10 April, Tuesday. We get the first news about the English victory around Arras.[21] 10,000 prisoners of war.

11 April, Wednesday. Such miserable weather for the time of the year. It snows almost all day long. Not a single trace of green anywhere. At 10 p.m. there's the solemn funeral of Mr Six, the mayor. A lot of people were present, including Monsignor De Brouwer. At 5 p.m. Her Majesty the Queen of the Belgians arrives here to attend a film show organised by the English to raise money for the Belgian Red Cross. The show takes place in a very fine wooden building that has been erected in Pieter Cambron's meadow along the Zevecote road. It has three wings: a wing for the cinema room, one for the officers' mess, and one for the games room and bar for the soldiers. The inhabitants of Poperinghestraat were asked to put out their flags. The queen arrived in a motor car, accompanied by Prince Charles. Because of the terrible weather, there were only a few curious people on the streets. Only soldiers were allowed to see the screening. Seats at 10, 5 and 1 francs. A schoolgirl presented a bunch of flowers, another read a little ode. The Queen stayed for dinner with the General of the 41st Division in the house of Mr Achiel Camerlynck.

12 April, Thursday. A French priest and interpreter is staying at Cyriel Lamerant's farm. There were still a lot of Easter communions this morning. Butter is allowed to be sold at 5.50 francs on the farm and at 6 francs in the shops. Before the evening a German aeroplane glides above Cyriel Lamerant's farm and drops a flare as a signal.

---

21 This is the Battle of Vimy Ridge.

Father Peeters, chaplain, staying at Lemahieu's farm, gives the last rites to Alderman Doom, since I can't get there with my painful foot. We hear the good news of Brazil's rupture with Germany. However, what pleases us less is the goings-on in Russia, which is torn by political division and not much engaged in the war but rather inclined towards a separate peace. We hear that an army of Portuguese has arrived in France, and that Portuguese officers have been spotted on Scherpenberg.

13 April, Friday. Around 4 p.m. the Germans start shelling, first around Doom's farm, and soon afterwards around Planckeel's. A lot of shells fall on the wood, two of them hitting the stables. Several soldiers and horses are killed. Soon the bombardment is extended, and shells are dropped on all sides along the stream and in front of Cyriel Lamerant's farm, on Cyriel Onraet's farm, and at Henri Vermeulen's place. The shelling continues along the railway, at the Delporte station and the Verhaeghe-Cossey unloading quay. It's very fierce and a sort of bombardment that we are not used to, the shells flying so fast that we barely hear them approaching. We can hear the big German gun very well, it's as though it's only an hour's walk from here. Then a very brief whoosh, and a dull explosion, sometimes almost inaudible. Near Delporte's farm a train has been stationary for several months, its wagons serving as housing for the staff of the railway station. 2 wagons are shattered to pieces, and 2 officers and 4 soldiers are killed. After that the train takes itself off to the village square of Reninghelst. Shells have fallen right up to De Brikke, 5 minutes from the square. On the rough and bumpy gravel track next to Henri Desmarets' farm an ammunition cart was approaching towards evening when suddenly, probably as a result of the shocks, there was a terrible explosion. The entire cart flew into pieces and the man on it was blown into the air. The poor man was torn into 50 pieces or more.

14 April, Saturday. In the morning 2 German aeroplanes drop flares above the farms of Henri Lamerant and Widow Derycke. In the morning shells fall around Alouis Adriaen's farm. Around noon Dickebusch village is heavily bombarded. Several shells fall on the buildings. 3 big ones drop on the cemetery. A family vault next to that of the Ghyselen family is blasted open. That vault belongs to the Malou family, but served only as a provisional burying place, and no one was in it. Several gravestones are broken. Also a very deep hole next to the tombstones of the Onraet and Coene families and an equally deep hole near the church wall where the French soldiers lie buried. The holes are 2 metres deep, and I have heard that several corpses had been thrown out of them. The soldiers buried them again immediately and when I went back some days later, I only saw a few little bones. Around 6 o'clock 2 shells along the railway line near the Delporte station (Ouderdom).

15 April, Sunday. Bad weather all day, it's mid-April and one cannot yet see the difference between rye and wheat, so behind is everything. Nature looks the same as it does in February. No green to be seen anywhere yet. Another 40 people take the Easter communion. Thus I count 240 Easter communions altogether, which is the number I expected, taking into account that ¼ of the population take the Easter Sacrament at La Clytte. Later on another 20 communions to the sick and the feeble-minded. This year it has been impossible to know whether all parishioners and refugees have taken the Easter Sacrament. Nevertheless, I fear that there are 2 or 3 who have not done that duty.

Shells fall around the lake. News reaches us that Liévin has been taken by the English. The Belgians who are in Dickebusch have to collaborate with the English there to prepare positions for the guns.

16 April, Monday. Shells land in the morning, first around the mayor's farm and then on the village square and around the dairy. One falls on the house of the local policeman, next to the council hall, and kills a sentry who is standing guard at the corner there.

17 April, Tuesday. They expect an English offensive here soon. In the presbytery, space has been made ready for a general commanding an army corps. Shells fall near the Delporte farm (Ouderdom railway station). Yet another spy has been arrested in Dickebusch! Farmer Arthur Cafmeyer. The reason? A few days ago Cafmeyer had ploughed a piece of land to sow oats in it. Unfortunately, the soldiers had walked across it to go to their guns nearby so that here and there the soil had been compacted into paths. Today Cafmeyer went and loosened them with a harrow, leaving untouched what had remained untrodden. But lo and behold a cocky young officer berated him for giving signals to the German aeroplanes by not harrowing his land uniformly. However hard Cafmeyer tried to explain his agricultural theories to him, it was of no use and the last he heard was: 'By tomorrow morning the entire field will be harrowed, or we'll know where to find you.' It was evening and Cafmeyer intended to comply the next morning. Unfortunately, it rained heavily the next morning, which made harrowing impossible. That was enough. The following night they got Cafmeyer out of his bed, and all the soldiers of Reninghelst and surrounding area soon knew that a big spy had been arrested in Dickebusch. Cafmeyer was detained for 3 days in Reninghelst, was questioned several times, and returned home just like almost all the other spies. This is just one case among thousands. There was also that farmer in Reninghelst who began spreading manure on a 3-acre piece of land. He had barely dropped little heaps from two cartloads when an English officer joins the party and claims that the man is signalling to the Germans using the little dung heaps. The man explains what their purpose is. The Englishman doesn't trust this, but allows him to continue on one condition, which is that the entire field must be covered by the evening. A farmer from Westoutre wants to plough a field and starts by filling up the furrows. This was likewise a way of signalling, and the man was arrested. The parish priest of Reninghelst is arrested and questioned by officers about why he's wearing a soutane. When he explains, they tell him that this is very careless, and they advise him to dress just like other people.

18 April, Wednesday. Snow. A lot of Kemmel inhabitants and also some farmers are warned that they must move out before 4 April[22]: from Dickebusch, Honoré Indevuyst, Henri Doom, Widow Dewilde and Alfons Cordonier. Widow Dewilde lodges an appeal and is allowed to stay. We notice that the army horses have lost a lot of weight.

The English who have replaced the Belgians on the farms of Lamerant, Decrock and Desmarets accuse their predecessors of espionage. This is, of course, no surprise.

Today the Dickebusch mayor is summoned for Cafmeyer's interrogation by the British. The questioning turns into a farce. There were aggravating circumstances, so it seems. 'The father of the accused is also a spy,' the judge said. 'That is very well possible,' says the mayor, 'it's just that he has been dead

22 This date must be wrong, since it is already 18 April. He may mean 4 May, but we don't know the correct date.

81

these last 25 years, and I didn't know him very well.' 'No, no,' is the reply, 'he's alive, and we arrested him last week. He's on the farm almost all the time.' It turned out that they were referring to Jules Perdieu, Cafmeyer's farm labourer, a simple soul who was arrested while he was filling up shell craters on the mayor's land and unfortunately hadn't got his permit in his pocket, which resulted in him being detained for a whole day. 'Now then,' said the judge, 'in any case his mother is a spy.' The mayor started laughing again and said she had been dead for 8 years. This time it appeared to be Sidonie Capoen they were talking about, an old woman who can often be seen doing her rounds as a midwife and a nurse and who was staying at Cafmeyer's place.

The greatest asset we have found in the English so far is their endless patience, which truly deserves our admiration, and their tough discipline, which remains intact in spite of the long duration of the war. Without being too severe the officers have a lot of authority over their men, and one never hears these speak ill of their superiors. It's a pity that it's not like that in the Belgian army.

19 April, Thursday. The 41st, 47th, 23rd, 39th and 19th Divisions are here.

20 April, Friday. Big bombardment around the lake. Funeral of Widow Saelen in our war cemetery. In the evening, a terrible attack in the Wytschaete area by the Germans, who got into the English trenches and have probably taken some prisoners of war.

21 April, Saturday. Heavy shelling around the lake.

22 April, Sunday. 5 minutes before the 1st mass a shell falls between the farms of Cyriel Onraet and Cannaert. It passed above the church. High mass is celebrated by a French priest who is also an interpreter. I make use of the opportunity to go to the centre of the village after the 1st mass and visit the sick Alderman Doom. Along the road and around the village I can see new gun positions on all sides. There are such gun positions along all hedges, except those right next to the cobbled road. Even elsewhere gun positions have been prepared with wire netting into which twigs had been woven.

At Dalle's unloading quay I can see even more material than ever before. I notice that several more houses have disappeared: in Kerkstraat, the houses of Constant Ryckaert and René Van Ackere, and the *De Swaene* inn, so that only one house remains in this entire street. It belongs to baker Coene, but is in such a state that pulling it down is the only sensible possibility. What remained of the presbytery has been blasted down with dynamite, and they are now removing the rubble. At the dairy Constant Vandenbussche's three-family house has disappeared. Of Klein Brussel nothing remains. Perdieu's house is likewise gone. Everything has been pulled down by the soldiers. In the cemetery I can see 4 big holes. More damage also to our church tower. A shell has struck it below the level of the bells, blasting off the two south turrets. A 2nd has hit it a bit lower down at the level of the gutters, likewise on the south side. An English officer I met at Noyelle's house told me that the bells were still hanging intact in the tower. He was at that spot yesterday, because they have an observation post in the tower. And indeed, I had observed telegraph wires that led to the tower. It's a pity that there's no way of lowering the bells. It's impossible because such work cannot be done by night, and by day one is too visible to the enemy. After that I go to Doom's farm. It's in a terrible state, just one hole after another. There's not a single spot the size of a normal house without craters. And this over an area of more than 3 acres. It's hard to believe that the inhabitants are still living there. Even a sick old man. Their house is dearer to them than their lives. I find Alderman Doom on his deathbed, but he still recognises me. I read some of the prayers for the dying, and hurry back to high mass, but too late for my little sermon. At Cafmeyer's farm I see some new guns. At Comyn's farm I notice the new railway, which is narrower than the usual one, coming from Ouderdom, veering off to the left of the mill and Henri Desmarets' farm, then alongside Oude Wal splitting into 3 branches, one next to Amand Heugebaert's wood, one next to Planckeel's wood, and one further on alongside the big railway beyond the lake towards Voormezeele. This railway is for the supplies of the guns, and munition trains keep coming in constantly. How our Dickebusch has changed! It makes one's heart sink. No one asked for my permit and I wasn't troubled by the shelling.

After high mass I baptise the 3rd war child of farmer Arthur Deraedt. On leaving the barn I see a German aeroplane fly straight towards the English observation balloon at Ouderdom. It isn't even 100 metres above the ground. English artillery and machine guns are shooting like mad. The German likewise uses his machine gun. At any moment I expect to see the balloon on fire, or the German aeroplane crash. Neither of these happens. Soon I see the men descend by parachute, the balloon is pulled down, and the German manages to slip away, still flying low as before. The balloon men land alongside the stream between Ouderdom and the village, having first scraped through the barbed wire with their parachutes. Two Belgian soldiers who were first on the spot and helped the men were given a 5 francs tip each.

23 April, Monday. At 5.30 I celebrate mass at Cyriel Lamerant's place and do my first round with the Easter Sacrament to the sick and ailing in *De Hert*: Widow Ghesquiere, Charles-Louis Charles, Widow Braem, Jules Spenninck and Widow Dewilde. A shell and two shrapnel shells explode in Cyriel Lamerant's fields just after I pass by. To get from *De Hert* to Widow Ghesquiere the shortest way is via *Het Zweerd*, but since the right hand side of the main road has been fenced off with wire netting, there's nowhere I can get through and I have to go through the centre of the village. Beyond *Lake House* there's rapid fire on an English battery. At the beginning of the war we had no inkling of the ferocity of that kind of bombardment. Shell follows shell without pause. For whoever is in that hell, there's no escape, at least 500 shells drop from 6.30 to 7.30, and all of this on an area of no more than half an acre. They know for certain that they'll hit guns and kill men. And to think that such shelling is now a daily occurrence! I notice that the English cemetery is now full. It's being widened by a few metres on the Kemmel side. On the farm of Widow Alouis Ghesquiere I can see 5 guns that have been firing for a few days already. That Rose Ghesquiere is not too pleased with these guns, is clear from what she tells me. 'At the first shot,' she says, the little statue of Our Lady that was hanging in the tree was flung off and fell to the ground in pieces. I couldn't stand such blasphemy and I said: 'If I were the Blessed Virgin I would make their guns sink into the ground,' and lo and behold, my prayer was heard. Their gun has sunk twice already, and they had to dig it out again. But they have no idea that I'm behind this.' At De Razelput a shrapnel shell explodes just after I've passed the spot. I notice that guns have already been positioned around Charles-Louis Charles, and in the hedges around Vijf Geboden, Braems, Adriaen and Hallebast. From there, to La Clytte and with the parish priest and curate of Reninghelst we drive to Poperinghe, get the holy ointment from the Dean, and have a meal in the secondary school. There news reaches us that this morning in the areas of Proven, Watou and a part of Poperinghe, asphyxiating gas was smelt. Later on we hear that it has blown over from Nieuport, where the Germans carried out a gas attack on the French.

In the morning the village is shelled, and 3 shells are dropped on the church and 1 on Noyelle's house. 2 shells also in Ouderdom at Delporte's railway station.

An eerie event took place this afternoon on Doom's farm. Alderman Doom died yesterday a couple of hours after my visit, and now his farm has been shelled with rapid fire, just as fiercely as I witnessed this morning at *Lake House*. A shell fell on the house and Doom's corpse was flung onto the ground and buried under the rubble. The old man had died just in time to escape being killed by the shelling.

24 April, Tuesday. A lot of firing last night. It's a clear sky and the aeroplanes are in the air early. A painful accident happened in Locre. At 6.15 a.m. a German aeroplane was gliding above the village when it was targeted by the English. Unfortunately, a shrapnel shell that failed to explode in the air fell back down on the house of Mr Cuvelier, the sexton, schoolteacher and secretary. The good man was still in bed and his legs were ripped off. The shell exploded in the kitchen and wounded the daughter as well. Master Cuvelier lived for another hour or two and died in the Bailleul hospital. At 8 a.m. I conduct Alderman Doom's funeral. The mayor and 3 members of the council are present. The daughter and granddaughter have to attend in their weekday clothes, their other clothes being in shreds because of the bombardment.

In the morning an English battery near Remi Lamerant's farm is heavily bombarded. Later on a shell drops between the farms of Delanotte and Deraedt.

There's an explosion in the boys' school in Reninghelst.

A boy called Belpaire, a refugee from Voormezeele, was poking into a little tube he had found on the side of the street. Suddenly a blast and the boy lost 4 fingers. In an instant all the boys were running around on the street crying.

On Saturday there was a farmers' meeting in Poperinghe as a protest against the unreasonable taxes. Slanderous letters appear in the *Vingtième Siècle* against the farmers in unoccupied Belgium.

Fertilizers are extraordinarily expensive. The mayor paid 90 francs a kilo for his sulphate and 81 for his salt.[23]

Since Low Sunday a new tariff has appeared for the innkeepers. The glasses must be of a certain size. Ordinary beer can still be sold at 10 cents a glass. Special at 15 cents. Stout 80 cents a litre. At the brewery we now pay 22 cents for half a barrel of special, its quality being no better than that of ordinary beer before the war – quite the contrary. The brewer now pays 120 francs for his malt. These measures cause a lot of discontent among innkeepers, and all agree to close their inn on a fixed date. But come the day most of them carry on serving beer, allegedly because the barrel wasn't empty yet, or because a neighbour continued to serve customers, and soon all the inns are open again. Nevertheless, the innkeepers claim that they cannot make a profit anymore, and that it's all out of love for the soldiers. But even though not much stout or English beer is sold any more, they sell as much ordinary beer as they can get, and the brewer can by no means keep up with the demand. In addition, quite a lot of sweet wine is served in the inns. One can now get an idea of how much the innkeepers must have earned earlier on, when the prices they could charge

---

23 'Salt' ('zout' in Van Walleghem's dialect) was the term used for a nitrogen-based fertilizer that had immediate effect on the growth of crops. Its drawback was that the crops might grow too fast and become less productive.

were higher or unrestricted, and the purchase price from the brewery considerably lower. Ordinary innkeepers mention a profit of 50,000 francs, and people who needed assistance before the war can now afford to send their children to a secondary school.

25 April, Wednesday. A lot of shooting all night. It's an English artillery attack on the Hooge to Saint Eloi front. I take the Easter Sacrament to 4 old people and celebrate mass on the Feast of Saint Mark in the barn. 35 attend the service. More and more we expect the English offensive here on our Ypres front. They say it's imminent. Together with the curate I pay a visit to Private Van Steelandt, of Stukje, who was a prisoner of war in Germany but has escaped from there. The lad tells us of his adventures, which are fascinating. Now he has been given a month's leave.

At 9.30 p.m. Henri Lamerant's barns go up in flames. There's not the slightest doubt that the fire was caused by the carelessness of the soldiers. On the farm there were 2 aircraft guns and a part of their ammunition was in the barn. They used another part of the premises to sleep in and keep house. Several times already Henri had complained about the carelessness of the soldiers and even extinguished the beginning of a fire. He had even filed a complaint with the police, but it didn't help. This evening huge flames suddenly shot out of the small barn. It was clearly too late to try to put them out. What was now most urgent was to protect the house and the big barn, and to salvage whatever one could from the small barn. Alas, none of this was possible. The fire had reached the ammunition, and the shells were exploding one after another. Neither civilians nor soldiers could do anything but run away from the fire. The only exception was that some civilians, at risk to their lives, managed to drag the big wagon with several boxes on it out of the big barn. The house was spared, but the big barn fared worse. It caught fire quickly, probably because of the explosion of the ammunition. The damage was immense. 4,000 sheaves of unthreshed wheat and oats, the carriage etc., and the belongings of 5 refugees, Widow Mahieu, farmer Van Steelandt, Jules Devos, the mayor, as well as three ladders and the baptismal font of our church. I apply for compensation and estimate the ladders at 102 and the font at 380 francs.

26 April, Thursday. Took the Easter Sacrament to 6 old people. Heavy bombardment around Hemelrijk. The commander of the 2nd battery of Belgians has moved with his officers from Camiel Ollevier's house to Jules Verschelde's farm.

27 April, Friday. A calm day. Across Pieter Cambron's farm there are already 4 railway tracks towards Westoutre.

28 April, Saturday. With the curate I go to Locre to Mr Cuvelier's funeral, which is attended by a lot of people. A calm day.

29 April, Sunday. It's the first summery day of the entire year. Until now everything has still felt like winter, without the slightest bit of green. At 3 p.m. shells fall along the railway. It's worst between the cobbled road from the village square to Ouderdom, and the gravel road from the square to *Het Prinsenhof*. But also on the other side of these roads. The shells are fired from Wytschaete. The bombardment is very heavy. They are fast flyers that make little noise when they explode but make very big holes. By 5.30 p.m. more than 160 had been counted already. The barn of the Deryckes is pierced on the side of the cobbled road, and also the façade of the Barroo house near Widow Steen's farm. The nearest one fell only 7 minutes' walk from Reninghelst church. At 7.30 p.m. the shelling starts again, this time on Stukje, between Kasteelmolen and the La Clytte road. 15 of the fellows are sent our way from around Boesinghe. How strange, these shellings: on Stukje from Boesinghe and at the railway from Wytschaete. If the bombardments had taken place at the same time, the shells would have crossed each other!

Fritz was clearly bent on continuing his wickedness. At 9 p.m. he sends his cigars to the sawmill on the La Clytte road and smashes a hut there. And in the course of the night 3 separate bombardments at Delporte's unloading quay. These didn't last long, but there was no pause between the shells – about 30 in just a few minutes. The façade of Delporte's house was pierced. The inhabitants had a lucky escape. Thank God we need not mourn the death of any civilians in the course of this entire bombardment, and not even of any soldiers, as far as I have heard.

Apart from this bombardment, there was a lot of shelling on Reninghelst. News has reached us that south of Ypres the English made a raid and captured 18 prisoners of war.

We also hear that the 2ⁿᵈ Belgian group of the 13ᵗʰ artillery, which stayed in Dickebusch for nearly 2 years, has now arrived in Woesten and has thus been transferred to the Belgian front. The 1ˢᵗ group is still here.

30 April, Monday. The fear among the Reninghelst population because of yesterday's shelling is very great. This evening already the priest of Reninghelst is going to sleep at Mayaert's farm, 12 minutes to the north-west of the village square in Reninghelst. Some people from Ouderdom are likewise going to sleep elsewhere. 2 or 3 households of Ouderdom flee.

At 10 a.m. a German aeroplane that is flying above the square in Reninghelst is fired at, and the case of a shrapnel shell that has been fired falls through the roof and into schoolmaster De Canter's bed. Fortunately, the teacher had already fled from his nest, or else he would have undergone the same fate as his colleague in Locre. One might think that the Germans are targeting those in charge of the young. General Gilson, who has been staying in the curate's house for a few weeks, is leaving today and is coming to offer his thanks and say his farewells. This is worth mentioning because it's only the 2nd time that such a thing has happened. At 7 p.m. a big shell falls along the gravel road to Ouderdom.

1 May, Tuesday. Heavy gunfire practically all day. 2 aeroplanes that have been shot down pass by here on lorries, an English and a German one. The latter was shot down above Elverdinghe after a tenacious fight against 4 English ones. Chaplain Dumon, who was on the spot, gave the last rites to the dying pilot. The English pilot who had been shot down was unharmed.

Leroye, who lives across the lake, is leaving his farm at last. It's amazing how long those people have been able to stay there so close to the enemy. Admittedly, with the exception of the first week and the last few weeks, they haven't been shelled all that heavily, mainly thanks to the woods that more or less hide the farm. The man's purse must have grown considerably fatter over there. With him were evacuated another 30 families from Kemmel and 4 from Dickebusch. The Reninghelst tax collector has fled to the remotest corner of West Flanders. He holds office twice a week in Reninghelst. Ordinary leaves of absence for the Belgian military can no longer be applied for, but a lot of soldiers are at home on work leave. The entire left-hand side of Pastorijstraat is without officers at the moment. Some of the Dickebusch artillery has left, probably for the Somme. There too there are fewer soldiers. People are beginning to realize that the general offensive planned by the allies on the western front has failed. The English have had some modest success in Artois, but the French have done less well in Champagne. Some blame the lack of solid leadership, others talk about treason, but a very important reason is probably the strong resistance of the enemy. Because of the Russian lethargy that is the result of its internal difficulties, the Germans had nothing to fear on the Austrian front, which enabled them to transfer at will a large number of divisions from the eastern front to strengthen the ones in the west. It's a pity about Russia. Because of this, the offensive that was supposed to move forward on the rest of the front collapses as well. In Boesinghe the grenadiers and riflemen who were meant for the attack have been replaced by the 4th Division. This means we need to have patience again here for a while.

2 May, Wednesday. Every day, heavy shelling on Dickebusch. In the afternoon, shells on and around Cafmeyer's farm. Cafmeyer's farm labourer, Jules Perdieu, 67 years old, was in the loft binding hay when he was hit in the spine by a shrapnel bullet. The poor man was instantly paralysed in both legs and his situation was hopeless. After having been transported to Couthove hospital, the unfortunate man died of his wounds after 6 days of terrible suffering. He's the 21st civilian victim in Dickebusch.

In Poperinghe shells fall around the dairy.

3 May, Thursday. Beautiful weather already, for the entire week. Without any transition we move from deep winter to the heart of summer. Shells fall on the village in the morning, and in front of the local policeman's house 2 soldiers are killed. In the morning constant shelling between the farms of Widow Forceville and the mayor, near the 2nd Belgian battery.

In the afternoon near Celeste Planckeel's wood, where several soldiers are wounded. After my mass at Lamerant's farm we become aware of a faint smell of asphyxiating gas. In the laundry the women now need to do the washing with pure creosote, and this because of their eagerness to annihilate the charming little beasties that the English call the 'itchekos,'[24] which are teeming on the soldiers' underwear and couldn't be destroyed by the laundresses' previous heavy fire. Among the Belgian soldiers these little fellows seem to be more or less under control at the moment. On the door of Door D'Hellem's house someone has written 'Itchekos farm.' It's probably Belgian soldiers that have done this to keep the English out of that house and keep possession for themselves.

4 May, Friday. Towards evening 3 shells fall on the farms of Camiel Derycke and Verhaeghe-Cossey in Reninghelst. An accident happens on Achiel Vandermarliere's farm. Paul Fournier, the gravedigger of Comines Ten Brielen, who has taken refuge with Henri Depuydt, was working on the aforesaid farm. After their sandwich break at 4 p.m. he was smoking a pipe with 2 other men. Above them there was an English aeroplane that was being shot at by the Germans. A shrapnel shell that missed its target landed on a tree right next to them and exploded. One fragment hit Fournier's arm, which was sliced off almost literally. Immediately he was taken to Couthove hospital. There the arm was cleanly amputated and 2 months later Fournier was allowed to return to his friend Depuydt. What is most strange in this story is that Fournier

---

24 The Belgian scholar Tony R. De Bruyne points out that 'Hitchy Koo' was a popular song which was successful just before the war. It was written by L. Wolfe Gilbert, Lewis Muir and Maurice Abraham. It is to be assumed that the British soldiers jokingly referred to their lice as '(h)itchy koos' and that in fact it was the Belgian soldiers who rendered this as 'itchekos.'

did not feel the slightest pain – either when he was hit or when the arm was amputated.

5 May, Saturday. In the morning fairly calm. Around 4 p.m., heavy firing which lasts until 4 a.m. and becomes more and more frightening. A tremendous amount of heavy artillery. In the evening shells fall at Millekruisse, and later in the night again at Millekruisse and at the La Clytte unloading quay and on and around the hamlet. They come thick and fast. Jooske De Wilde's house is hit. In the first half of the night also a lot of shells on and around the farms of Planckeel and Marcel Coene, and the wood between them. 1 falls on Celeste Planckeel's house. Celeste and Henri Rubrecht, who were both in their bedrooms, remained unharmed, but Henri's wife, who had just got up, and her 4-year old child were both wounded. The child slightly, but the mother much worse. Her right thigh was blasted off and her entire right foot was in a terrible state. She was taken to Couthove the same night. The poor woman, a mother of 7, suffered terribly. At first the doctors were hoping to be able to heal her foot without amputation. Alas, after a few days they were forced to proceed to that painful intervention. The wound continued not to heal and for some time they even feared for her life. At last after 6 weeks came some improvement and after two months the healing was well on its way. This was the second accident to befall Celeste's house, and it is now totally destroyed and uninhabitable. The good young man is moving in with his friend Cyriel Lamerant.

6 May, Sunday. Unfortunately, another painful disaster was to take place in our parish last night. In the attic of *De Koevoet*, the men of the 3rd battery of the Belgians were sleeping, with among them Abbé Jan Coveliers, from the Malines seminary. Suddenly a shell exploded at the east side of the attic, where

Jan was lying. The result was terrible. The driver and the telephone operator killed instantly, Jan dying and 3 other soldiers wounded. Rev. Peeters, the chaplain, who has never had any sense of danger where his duty was concerned, and deserves more than one medal, was on the spot immediately and gave the good Abbé the last rites. It took more than an hour before they were able to transport the wounded, and this because they first had to find an English car, since the driver of the Belgian one had been killed. Mr Coveliers died on arrival at Couthove. One of the 3 others was wounded seriously but not fatally, and he too recovered. The other 2, one of whom was Vandenberghe, the student from Oost-Roosebeke, were wounded only lightly.

It was after high mass that the mayor came to tell me the sad news about 'Little Jan.' Following custom, mass was going to be celebrated at the mayor's farm, and the good man, who slept at the farm of his son Marcel, had gone over to his own farm with the sweet loaf that they always put aside for the breakfast of the chaplain and the Abbé. How shocked he was when he heard about the sad event. The Abbé was so much at home there, and the mayor told me how, when farm labour was scarce, Jan had asked the men of the 3rd battery to lend a helping hand. Throughout the entire Saturday afternoon the Abbé and 3 of his pals had planted potatoes. In the evening Lucie wanted to pay them. The Abbé refused saying 'I'd rather you gave my share to the brewer' (which was a nickname for one of the soldiers). I too was very moved when I heard the sad announcement. Rev. Coveliers was born and lived in Turnhout, and was the only son of a widow. After 2 years in the seminary he had only just been ordained a subdeacon when the war broke out, and he was now 24 years old. In February 1915 he had arrived at the Ypres front, first in Brielen, then in Vlamertinghe and Ypres, and then from

June 1915 to January 1916 near the Verschoore chateau, where he lived for several months in the beer cellar. After this he stayed at the farms of Cyriel Claeys and Theophiel Dauchy, and from 16 November onwards near the guns at Dickebusch lake dam. For more than a year Jan had been our good friend and was rarely absent from our fortnightly priests' meetings in La Clytte or Reninghelst. During his stay with Theophiel Dauchy he had breakfast every day after mass with the priest of La Clytte, and whilst smoking a pipe they discussed literature and other subjects of study. There Jan forgot time and place, and more than once I saw him arrive all sweaty at Cyriel Lamerant's farm, where he was expected to find the doctor for the medical report. He was a bright young man and a true Fleming: God-fearing, simple, calm, determined, brave and good company. Later on he would certainly have become a good priest. May he rest in peace. *De stem uit België*[25] has published the following beautiful article about him:

In memoriam Rev. Jan Coveliers

From a letter from the chaplain of Rev. Jan Coveliers, we have selected the following, an account of his last moments, an homage to his courage and self-sacrifice, by someone who witnessed his work from close at hand.

'I am still deeply affected by the painful shock I received last night. I had barely fallen asleep when I was woken up at half past midnight by a heavy bombardment, very near to our house, but which I understood to be in the immediate

25 *The Voice of Belgium (L'écho de Belgique/ De stem uit België)* was published in London and had articles in both French and (Flemish) Dutch. The text that follows here was published in French and is quoted in that language by Van Walleghem.

neighbourhood of the battery of Jan Coveliers, the stretcher-bearer and seminarist. Soon we received a telephone call that people had been wounded at the battery. I left with the doctor and soon learnt that the good 'Little Jan,' as he was called by his friends, was gravely injured. A shell had exploded above the garret where he slept with the driver, the telephone operator and several others. The operator and the driver had been killed instantly. Little Jan had had his legs crushed and two fingers torn off. Fortunately, a strong and very devoted fellow was there who had escaped as if by miracle. With some difficulty he managed to take Little Jan on his back and to descend, not without difficulty, the stairs that were covered with plaster and debris. Unfortunately, the rescuer had been unconscious himself for a few minutes and before tourniquets could be applied, Jan had lost a large quantity of blood. When the doctor and I arrived, all we could do was to hold death off for a few hours. While they tended his legs, he made his confession calmly, as he always did. I still encouraged him, but soon the pain became intolerable and he began to weaken. I gave him the last rites while he was fully conscious. Oh, he accepted God's will perfectly, and it was with joy that he received everything from the hand of the Master he loved so much. After an hour the shelling diminished. They picked Jan up together with the other wounded men. I was still able to give him a last absolution and a full indulgence *in articulo mortis* and then had to leave him. Jan died as he arrived at the hospital.

(…)

Even though he was 25 years younger than me, Jan was a companion and a helpmate to me. He was very straightforward and had a judgement of people and things that is rare in someone of his age. He always served at mass for me and received holy communion. He had a firm and clear vocation with zeal for souls and a sense of duty. His example and his good cheer made him loved by all, and his commander as well as his comrades have borne witness to this: "He was an admirable and brave man."

I have wanted to give you all these details because I owe this to the memory of a hero. Others have shown bravery with less modesty and with less clear-eyed reasoning as to their actions.'

One may add to this what Jozef Cos has written about his friend.

'Several witnesses have confirmed to me the exceptional courage that our friend showed, in spite of his severe pain. To his commander, who was trying to keep his spirits up, he replied that he knew very well he was going to die, but that this didn't discourage him, because "I die for the fatherland." These words were repeated with a lot of emotion by the commander who declared in the funeral speech yesterday that Jan Coveliers was "one of the regiment's greatest heroes."[26]

Coveliers was a man with a will of iron and a sharp intelligence, a seminarist with a deep and true piety, full of self-sacrifice, a stretcher-bearer who in the many highly dangerous situations in which the third battery so often found itself always did his duty fully, and often more than his duty. Little Jan or Jean, as his boys used to call him, was also loved and highly esteemed

---

26 In the original text the quotations in the last few lines appear in standard phrases in French: 'Je meurs pour la patrie' and 'une des gloires les plus pures du regiment.'

by all. His gunners and officers cannot sufficiently praise their sadly missed friend.'

That night Poperinghe was also shelled, mainly at Werf. In Kemmel the stables of the Dambre Brewery were set on fire. It was one of the most frightening nights of the war.

A lot of people from Millekruisse and La Clyttte are leaving.

After high mass I baptise a child of Cyriel Gontier born between Dickebusch and Vlamertinghe in the midst of the guns and under daily bombardments. Everything went well. But it was rather imprudent of the mother to carry on living at such a dangerous place under such circumstances. Alas, there was no way that she could be got away from her farm.

7 May, Monday. Another frightening night. The shelling was very heavy on La Clytte and Millekruisse. At La Clytte a shell falls on Benoit Tanghe's house. Another 1 falls in the grounds of the deanery. 1 fell just in front of the door of Verkest, the farmer, just one hour after the birth of a child. It's a miracle that no one was hurt. It seems that in the course of this dangerous night no fewer than 400 shells were dropped on La Clytte. Almost everyone is now fleeing, and only the parish priest and another 2 or 3 people stay and sleep in their houses. The staff of the army headquarters are fleeing to Scherpenberg. The shelling was also very heavy between the farms of Celeste Planckeel and De Potente, and shells fell on the farms of Marcel Coene and Lievens. In Poperinghe a lot of shells fell on Werf. Eyewitness accounts from the surrounding area tell us that for the last few days the bombardment has covered the entire region. Also Vlamertinghe, Kemmel and Neuve-Eglise are hit by shells. There are a lot of firebombs among them. In Millekruisse some bomb craters went on smoking for a whole day. What can be the meaning of this intense shelling? Do the

Germans fear an English offensive and want to prevent it, or are they preparing an offensive themselves? Nobody knows, but we fear the latter, while at the moment the English seem to have given up their plan for an attack on this part of the front in the immediate future.

I go with the curate to Poperinghe and in the military cemetery we notice 3 open graves ready for Mr Coveliers and his unfortunate companions.

8 May, Tuesday. Yesterday evening and last night the English launched 3 counter-attacks of half an hour each on the entire German front in this sector, and the area behind it, in order to revenge themselves for the daily heavy shelling by the Germans. All the guns of the entire area were active. The Germans fired a lot of shells towards Ouderdom, and in Widow Bernaert's meadow 6 soldiers and 11 horses were killed.

In the Church of Our Lady in Poperinghe the funeral took place of the 3 gunners that were killed. It started at 11 a.m. and was very beautiful and moving. A lot of officers and more than 100 soldiers were present. Count Dumonceau, the commander, did a very beautiful funeral speech, with a word of praise about each of them, but most of all about Coveliers. In the afternoon I went with the curate to La Clytte and found Father Cos there and 2 or 3 other friends, who were returning from the funeral. It was they who told us everything. The Dickebusch mayor likewise attended his friend's funeral. We were unable to because of a funeral in Reninghelst.

Commander Dumonceau, who gave the funeral address, was himself an example of courage, and never ran from danger, and before dying Mr Coveliers had praised him for his valour.

Father Higgins, chaplain of the 41st Division, is coming to lodge in the house of the curate.

9 May, Wednesday. A lot of violence again last night. Relative calm in the morning. In the evening, around 9.30, the Germans start an extremely heavy bombardment. The English don't fail to take up the challenge. For 1 ½ hours the firing is terrible. Later on we hear that the Germans penetrated into the English trenches and took some men captive.

In the afternoon I go to Couthove hospital to visit the wounded Dickebusch inhabitants. Jules Perdieu has just died. Paul Fournier is on the mend. Mrs Rubrecht is suffering a great deal. I notice that the wards are very hygienic and hear that the wounded are taken good care of there. Rev. Henri Callewaert, the curate of St. Martin's parish in Ypres, is the chaplain there.

During the shelling in Celeste Planckeel's place all the furniture was blasted to pieces, except for the crucifix that remained hanging in its place unharmed. The protestant officers who were staying on the farm were very moved by this occurrence and offered Celeste a lot of money for that cross. But to no avail, Celeste would not part with it at any price.

There are still Canadian and Australian troops in the area, nearly all of them engineers, but there aren't many of them.

10 May, Thursday. In the course of the night heavy firing again. In the morning shells fall between Dalle's farm and *De Hert*. In Dickebusch I hear more details about the last shellings. It was especially on Sunday and Monday that the centre of the village was heavily bombarded. Several more of the best houses were shelled, among them those of Thevelin, Goderis, Noyelle, Delforsche, Opsomer, Theophiel Debaene, Delanotte, Leeuwerck, and also the *De Lustige Boer* inn. The English chaplain Father MacHavy of the 41st Division intended to say mass in a house in the village centre. Everything was ready, but only one soldier was present. This made him decide to celebrate mass elsewhere, where there would be more soldiers. He had scarcely been gone from there for 10 minutes when the house was hit by a shell. The mayor told me that he had prepared a field of a bit more than an acre in front of *De Koevoet* in order to sow it in the next few days. He went and had a look at it yesterday, and counted no fewer than 48 shell holes. The children of the Vandepitte family of Het Hemelrijk have now, also, finally fled, and about time too.

In Reninghelst, in the course of the 7.30 mass, a German aeroplane was being shot at. In the church the priest was performing a churching and he was walking with the woman from her seat towards the altar, when suddenly the case of a shrapnel shell that had been fired at the aeroplane pierced the roof and landed on the chair that the woman had left only a few moments earlier, smashed it into matchwood and destroyed the flagstone underneath it. What a lucky escape!

11 May, Friday. A day of calm, which we are no longer used to. In the morning a German aeroplane drops five bombs at Werf in Poperinghe. My presence was requested at Henri Lamerant's farm, where there was an investigation of the fire (its causes and the damage that was done). I was given an opportunity there to improve my patience. I was told to be there by 10 a.m., but it was 1 p.m. by the time I was called to appear in front of the committee of investigation. The mayor and Jules Devos had to wait for yet another hour. The questioning of Henri and his wife took 3 hours altogether and was resumed several times. If the case had not been crystal clear, I believe the army would have got away with it, but there couldn't be any doubt at all and what was more, they were at fault in more than one respect. It was forbidden to have any ammunition or fuel in the buildings, and there was a large quantity of both. The fire had started 16 days before, and the wheat was still burning.

A new order has been issued stating that ordinary beer is to be sold at 15 cents a pint and 25 cents for 2 pints. The Belgian Official Gazette announces that the 2nd half of Class 18 must join the army on 1 July.

12 May, Saturday. This morning from 6 to 8, a heavy bombardment at the *De Hert* inn. The guns in the hedge of Goethals' meadow, as well as the inn and adjacent houses, were the target. Several soldiers were killed right next to their guns. 1 shell fell on the courtyard of *De Hert* and Prudence, Pé's wife, was hit by the fragments. She received deep flesh wounds on her arms, though they weren't life-threatening. They rushed her to Jules Ooghe's house, and scarcely had they gone 80 metres when another shell fell and the entire inn was destroyed. Prudence Van Elstlande was taken to hospital in Couthove and stayed there for 2 months. By the afternoon, they were already frying eggs for the soldiers again in the next house, which belongs to Arthur Dury, and in the shop, too, it was business as usual. In the afternoon the shelling was just as severe around the farms of Claeys and Doom. Arthur Cafmeyer was harrowing his land. His harrow was blasted to pieces and his horse remained unharmed.

13 May, Sunday. In the morning the Germans fire shells in various directions. A treacherous bombardment.

It's very hot today. We have had a whole unbroken fortnight of beautiful weather, and it's unbelievable how everything has grown.

Hector Coene protested about his rye field on which the English pitched their camp last winter. An officer of the claims committee had the nerve to answer him that he shouldn't have sown that early, and ought to have waited until the spring. In the end the officer suggested the following: 'Prepare your account, and we will pay you 1/12 per month.' In this manner, having been there for 4 months, they got off with paying a third of the damages.

14 May, Monday, 1ˢᵗ rogation day. 32 people attend mass at Cyriel Lamerant's place. Several shells drop on Hallebast. More troops than usual are at the line. At Ouderdom along the road to Vlamertinghe there's a lot of ammunition for heavy artillery. A Belgian observation balloon is shot down in West-Vleeteren. I climb on top of Mont Rouge and again see smoke coming from the factory chimneys in Armentières.

15 May, Tuesday. Last night 2 big guns were positioned, 1 at Paddebroek and 1 in front of St. Hubertus in the painted sheds that have been ready for more than a year.

Early in the morning already Fritz is throwing them around. First at *Het Zweerd*, then a bit closer to Reninghelst. On my way to Dickebusch I had a lucky escape. When I was close by Widow Derycke's farm, I saw a shell drop near the barrier of the railway just on the edge of the road, and when I reached that spot 7 minutes later another fell next to Mathilde Derycke's farm, at the very spot where I had been when the first one landed. In the course of my mass and immediately afterwards several others passed above the barn where the mass was being held and exploded near Ouderdom and at Theophiel Dochy's farm. In spite of the danger 37 people attended. Then, on Comyn's farm, the heaviest shelling started that I've ever seen. Between 8 and 10.30 a.m. no fewer than 600 shells exploded. It was the guns that had been placed in the hedge and the buildings that were targeted. It didn't stop for even a moment. The first shell hadn't exploded yet when you could already hear the next approaching. Several fell on the buildings, and at 8.30 a.m. the barn caught fire, and still we saw shells drop into the flames. 3 guns were blown to pieces and the colonel and 4 men were killed and 6 wounded. Almost the entire hedge was ripped out, and the next day Celeste Planckeel found several hawthorn bushes on his farm, which is at least 5 minutes from there.

With the dean of La Clytte and 3 other friends I go to Scherpenberg in the afternoon to see the scale model of Wytschaete in its current state. Behind the *De Zonne* inn, on the slope of the hill, on a scale of more or less 300 square rods, the whole of Wytschaete has been represented, everything in relief and exactly the way it has been observed by the aeroplanes. Some bricks show us the debris of the village, others point out where the farms are that have been shelled. One sees both the main and communication trenches, clearly delineated by cement borders, of which there's a very large number. Also a lot of stretches of barbed wire, and furthermore the streams, the main roads and smaller roads. Some little sticks and branches indicate the woods. One also sees a lot of small tags mentioning the name of the farm, trench or wood. In most cases these are in English and attributed by the English themselves. Those who know the area say that it's all very accurate. But when one sees this model, one has to admit that Wytschaete has become a genuine fortress and will be hard to capture. It's here that officers and soldiers come and study the place they need to conquer. They can walk around in it, and take a good look at it all. This is forbidden to civilians and we have to content ourselves with looking from the outside. However, this offers a fairly good view too. We were very satisfied with our walk. We hear that in Dranoutre the village of Messines has been represented in the same manner.

Again a lot of troops arrive in the area. On Cyriel Lamerant's farm 3 batteries have arrived and 2 at De Crock's. This raises our hope again that the English will soon launch an offensive here.

16 May, Wednesday. A calm night. In the course of the day shrapnel shells explode above Cyriel Gontier's farm. After my mass in Dickebusch I walk along the country road to Westoutre, to the funeral of Mrs Vanderhaeghe, the curate's mother. This road passes Kasteelmolen and goes on across the fields of Rozenhil, from there again through the fields and via Theophiel Dochy's place straight to Paddebroek. It leads to our cemetery and then in front of *De Hert* to the house of Angillis. This road is very practical in the summer and is for walkers, horses and carriages, but not for motor cars or lorries. It reduces traffic on other roads, and one is less in danger of being shelled on it. In Westoutre we pay a visit to the priest of Kemmel, who is living in the parish hall converted into a home.

17 May, Thursday. Ascension Day. Rain. A lot of firing in the night. In the morning the first group of Belgian artillery leaves after having stayed for more than 2 years in our region. They pulled their guns away the day before yesterday, and yesterday Father Cos and Chaplain Peeters came to say goodbye to us.

It's a pity that our friend Coveliers was taken from us when he too was about to leave with them. They are going to the training camp at Eu. A couple of months later we would hear that they had come back to the Belgian front. In all honesty it should be said that for the good morals of our area it is a good thing that the Belgians have left and will stay away for good. Especially the older soldiers among them were by no means shining examples, and what's more, when the same soldiers stay on the same spot for 2 years, quite a few among them get involved in a relationship, and the courting is often far from decent. A lot of young women, and even married women, in the area, were corrupted by the Belgian soldiers, though there were also soldiers who were corrupted by loose women.

The newspapers bring us more and more bad tidings from Russia. Such a pity!

18 May, Friday. A lot of firing in the course of the night. During the day a lot of new English observation balloons have been added in the area. There's a new one in Reninghelst above Durein's wood. On this front one sees an English balloon every 4 kilometres. The Germans have far fewer of them. A German one was shot at and went up in flames behind Wytschaete.

The soldiers are growing vegetables all around the place in their camps. Some of the gardens are very well kept. Others aren't. In Micmac camp, on Hector Coene's farm, they plant potatoes more than a foot deep in the ground and 10 days later they are surprised that they haven't surfaced yet.

19 May, Saturday. At 3 p.m. the Fritzes of Langemarck shell Dalle's farm and further on towards *De Hert*. A hut is blown to pieces next to Jan Plak's[27] oven shed. 'Not too much of a disaster,' Mrs Plak said to me the next day, 'they missed our shed,' and promptly put the shelling out of her head. At 6 p.m. shells on Theophiel Huyghe's farm, with one of them landing on the chicken coop, this time from Wytschaete.

I go for a walk to Mont Rouge and Scherpenberg. Access to the top of Scherpenberg is forbidden, but not to the area a bit lower down the hill. There was a bright sky and I had a clear view of the German lines. I saw that the German trenches were constantly being shelled by the English. The whole place consisted of bare and dead land with a lot of smoking shell holes. From their side the Germans were shelling the farm of Henri Goudeseune from Kemmel. I encounter civilians from Dickebusch who are returning from their work behind

---

27 Jan Plak is the nickname of Jan Gotenaere (see 27 February).

107

the village of Wulverghem, less than 2 kilometres from the German line.

20 May, Sunday. 67 people in the first mass, 100 at high mass. I notice that ammunition has been stacked next to Benjamin Haelewyn's house. This means we can soon expect the guns in Baes's little wood in the positions that were prepared last summer.

Near Leroye's farm the English had taken over the position of the 1st battery of the Belgians. Around noon, from his farm, the mayor saw that the men were playing football in the open field, without the slightest forethought. On the basis of his past experience he said to his wife: 'It won't be long before we see things happening at Pé Leroye's, and the Belgians will be called spies again.' Alas, it took less than an hour before the English had to pay a heavy price for being as stupid as asses. The shells rained down on the English batteries, and several men, more than 20 in fact, were wounded. When at last will they stop being so arrogant! The same afternoon, shells at Millekruisse, at Theophiel Huyghe's farm, and again at Dalle's, where the batteries and the ammunition dump exploded, a terrible crump that shook us in Reninghelst.

I do a tally of the civilian population in Dickebusch and count 208 civilians who are still living in their own houses, 63 from Dickebusch who have left their homes but stayed in their village, and 67 refugees from elsewhere, making a total of 338.

21 May, Monday. Last night large-scale movement here of heavy guns. Shells towards Boesinghe around Oudewal and the farms of Theophiel Huyghe and Cyriel Gontier. In the afternoon I go to the aid post of De Leene (Lijssenthoek). It has become even bigger since last year, with flower and vegetable beds on all sides. At the cemetery at least 3,800 soldiers[28] have already been buried. 1 hole serves as a grave for 2 soldiers.

The chaplain who is staying here is an impetuous Irishman, Father Higgins, the kind of fellow who by his boisterousness does more harm to his own cause than good. For the rest, he makes life very easy for himself and begins his mass half an hour before 12. As regards his zeal he very much resembles his predecessor, Father Bull, who was excessively English. A remark we are entitled to make after 2 ½ years is that the English chaplains are by no means as hard-working as our Flemish priests, or the French chaplains. There are, however, some exceptions. Some are exemplary, such as the Redemptorists O'Connor, Aherne and Bowes; the Jesuits Gill and Tighe; and Father Daniel of the Canadians. But these are and remain exceptions. We didn't have a high opinion of the English clergy before the war, and it's even lower now. As a rule, the Irish are hardly any better. They cancel their mass more readily than our priests their rosary. One has to admit, however, that here in Reninghelst the nagging of our priest is partly to blame. He keeps moaning about the wine and candles they are using and all their other expenses, but forgets that he collects at least 50 francs each Sunday in the mass for the soldiers. And yet in most cases the English chaplains are fairly good-natured. Some are even agreeable to deal with, but quite a few are too bold and unembarrassed to pass as polite. Amongst themselves they are not very well-organised and they don't plan ahead much. As regards courage there are huge differences between them. Most of them are truly brave, whilst some are more frightened than the civilians, so that in some cases I wonder: 'How on earth

---

28 According to the Commonwealth War Graves Commission, in Lijssenthoek Cemetery 3,339 soldiers are buried who died before 21 May 1917. Van Walleghem's estimate comes close to the actual figure.

did that fellow become a chaplain?' There are also several priests here who are at the same time interpreters. Most of them are missionaries or teachers of English from French secondary schools. They also have very different ranks. Most of the chaplains have portable altars, and mass has been said in each and every corner of the village.

22 May, Tuesday. I bury little Margriet Braem in our war cemetery. More and more one sees preparations for the imminent attack on the Wytschaete front. Behind the front, along the main roads, one can see the guns on every side ready to take positions within the next few nights. There are also a lot of new camps. Commander in Chief Douglas Haig was in Reninghelst today. German shells fall on Poperinghe today in the neighbourhood of Vogeltje.

23 May, Wednesday. Last night again large-scale movements of artillery that is being taken to the front. I go to Poperinghe in the afternoon. While I'm in the house of Mr Nollet, the schoolmaster, in Statiestraat, the town is shelled. In Dickebusch 3 English aeroplanes are shot down today. It rarely happens that we see a German one being shot down. And yet the official English statements claim that the Germans are losing more aeroplanes than they are.

24 May, Thursday. On my way to Dickebusch I notice that a lot more field artillery has been added around the farms of Henri Lamerant, Charles Cannaert and Cyriel Onraet. Their guns haven't been positioned yet. 1 big gun has been installed at Baes's little wood. They say that tanks have arrived already and are standing in special shelters – huts with covering on top – on Cyriel Jacob's fields at Ouderdom. They are making new water reservoirs all the time. It seems that all the railways are now ready. At the office of the camp commander an order is on display telling the English soldiers to avoid doing needless damage to the crops of French farmers, bearing in mind the scarcity of provisions and the sacrifices made by France for the war. No mention of Belgian crops and Belgian sacrifices. Do these people know that they are in Belgium here, or has Belgium been abolished already?

25 May, Friday. In the night and the morning once again shells on Poperinghe, a lot of them, and very big ones. 2 of them land on the chapel of the secondary school, most of the others fall on the parish of Our Lady. A curate tells me that these recent bombardments have caused considerable damage, in the school alone to an amount of 25,000 francs. Last night a lot more artillery arrived on the sown fields of Cambron, Spenninck and the Verhaeghes. Cambron's farm has a surface of more than 90 acres, and he cannot use more than 15 of them, all the rest being occupied by troops or having been transformed into railway. The people who notice all these preparations usually see the situation as much more dramatic than is necessary. A lot of them scare each other and are convinced that everything here will be levelled to the ground. For days on end one sees furniture being loaded and carted further away. In Reninghelst the most prominent people set this example and needless to say, the others follow. The parish priest is now loading his 8th lot and hasn't even got a bed to sleep in left in the house. The curate isn't moving anything at all, and I cannot disagree with him. In Dickebusch they find it hard to understand why people in Reninghelst go to so much trouble and spend so much, taking into account the costs for transport – 30 francs if you please for the journey both ways, with a light wagon and one horse, from Reninghelst to Rousbrugge – as well as the damage and wear and tear of the furniture, and on the

111

other hand seeing that the risk that the furniture will be hit by shells and damaged is so slight. I say to myself that if I had the money, I would gladly take over a 7% insurance on those pieces of furniture, whilst those that remove them don't get away with spending less than 15% of their worth.

Shells around the farms of Doom and Theophiel Huyghe. Douglas Haig in the Westoutre presbytery today. In the afternoon I go to Mont Rouge and see that the Germans are undergoing terrible shelling again.

26 May, Saturday. More and more guns are positioned in Dickebusch. In Baes's little wood there are 3 already (220 mm ones[29] with very long barrels), and their gunners are Australians. A lot of guns have also been placed around Hallebast, Vijf Geboden and all along the hedges of Charles-Louis Charles, a lot of them also at *De Hert*, Klein Brussel, Dalle, Planckeel, and Amand Heugebaert's wood. They cover the guns with iron netting with green ribbons woven into it, which makes it more difficult for the aeroplanes to spot them. Guns also on Jules Spenninck's farm. Most of these guns have been firing already. More tanks arrive at Ouderdom, but only by night and well hidden, so that nobody can see them. On Alouis Adriaen's farm and Drie Goen negroes have arrived from Jamaica in the West Indies to work. They are dressed like the English, are civilised and speak with a soft voice, but are not very welcome because of their light fingers, and the civilians prefer to see their heels rather than their toes, for when they go into somewhere for a cup of coffee, they may very well sit there for a couple of hours rather than 5 minutes. I have found a letter of one of those negroes written to him by his mother. Such honest and

---

29 This is a French format. Van Walleghem is probably referring to 8 or 9.2 inch guns.

112

Christian motherly feelings! Not one of our own mothers would speak more aptly.

The negroes are extremely frightened of the firing. They have a timorous and savage stare in their eyes when they hear a shell approaching and if it drops rather close, they flee like madmen. There are railways on the other side of the lake and in daylight the train travels up to Madame De Gheus's chateau (Elzenwalle), which is 1 ½ kilometres from the Germans. It's an engine without smoke, which is nevertheless sometimes seen by the Germans. They aim at it from time to time, but that doesn't prevent them from carrying on with their work. On the other side of the lake there's ammunition everywhere, all of it stacked in small heaps, just like the dung from the stables when it has been distributed over the fields. In Dickebusch a lot of meadows and cultivated fields are occupied, whilst many abandoned fields that lie next to them are left alone. But no one gives this any thought.

The security service is very suspicious about the doings and conversations of civilians and soldiers. One has to be very careful about what one says. Everywhere agents of the Poperinghe Intelligence Office are walking around nosing into everything and eavesdropping on everyone, most of the time dressed as simple soldiers. Sometimes they mix among the civilians and soldiers, covered in mud as though they are men from the trenches, or they enter an inn or another house to order a beer or a cup of coffee, and try to sound people out. They all understand French and quite a lot of them Flemish, which means that people have to be on their guard. The secondary school of Poperinghe has moved to different premises again because of the danger, and the lessons have been resumed.

27 May, Sunday. Whit Sunday. 43 communions. From 5 to 7 a.m. Alouis Adriaen's farm is shelled terribly. 2 shells fall on the cowshed and 1 on the house. The inhabitants have a lucky escape. When the shell landed on the house they were in the cellar and got off with just a bit of smashed masonry, and when the others landed on the shed the animals had just fled to Hallebast. The negroes who were billeted there fared worse. 4 were killed and 3 wounded. The iron fragments flew as far as De Canada.[30] How that farm was changed by a single bombardment! A lot of shells also around the farms of Claeys, Theophiel Huyghe and Doom. Whilst I'm saying my masses the Oudewal guns are firing furiously. Between the masses I went for a walk. I was between the farms of Marcel Coene and Henri Desmarets, when all of a sudden I saw a column of thick smoke billowing into the air from Celeste Planckeel's wood. I didn't have the time to guess what it was before I heard a terrible blast. It was an ammunition dump going up. The shock was so enormous that in Reninghelst people thought that it was a shell landing within a few metres of where they were. A few days later I went to Abeele and people there talked to me about that shock, which had upset everyone. In Westoutre a painful accident happened, a stray anti-aircraft shrapnel shell landed and exploded near the road in front of the mayor's house. 3 people on their way to high mass were seriously wounded, 2 of whom died the next day – one a man from Locre and the other a refugee from Wytschaete. In the evening shells from Boesinghe. An ammunition dump explodes near Hector Dalle's farm, a shell lands on the shed of Omer Verraest of Vlamertinghe. A lot of firing all afternoon. At noon we receive a visit in the curate's house from Major O'Riordan, a grandnephew of Daniel O'Connell, the great Irish leader.

---

30 'De Canada' is a hamlet of Dickebusch.

28 May, Whit Monday. 13 communions. Yesterday at 9 p.m. the Germans started an extremely heavy artillery attack. Its intensity is truly unprecedented. Shells on all sides, around Leroye, Het Hemelrijk, Amand Heugebaert, Dickebusch village centre, La Clytte, Charles Maes, 3 Goen (Reninghelst), Dranoutre, up to half way through Bailleul, Lindegoed and a lot of other places. What a deafening noise! Around 2 the gas alarm is sounded (both bells and horn) and indeed gas shells rained down in some places. In the Scottish Wood a lot of soldiers were poisoned, and on Cafmeyer's farm soldiers were killed by gas. Not until 4 a.m. did the roaring of the guns begin to quieten. Such a terrible night. Nevertheless, we are glad to hear that the German attack has failed. The English have even taken some prisoners of war. About 30 Germans passed through Kemmel. In Reninghelst around 4 a.m. a very large shell landed 5 minutes' walk to the north of the village, near Dehouck's farm. This tells us that the Germans expect an English offensive, and want to disrupt the plans of the allies by their attacks. That's why we think the sooner the English start their offensive the better, provided of course that they are ready for it.

Several large sawmills have been started up in the area. There has been one for more than a year along the Poperinghe road, near Legache's farm; for 8 months at De Potente; for 7 months at Busseboom, and for a month on Vandenbussche's farm, on the La Clytte road. A lot of civilians, including women, are working in them. The English also buy a lot of trees in the area which are processed in them. Last year there was also a sawmill here near the village square in Cambron's meadow. Legache's sawmill will soon close its doors.

29 May, Tuesday. Yesterday evening around 9.30 the Germans start firing a lot of shells again, but they get even more back, and again the game continues all night. Shells and shrapnel on Dickebusch, Razelput, Micmac camp, Delporte and Ouderdom. In Westoutre there are also a lot of horses, unusually along the road to *De Volksvriend*. On the hill I see again how heavily the German lines are being bombarded. In the evening I see a lot more guns being added.

30 May, Wednesday. Again a lot of firing all night. The shelling is very heavy along the main road from Ouderdom to Hallebast, and also from Vlamertinghe to the *Café Français*. One can see that the principal aim of the Germans is to disrupt the transport. 1 shell falls on Behaegel's cowshed in Ouderdom. 1 soldier is killed behind the house of Widow Vermeulen, 1 at Marie Baeke's house and 4 in front of August Hennin's house in St. Hubertus.

In the curate's house, where there haven't been any officers for almost a month, 3 colonels of the 24th Division have arrived.

31 May, Thursday. Again a terrible bombardment on the transport. Last night most of all around Warande and along the cobbled road to the *Café Français*. It was terrible around *De Zorgvliet*. Mrs Jules Goethals, who lives there, tells the story of how they fled in the night, and how when they came back in the morning, their inn was full of blood, with several dead bodies of soldiers lying around their buildings. In the afternoon they were still lying there, from *De Zorgvliet* to *De Groene Jager*, 3 minutes further away. 13 dead horses there as well, and 30 from there to the *Café Français*. This evening they are going to change the hour of the transport, to deceive the Germans. Ammunition will also be transported without wagons. Each horse will carry 8 shells. That will make it no longer necessary to come to a halt in order to unharness dead or wounded horses, and in the event of shelling it will be possible to carry on through smaller roads or fields. Last night Dranoutre was likewise shelled heavily. In the morning several shells land on the territory of Meteren, more than 15 kilometres from the front. These were very big (380 mm).[31]

I pass De Potente and see that several stables have been blown to pieces, and that some of the camps have been abandoned. Next to the centre of Dickebusch a large gun is smashed to pieces. At 9 p.m. an English balloon is shot at and goes up in flames. Constantly one sees people taking away their furniture and animals. In Ouderdom there are hardly any civilians who still stay there overnight. Before 8 a.m. all transport of civilians is forbidden, a measure that is hard to understand because that is precisely when there is least army transport.

1 June, Friday. Last night, shelling over Ouderdom and along as far as Schaapstal. At 3 o'clock we were shaken out of our sleep by the explosion of a munitions dump by the stream behind Henri Baes's place. When I was on my way to Dickebusch in the morning a shell exploded 50 paces from me in one of Henri Lamerant's corn fields. During my mass, more shells in the same place.

After my mass I go to the day of prayer at La Clytte. At Hallebast I notice 3 Belgian soldiers from the requisitions guard who had been set to checking the traffic. One of them was Wyckhuise from Pitthem.[32] The day of prayer at La Clytte went relatively well; there were some communicants, though not many people in the mass and at vespers, which is understandable given the fact that because of the dangerous situation here a lot of people have fled. For the 3rd time since the beginning of the war Father Serruys of Poperinghe comes

---

31 This is the famous gun the Germans called 'Langer Max.'
32 Pitthem is the village that Van Walleghem comes from.

to preach and hear confession. All day we hear the guns thundering nearby. After lauds we go to the high ground next to August Verhaeghe's farm to have a look at the shelling. In the valley before us and on the slope of Kemmel Hill we see a hundred or so guns firing almost constantly. It is a continuous barrage of flashes and loud thumps and whizzings, and on Wytschaete and its surroundings where the shells explode, a very hell of smoke. But one gun particularly attracts our attention. It is a 380[33] with a fairly long barrel and it is on the slope, about 150 paces from us and a little to the right. We see how the men load the shell, then how the barrel goes up, a brief signal, and the men take a few steps back. The gun fires and for the first time I see clearly a shell go into the air. It looks like a bottle flying forwards at lightning speed; I can follow it for at least 2 to 3 kilometres, and by then it is perhaps 800 metres high. Yet all this takes just a moment, when you consider that the shell travels 800 metres per second. While we were there every 3 minutes saw another such customer sent up into the air. Whether Fritz is partial to these sorts of cigars I don't know. Meanwhile, the Germans were no timid lambs either and kept up a heavy bombardment of the area around the Dambre brewery.

In the morning a munitions dump on Pé Leroye's farm was set on fire by the guns and as a result the buildings caught fire and the whole farm burnt down. (It was the only farm across the lake that was still standing.) Shelling too on Bailleul, and in the afternoon on the farm of Arthur Desmarets (Hallebast). The observation balloon from Ouderdom has progressed as far as Henri Breyne's farm and sometimes even as far as Cyriel Lamerant's farm. The people here call such balloons 'pigs' or 'sausages.'

---

33 Probably a 15 inch howitzer.

2 June, Saturday. A lot of shelling in the first part of the night, in the second part not much. In the morning I go with Jules Maerten's cart to Abeele to take our silverware to safety there. I had some of the silverware with me at the curate's house in Reninghelst, the rest was hidden at Jules Maerten's. He had conscientiously looked after it for the whole war and is owed much gratitude. I judged it to be dangerous to leave it here with all the fighting that is expected because we couldn't tell what might happen. The sisters of Voormezeele, who were living in Abeele, willingly agreed to take care of it for a while. The most notable objects which we entrusted to them were the following: our 2 monstrances, our reliquaries, golden chalice with paten, silver chalice with paten, silver incense burner with boat, silver wreath of Our Lady with gold-work, silver cruets with platter, ciborium, ex-votos. When I arrived home, to my great pleasure I found my brother Joseph, who had come to spend several days' leave with us. On my way I saw an English airplane come down about 50 metres from me. The man was wounded very badly by a German bullet. The German positions at Wytschaete come under heavy shelling again. In the afternoon Hallebast and Kapelstraat are shelled from near Wytschaete and in the night shells coming from around Boesinghe fall at *De Hert*.

3 June, Sunday. A very violent night: 1 shell falls at Henri Breyne's farm next to the observation balloon. A lot of shells at the farm of Jules Lamote (La Clytte). At Kemmel the Wildemeersch farm is set on fire, near the Dambre brewery. Yesterday evening and early this morning shells land at the farm of the Verhaeghe siblings in Ouderdom. In the morning, many shells on Poperinghe (the parish of St. Jan), mostly in the fields. One shell falls on the house of Deausy, the farmer, and both mother and daughter are burnt to death under the rubble. At noon, Hallebast is shelled. At 6 o'clock in the evening 8 shells fall near the village square in Reninghelst and along as far as Pastorijstraat, then shelling at Ouderdom. No one is injured, but there is much terror.

I thought to see few people in my masses, given the increasing danger. How amazed I was to see the usual number present. Today for the first time I see a triplane. The English artillery was once again shelling fiercely the whole day and the sky above Wytschaete was nothing but one great cloud of smoke. 17 German prisoners of war pass through Westoutre.

It is unbelievable how many soldiers are stationed here in Reninghelst now. I estimate that there are not fewer than 45,000 men, and at least 15,000 horses. At least 250 motor cars and lorries go past the church every hour (except early in the morning). There is more bustle and commotion in the streets of Reninghelst now than there was in peacetime in the busiest streets of Brussels. No need to ask whether these are good times for innkeepers and shopkeepers! Every day, 3,000 horses go along the gravel road from Kasteelmolen to Pieter Cambron's farm, where they go to drink; 3,000 horses, three times a day, there and back, that makes 18,000 horses. That street has already been christened 'Horse Dung Street.' In Dickebusch now there are more guns smoking than there used to be chimneys.

4 June, Monday. Last night was less violent than usual, but the enemy nevertheless shelled the Ouderdom area, *Boerenhol* and St. Hubertus. 1 shell falls on Charles Breyne's house, which is now inhabited by Louis Ghys. The latter's wife is wounded in three places. Her injuries are quite serious, but not life-threatening. Her nephew Gaston Lesage, who happened to be there at the time, is also slightly injured. Mrs Ghys is taken to the hospital in Proven where she will have to stay for several weeks. In the morning at 9.30 Reninghelst village square is shelled. 5 shells explode in the meadows and gardens around it, 1 in the meadow behind the presbytery, 1 in the meadow in front of the mayor's house, 1 behind the dressing station at the boys' school. People are very frightened because everyone can see that the enemy is targeting the village square. Some people will seek more safety in the countryside. Poperinghe and La Clytte are also shelled.

In the afternoon with my brother Joseph I go up Mont Rouge to take a look at the bombardment of Wytschaete. It is more terrible than ever. There is nothing there but bare earth, fire and smoke. It is hard to imagine that there are still people living in that hell. The German positions must be near enough destroyed, yet the German artillery is not silenced and continues to pound Kemmel Hill and the English trenches, even though the English fire is at least 5 times heavier than that of the Germans. The flashes and the thuds come thick and fast. What a strange, cruel and in a way impressive spectacle it is when one stands on a hill and looks at that artillery battle raging just 2, 3 or 4 kilometres away, with even an occasional German shell whizzing over your head on its way to exploding in an English camp. Just as that time when at least 50 shells landed around the chateau of Mr Behaegel on the border between Locre and Bailleul: however dreadful it is, one could watch it for hours.

At 10 o'clock in the evening the shelling grows even heavier and it lasts more or less the whole night. It is so intense that we really think that the offensive is already fully underway. Shells fall at Drie Goen. Today's English communiqué reports 47 German prisoners taken at Wytschaete.

5 June, Tuesday. The English shelling is less fierce than yesterday. The Germans shell ferociously the whole morning around Hallebast, where the big guns are very numerous; they are all 220mm. 1 shell falls on the house of Charles-Louis Charles, who had only fled a few hours before. Another explodes in the wall of Charles-Louis Hoflack's house; he too had fled just a few days ago. Poperinghe is also shelled, mostly over the town but even as far out as 2 kilometres from Abeele. A lot of shells on Bailleul, too, an ammunition train is hit near the airfield and 14 wagons are blown up. The damage in the town is very great, almost every window has been blown out. The Germans have waited an incomprehensibly long time to turn their guns on Bailleul, but now it is getting its share too, and it is suffering terribly.

Several households from Dickebusch are obliged to vacate their homes temporarily, among them Widow Forceville and the mayor. I hear that during the night several tanks from Ouderdom have already left for the front, crossing the fields and streams in front of and behind Cyriel Lamerant's farm. Wherever those monsters pass everything is pushed into the ground as if into butter. We are expecting the attack any day. The English communiqué reports 1 German officer and 75 soldiers taken prisoner at Wytschaete. Every night the English make a raid.

6 June, Wednesday. In the evening and during the night there is again a very great deal of shelling. The Germans bombard the English batteries ferociously. In the night, German aeroplanes fly over Westoutre; they drop bombs next to Sulferberg, 2 land in a group of officers' horses and 55 of them are killed. There is also shelling in the night round La Clytte and round Drie Goen. For 2 nights already the nearest balloons have remained out through the night. In the morning, shelling on Locre and almost all day on Poperinghe. The horse of Widow Vermeulen from Dickebusch is killed by a shell in Poperinghe. In Emiel Gesquiere's farm yard, 4 artillery officers are killed by a single shell.

We hear from an officer this afternoon that the attack will take place early tomorrow at 3 o'clock. It was of course told us in all secrecy, which didn't prevent my hearing the story from several other people the same afternoon. The evening was fairly quiet: the calm before the storm.

7 June, Thursday, Corpus Christi. Full moon and a beautiful summer night. The first part of the night is fairly calm. I hear a few whistlers which explode around Achiel Jacob's farm in Ouderdom. I awoke a few minutes before 3 o'clock and my first thought of course was whether the attack would begin soon. My room was in a very good position to see the battle. It faced south-east and no houses and few trees interrupted the view of Wytschaete. I would be able to see part of the artillery battle from my bed.

It was just 3 o'clock and the first glimmers of dawn were appearing when all at once I saw the most enormous and also the most horrifyingly beautiful firework display that was ever set off in Flanders. It was extraordinarily intense above Wytschaete, a little less so on either side of it: a real volcano, it was as if the whole of the south-east was spewing out fire. There was no doubt that it was the mines of Wytschaete, Messines and Hill 60 which were exploding. It was a few seconds before we felt the shocks. This was a real earthquake which lasted a good minute. And meanwhile all the guns on the whole front (perhaps 1,000 in number) were firing. What hellish music, what a gruesome spectacle! Thousands of flashes and thuds per minute from the guns, under a rain of fire and the crashing of the explosions of shells and shrapnel. Ah, if it wasn't a slaughter of men, one would call it 'beautiful.' Yet one cannot resist looking at such a spectacle and would like to be even closer to it to get a better view. For us onlookers, it is nothing, but what must it be for the 100,000 men who are living and writhing in that lake of fire.[34]

When I got up I saw that there were already several sausage balloons in the air to observe the fighting and to spy on the enemy. The noise continued the same. Everything around me was shaking and trembling, but I finally managed to shave, though it took twice as much effort and twice as long as usual. At 5.30 I set off for Dickebusch, with the firing as heavy as ever. At Ouderdom I come across the first 2 German wounded who are going into Cyriel Jacob's first aid post. In the German prisoner of war camp at Hector Coene's farm I see 75 prisoners already. The Germans were not shelling the rear front much, but big shells nevertheless land around Theophiel Huyghe's farm and round Oudewal. There were 14 people in my mass; the altar shook throughout. After my mass I can already see that the attack is going well: on the cross-country route it is one long procession of horses making haste towards Dickebusch in order to haul the guns further forwards. The artillery which is on Henri Desmarets's farm is moving forwards to Monsieur Segard's chateau in Voormezeele. At least every fifteen minutes another group of prisoners of war arrives, usually 20 to 40 in number. I see few Red Cross vehicles with seriously injured English soldiers but I encounter several wagons with lightly injured English. At 8.30 the shelling begins to diminish and at 9.30 it is more or less over. At 8.30 the 3rd group of prisoners of war leaves the camp at Hector Coene's. It consists of 117 men. 2 other groups have already left, each of about 80 men, many of them with light injuries. The Germans are going in the direction of Westoutre. I got a good look at the Germans; on the whole, the ordinary soldiers didn't look sorry to have

---

34 The formulation of this apocalyptic event probably echoes the Book of Revelation 20, 14-15.

124

been taken prisoner, although some of their faces showed no emotions at all: one would have thought that they were used to being taken prisoner. The officers made a show of being aggrieved at being captured, but as to whether they really were, I have my doubts. They looked less tired and sick than some other German prisoners that I had seen in the past; however, it seems that they had only been in the trenches for a few hours. I saw one who opened a new little pot of honey and merrily dug into it. In the camp at Coene's farm they had to empty out their pockets and hand over all their papers. One officer refused, and kept refusing, and as punishment he was forced to kneel. How humiliating this was for him after all his swaggering. The Germans wear a grey helmet with a deep rim around it.

The observation balloons are tethered very close to one another. I can see them above the chapel, above Henri Lamerant's place, above Charles-Louis Cannaert's place and above Achiel Van Eecke's. At 9.30 we hear that Wytschaete and Messines have been taken. Later in the morning the Germans shell Micmac camp; the shells come from the direction of Warneton.

At 3 o'clock in the afternoon the shelling starts again, though not as intensely. After vespers we set off for Mont Rouge so that we would be able to take a look at the battleground from the hill. The whole of Wytschaete is bare earth and not the slightest trace of the village is to be seen. The guns of Dickebusch and Kemmel Hill are firing furiously; we see shrapnel shells exploding over Wytschaete and shells falling on St. Eloi. An observation balloon is already hovering above Kemmel Hill. Already 3 groups of prisoners of war have passed over Mont Rouge, each group consisting of about 400 men. We see another big group of them being brought into the camp at the *Volksvriend*. A brigadier general is also brought in. The man looks very cast down; we hear that he was much hated by his men, who are pleased to see him humiliated now.

Many prisoners of war made no secret of the fact that they were content to have done with the war. While we are there we hear that Oosttaverne, a hamlet half an hour's walk to the east of Wytschaete, has also been taken, and that prisoners of war already number 3,300.

At 7 o'clock in the evening the artillery fire once again becomes heavy for an hour, then diminishes somewhat in intensity, though it continues throughout the night. During the evening a good many tractors pass here, doubtless to be used to drag the heavy items further forward. Today we saw a lot of triplanes and from now on we shall see more and more of them.

The next day's communiqué reports that Messines was taken at 5 o'clock in the morning, after 1½ hours' fighting, Wytschaete at 11 o'clock and Oosttaverne at 3.30, and that there are 3,600 prisoners of war. All the objectives were achieved except for a small part at Zillebeke. The English losses are very few, fortunately, and far below all expectations. I understood this from the testimony of the chaplains, who said that they were not much called upon to deal with wounded men or with burials. In addition, we have seen very few Red Cross ambulances go by. This doesn't surprise me because I witnessed how superbly the artillery attack was prepared.

The most beautiful account that I have read of this battle, which the English and French call 'the battle of Messines,' is the article by Philip Gibbs in the *Daily Chronicle* of 8 June 1917, which I have translated as best I can below.[35]

[....] In the darkness queer monsters moved up close to our lines, many of them crawling singly over the battlefields under cover of woods and ruins. They were the Tanks, ready

---

35 Van Walleghem's translation is in fact largely accurate, with a few changes of format and the occasional error in translation. The text given here is the relevant portion of the original article by Gibbs.

to go into action on a great day of war, when their pilots and crews have helped by high courage to a great victory.

Last night all was ready. Men knowing the risks of it all – for no plans are certain in war – had a sense of oppression, strained by poignant anxiety. Many men's lives were on the hazard of all this.

The air was heavy, as though Nature itself were full of tragedy. A summer fog was thick over Flanders, and the sky was livid. Forked lightning rent the low clouds, and thunder broke with menacing rumblings. Rain fell sharply, and on the conservatory of a big Flemish house where officers bent over their maps and plans the raindrops beat noisily.

MUSIC IN THE DARKNESS.

But the storm passed and the night was calm and beautiful. Along the dark roads and down the leafy lanes columns of men were marching, and brass bands played them through the darkness. Guns and gun limber moved forward at a sharp pace. 'Lights out' rang the challenges of the sentries to the staff cars passing beyond the last village where any gleam was allowed, and nearer to the lines masses of men lay sleeping or resting in the fields before getting orders to go forward into the battle zone.

All through the night the sky was filled with vivid flashes of bursting shells and with steady hammerstrokes of guns and from an observation post looking across the shoulder of Kemmel Hill, straight to Wytschaete and the Messines Ridge, I watched this bombardment and waited for that moment when it should rise into a mad fury of gunfire before our men lying in these dark fields should stumble forward.

During those hours of waiting in the soft warm air of the night I thought of all I had heard of the position in front of us. 'It's a Gibraltar,' said an officer who was there in the early days of the war. 'The enemy will fight his hardest for the Messines Ridge,' said another officer, whose opinion has weight. 'He has stacks of guns against us.'

Such thought made one shiver, though the night was warm, so warm and moist that great wafts of scent came up from the earth and bushes. A full moon had risen, veiled by vapours until they drifted by and revealed all her pale light in a sky that was still faintly blue, with here and there a star. The moon through all her ages never looked down upon such fires of man-made hell as those which lashed out when the bombardment quickened. That was just before 3 o'clock. For two hours before that fires had been lighted in the German lines by British shell-fire – great rose-coloured smoke-clouds with hearts of flame – and all round the salient and the Messines Ridge our guns flashed redly as thy fired, and their shell-bursts scattered light against which the trees were etched sharply.

I could hear the rattle of gun wagons along the distant roads, and the tuff-tuff of an engine driving very close up to the firing lines, and above the great loudness of our gun-fire the savage whine of German shrapnel coming over in quick volleys. The drone of a night-flying aeroplane passed overhead. The sky lightened a little, and showed great black smudges like ink blots on blue silk cloth where our kite balloons rose in clusters to spy out the first news of the coming battle.

The cocks of Flanders crowed, and two heavy German shells roared over Kemmel Hill and burst somewhere in our lines. A third came, but before its explosion could be heard, all the noise there had been, all these separate sounds of guns and high explosives and shrapnel were swept up into the tornado of artillery which now began.

The signal for its beginning was the most terribly beautiful thing, the most diabolical splendour I have seen in war.

Out of the dark ridges of Messines and Wytschaete and that ill-famed Hill 60, for which many of our best have died, there gushed out and up enormous volumes of scarlet flame from the exploding mines and of earth and smoke, all lighted by the flame, spilling over into fountains of fierce colour, so that all the countryside was illumined by red light.

Where some of us stood watching, aghast and spellbound by this burning horror, the ground trembled and surged violently to and fro. Truly the earth quaked. A New Zealand boy who came back wounded spoke to me about his own sensations. 'I felt like being in an open boat on a rough sea. It rocked up and down this way and that.'

Thousands of British soldiers were rocked like that before they scrambled up and went forward to the German lines – forward beneath that tornado of shells which crashed over the enemy's ground with a wild prolonged tumult just as day broke, with crimson feathers unfolding in the eastern sky, and flights of airmen following other flights above our heroes.

GERMANS TAKEN BY SURPRISE.

Rockets rose from the German lines – distress signals flung up by men who still lived in that fire zone – white and red and green. They were calling to their gunners, warning them that the British were upon them. Their high lamps were burning as lost hopes in God or man, and then falling low and burning out.

Presently there were no more of them, but others which were ours in places which had been German. Smoke drifted across and mingled with the morning mist. One could see nothing, but a bank of fog thrust through with short stars of light.

The first definite news that I had was from German prisoners, who came down in batches, carrying our wounded when any help was needed for our own stretcher-bearers. They described how our men came close behind the barrage, some of them, by a kind of miracle, in advance of the barrage.

The Germans had not expected the attack for another two days, and last night were endeavouring to relieve some of their exhausted troops by new divisions, the 3rd Bavarians relieving the 24th Saxons and the 104th Infantry Reserve the 23rd Bavarians.

They lost heavily on the way up to the lines by our fire, and were then, after a few hours, attacked by our waves of infantry.

A GREAT VICTORY.

The story of this great battle and great victory – for it is really that – cannot be told in a few lines, and it is too soon yet to give exact details of the fighting. But from the reports that have now come in from all parts of the battle front it is good enough to know that everywhere our men have succeeded with astonishing rapidity, and that the plan of battle has been fulfilled almost to the letter and to the timetable.

The Anzac troops reached and captured Messines in an hour and 40 minutes after the moment of attack, in spite of heavy fighting in German trenches, where many of the enemy were killed. Irish troops, Nationalists and Ulster men, not divided in politics on the battlefield but vying with each other in courage and self-sacrifice, stormed their way up to Wytschaete, and after desperate resistance from the enemy captured all that is left of the famous White Chateau, which for years our soldiers have watched through hidden glasses as a far high place like the castle of a dream.

SALIENT WIPED OUT.

By mid-day our men were well down further slopes of the ridge, while our field batteries rushed up the ridge behind them to take up new positions. Further north along the shoulder of the Ypres salient our English troops advanced upon Battle Wood, south of Zillebeke, and now hold all but a small part of it.

I understand that the Germans are massing troops at Warneton and its neighbourhood, as though preparing a heavy counter-attack, and are shelling Messines Ridge with some violence.

For to-day at least, in spite of fierce fighting that must follow, our men have achieved a great victory, with light losses considering the severity of their task. The evil spell of the Ypres salient is broken. The salient itself is wiped out, and if we can hold the Messines Ridge, Ypres and its countryside will no longer exact that toll of death which for nearly three years has been a curse to us.

NEW ZEALANDERS HAPPY.

The roads and fields are under a glare of sunshine as I write, and down them, through the dust and fierce heat, come troops of German prisoners, exhausted and nerve-broken, but glad of life. And passing them come the walking wounded who attacked them in their tunnels at dawn to-day and conquered. The lightly wounded men are happy and proud of their victory.

'We New Zealanders can afford to be a little cocky,' said one of those bronzed fellows with eyes of cornflower blue. 'My word, I'm glad we had the luck.' He was wounded in the foot, but the man just hugged the news of victory. 'We shall be no end stuck up.' He said, and then he laughed in a simple way, and said, 'I'm glad New Zealand did so well, – that's natural. But they tell me the Irish were splendid, and the Australians could not be held back. It's good to have done the job, and I hope it will help on the sod.'

That New Zealander spoke the thought of thousands who have been fighting in this great battle. They have a right to be proud of themselves, for they have broken the curse of the salient and relieved it of its horror.

PHILIP GIBBS.

8 June, Friday. In the night the farm of Emiel Vandermarliere of La Clytte, near Millekruisse, entirely burns down. Once again thanks to the special understanding of the word 'careful' that the soldiers have. I notice that already one balloon has moved forward to above La Clytte and another to above Razelput. All day quite a lot of firing. Bailleul is shelled. In the afternoon I receive a visit from the chaplain Father Dumon, who had

132

returned from *Hollandsche Schuur*, the farm from where he had observed the battlefield. He describes the terrible destruction wrought by the English on the German trenches, the many still unburied corpses, and the unbearable stench hanging over the battleground. He heard our artillery firing heavily beyond Wytschaete. The Germans made little response. Our artillery is now where the German trenches were. A great deal of heavy artillery has already moved forward. The guns from *De Hert* and from Spenninck's farm are also already further forward.

Shells have fallen around Doom's farm. At 8.30 in the evening the Germans carry out a fierce counter-attack on a wide front, but heaviest around Klein Zillebeke and Messines. The ferocity of the guns is terrible, even though we are told that the artillery is no longer as near as it was. From some of them we still hear the shells shoot away, but only from a third of their original number. During the evening the Germans succeed briefly in taking Klein Zillebeke, but the English immediately launch a counter-attack and regain control of the hamlet.

Another 20 prisoners of war were captured in Wytschaete today, pulled from a cellar. The prisoners who passed through Reninghelst were mostly Saxons and Bavarians, with some Poles.[36]

9 June, Saturday. A fair amount of gunfire last night. In the morning little shooting, in the afternoon more, and in the evening quite a lot. We hear that the English are successful in fending off the counter-attacks, though a part of Zillebeke woods is not yet taken. The rumour is also doing the rounds that the Germans are still occupying ground up to St. Eloi. I have it on good authority that this is not true. The English communiqué today reports the spoils of the victory: 6,400

---

36 In 1900, there were approximately four million Poles in the German Empire.

prisoners of war, 132 officers and 21 guns, and all this thanks to the English 5th army under the command of General Plumer. 3 more prisoners of war pass through Reninghelst. The big prisoner of war camp is on Widow De Weerdt's farm, between Reninghelst and Poperinghe. From there this morning 45 wagons of prisoners leave for France. For a long time, I've been curious to know if the number of prisoners of war reported in the English communiqués is the true figure, and have wanted to put it to the test. Therefore, I have now tried by every means possible to find out approximately how many prisoners of war must have passed through the various villages and have come to the conclusion that the total must be near enough the same as the total stated in the communiqués. I conclude that the English communiqués are reliable.

10 June, Sunday. Quite a lot of firing in the night. In the early morning the Germans send shrapnel shells over to behind Razelput and during high mass to Marcel Coene's farm, probably aiming for the balloons. A fair number of people in the masses, in the high mass, however, rather fewer than usual. Between masses I go to the centre of the village. The guns have gone from *De Hert* and from the Onraet and Comyn farms. The guns behind Baes's farm and at Oudewal, the Planckeel farm, Commeerestraat and Vijf Geboden are still there and are firing hard above my head. The 60-pounder[37] from Dalle's farm left yesterday too. Our village is sadly changed since my last visit. The following houses have now joined the list of those that have been bombarded: the houses of Henri Dumortier, Henri Vermeulen, Henri D'hellens, Theophiel De Baene, Jules Noyelle, Justin Thevelin, Désiré Delanotte, Theophiel Leeuwerck, Maria Lauwyck, Jules Deraeve, Henri Van Damme, Désiré Van

---

37 Van Walleghem's text says '30er,' meaning a 30 kilo shell. We can assume this is a 60-pounder.

Achiel Van Walleghem as a young priest, photographed in Ypres, 1905.
(© In Flanders Fields Museum)

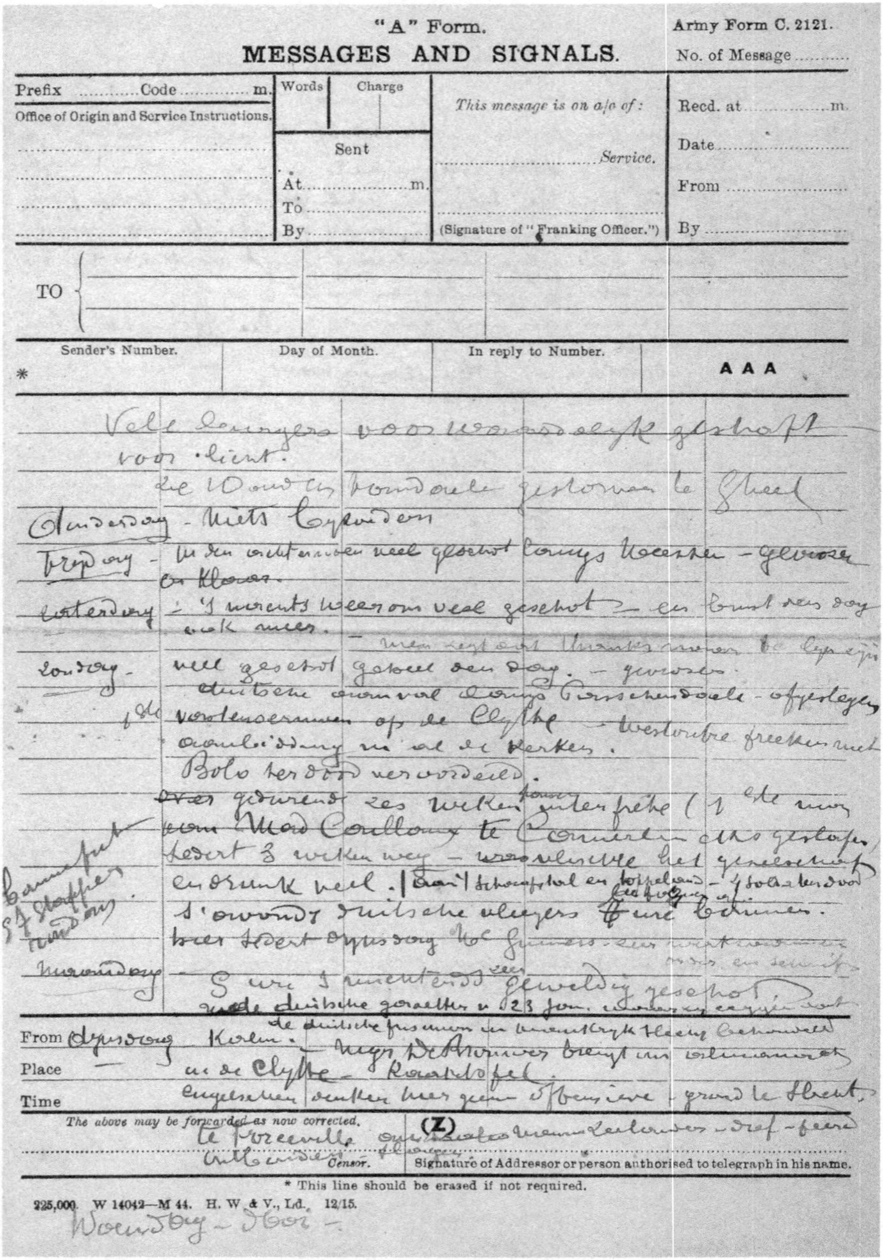
"A" Form.

MESSAGES AND SIGNALS.

Army Form C. 2121.

No. of Message ....

Prefix ....Code ....m.

Office of Origin and Service Instructions.

Words | Charge

Sent

At....................m.

To ....

By ....

This message is on a/c of:

..............................Service.

(Signature of "Franking Officer.")

Recd. at ....m.

Date ....

From ....

By ....

TO

Sender's Number. | Day of Month. | In reply to Number. | A A A

From

Place

Time

The above may be forwarded as now corrected.

(Z)

Censor.

Signature of Addressor or person authorised to telegraph in his name.

* This line should be erased if not required.

225,000. W 14042—M 44. H. W. & V., Ld. 12/15.

Van Walleghem's daily notes for February 1918, written on official British Army stationery. (© Archives of the Bishopric of Bruges)

The edited 'neat' version of the diary for the same period. (© In Flanders Fields Museum)

Achiel Van Walleghem with those members of his family living in unoccupied Belgium: his sister Hélène and his brothers Modest, Joseph and Remi. Vinckem, 9 Augustus 1916. (© In Flanders Fields Museum)

*Assisted by Germain Forceville, Achiel Van Walleghem celebrates mass in his temporary church in the barn of Cyriel Lamerant, 1916.
(© Germaine Forceville, Ieper)*

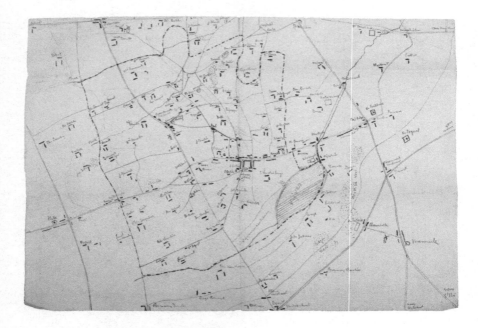

A map of the parish of Dickebusch and immediate surroundings, hand drawn by Achiel Van Walleghem, and indicating the farms and their owners. (© Archives of the Bishopric of Bruges)

A German aerial photograph of Dickebusch on 30 March 1916. The vast mass of Dickebusch Lake fills the bottom right-hand side of the photograph. The village itself is spread along the Bailleul-Ypres road with the church clearly visible to the south-west along the road towards Vierstraat and Wytschaete. (© In Flanders Fields Museum)

Dickebusch in June 1917: a YMCA canteen has been organised in the houses along the road from Ypres to Bailleul. (© Imperial War Museum)

The impact of the war on the landscape: a historical aerial photograph superimposed on today's landscape shows us the military installations in Melkerijstraat, north of Dickebusch. It includes an unloading quay. (© In Flanders Fields Museum)

A French officer in the remains of the church of Dickebusch, 1918.
(© Archives of the Bishopric of Bruges)

Members of the Chinese Labour Corps marching through Vlamertinghe.
(© In Flanders Fields Museum)

Reninghelst church seen from the ruins of the brewery, July 1919.
(© In Flanders Fields Museum)

A rare photograph of a British military laundry employing local women. To the right, two New Zealand soldiers.

In the neighbourhood of Dickebusch, September 1918. (© Imperial War Museum)

Renterghem, and the widower Francis Goethals. (The whole of Van Renterghem's house and a third of Goethals's were wiped out by a single shell.) The houses in best condition are those of Edward Lauwyck, Angillis, Leon Batteu, Maurits Devos, Benoit Leleu, and Mr Nollet (the schoolmaster), as well as the school, and then those of Bruno Van Wonterghem and Arthur Dumortier. However, of all these houses only one of them, that of Edward Lauwyck, could be restored at a cost of less than 1,000 francs.

Our church is in a dreadful state. More shells have fallen on the roof and one exploded in the wall next the altar of Saint Sebastian and has split the marble niche. Luckily our splendid central altar is still unharmed. On the altar I see a picture of Our Lady of Sorrows which I haven't seen before. It was probably placed there by the soldiers from Voormezeele or Ypres. I don't see any new shell holes in our churchyard. The English cemetery[38] in Justin Thevelin's meadow is full. I estimate that around 700 have been buried there. They are making a new cemetery[39] on the triangular field used by Jules Philippe, along the other side of the gravel road, and 25 soldiers have already been buried there. On and round about the village the soldiers are billeted only in houses and shelters. However, I see a lot of horses along the dam of the lake, and I notice that in the meadow in front of Monsieur Peirsegaele's brewery there are already a lot of tents where infantrymen are encamped. There is already a wide and very busy thoroughfare running through Thevelin's meadow and the lakeside marshes to Ridge Wood. At Hector Dalle's unloading quay I see more equipment than ever. At the dairy, where recently not a soul ventured, there is now a lot of hustle and bustle. There are a good many Red Cross motor cars and also 3 enormous shelters for the wounded.

---

38 Now Dickebusch New Military Cemetery.
39 Now Dickebusch New Military Cemetery Extension.

143

The people of Dickebusch are pleased about the good outcome and now think that they will have no more shells. The few who fled in recent days are quick to return. Some who fled earlier are already asking permission to return. But sadly the calvary of our people is not yet at an end. What bitter disappointments still await us? But in any case, the taking of Wytschaete is a very good thing for our village. Before that, the nearest Germans were just 37 minutes' walking distance from us, whereas now the distance is almost 7 kilometres. I reckon that the number of our civilian population has never fallen below 300.

All this afternoon there was a great deal of shelling. We hear that 1 officer and 40 soldiers were found in a celllar in Wytschaete today and taken prisoner. Both the soldiers and the officers say that there will probably be an attack to the north of Ypres and on the Belgian front. The Belgian communiqué, too, reports fiercer fighting and a lot of guns have been moved up to Vlamertinghe.

Here you can see a sketch of the current state of our church:

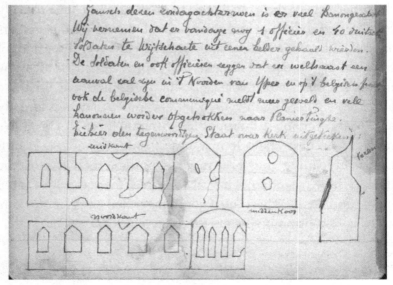

The Daily Mail says that in the battle of Wytschaete no less than 6,000 tonnes of explosive were used to blow up the mines (i.e. 6,000,000 kilos). The explosives consisted of one sixth ammonal and the rest dynamite and melinite. The digging, and the placing of the mines, had taken 20 months and was largely the work of Canadian engineers. There were 20 mines in Messines, Wytschaete and Hill 60. All of them went off successfully except one at Hill 60. Where the mines went off it was unbelievable how the ground was thrown out in all directions and ripped apart, and in a single moment hundreds of soldiers were buried under the eruption. They left appalling craters. An interpreter told me that at Spanbroekmolen one crater was so immeasurably huge that all 3 of the parish churches of Poperinghe could fit into it. I have heard others confirm this.

From questioning of the Germans it is understood that they did not know the time of the attack, although they expected it to come within the next two days.

In the battle of Wytschaete Major Redmond died. He was a member of the British parliament and brother of the Irish leader. He was 56. He was fatally wounded at Wytschaete and died a few hours later at Locre.

In such circumstances it is clearer than ever how impoverished the Protestant religion is, and how stark the work of its clergy. When a wounded Catholic is brought in, the Catholic chaplains give him the last rites if necessary; the Protestant chaplains do not know these sacraments and all they can do is offer their poor co-religionist a cigarette and promise that they will notify his wife or his parents of his death. Some of them try to ape the Catholics: so a Protestant chaplain was seen with a little bottle and a little brush, and all his wounded receive a little brushing. Father Brickford was in a dressing station not far from the Lille Gate[40] during

---

40 At Ypres.

the fighting, and he told me that at night, before he took a few short hours' rest, he asked a medical orderly: 'If wounded Catholic soldiers are brought in, please come and wake me.' The Protestant and the Presbyterian chaplains who were there heard this with consternation, but they didn't want to be outdone and very soon the Protestant made the same request of the orderly, and after him the Presbyterian.

The English newspapers say that the prime minister, Lloyd George, heard the sound of the explosion of the mines in Wytschaete in his home in London.

11 June, Monday. In the evening the enemy carries out a heavy attack; the shelling is exceptionally intense and lasts the whole night. It is worst around Zillebeke, but it is also heavy around Wytschaete and Messines. Fortunately, the English fought off the attack successfully. It seems that during their attack, the Irish came up against unexpectedly fierce resistance at 'Petit Bois,' 10 minutes' walk to the west of Wytschaete, a machine gun nest. The big guns were alerted and they sent over their costly cigars for an hour and a half, and when the Irish then went to look, it seems that there were still 3 or 4 Germans left alive there. It is said that there were Germans there who were tied to their machine guns to make it impossible for them to run away. The English soldiers are walking around with German helmets, weapons and all sorts of souvenirs. 'Come on Fritz' is the usual invitation from the English when they take a prisoner of war. When the English talk of going home on leave, it is 'to Blighty' or 'three Bs' (Bailleul, Boulogne, Blighty). It seems that 'Blighty' is an Indian word.

The prisoners of war who passed through La Clytte were mainly Prussians, and some Bavarians. They said that they had lost a great many men in the last bombardment. The

English communiqué says that on this stretch of the front line 100 German guns were blown to pieces by shells in the course of a few days. I can well believe this when I see how many English ones were shattered during the same days. A German prisoner of war who was brought into August Verhaege's farm at La Clytte said that he had lodged at that farm in October 1914.

12 June, Tuesday. Quite a lot of shooting in the night. We hear little news about the current fighting around Ypres. The German attacks are few now, and unsuccessful, but the English, too, make little progress. However, today's communiqué reports that the English have taken La Potterie farm at Messines.

Not much shelling this morning, in the afternoon rather more. Bailleul is shelled. In the evening an armoured train fires from the Ouderdom area. All day a lot of changing over of troops. At 5 o'clock in the afternoon, a thunder storm and welcome rain.

13 June, Wednesday. During my mass at Cyriel Lamerant's farm, shells explode between Dalle's farm and Depuydt's. They were fired from Boesinghe. Much of the Reninghelst army headquarters is moving up to Dickebusch. There are a great many horses along Kapelstraat, and also around Emiel Thuylies's place and the farms of Henri Baes, Oscar Ghesquiere and Achiel Vandermarliere, and even in the marshland by the lake. There are now a lot of French interpreters in the area, several of whom are priests. A French interpreter and an English chaplain who are staying in Micmac camp come every day to read mass in the barn church. This morning Father Sheridan read mass in Dickebusch church. No mass had been said there for almost 2 years.

A great deal of ammunition has been taken to the Canada. Every day, 40 civilians go to Voormezeele to work. They are paid 5 francs a day, 1 franc more than the ordinary workmen. No one is compelled to go. Those who have volunteered are nearly all Dickebusch men, or men who once lived there, and who are already used to the firing. They are loaded onto lorries at Ouderdom and driven via Vlamertinghe, *Café Français*, to their work. They have to repair the roads in the centre of the village and the ones on this side of it. The roads on the other side of the village are being repaired by English soldiers. At 5 o'clock already they are brought back to Ouderdom. They tell us that the narrow-gauge railway track has already been laid as far as St. Eloi. In the whole of Voormezeele not a single house is left standing except one half of a house, which is the De Coninck brewery. It is the only one which still has a part of its roof. For the duration of the war this brewery and the adjacent curate's house were used as a dressing station.

Today 2 shells have already fallen at the near side of the village. After 14 days the bombardments are so frequent that the civilians no longer want to go into the village centre.

Since the 17th of January we have had just 7 days of rain. However, because of the excessive numbers of horses and soldiers (and an Englishman is not content with just a little water), water is used in huge quantities and so now we are starting to have a great shortage of water, notwithstanding the many reservoirs and wells that the army has dug.

A lot of shelling around Messines this evening.

14 June, Thursday. The communiqué reports that the Gapaard hamlet at Messines has been taken. The Australians' guns have gone from Baes's little wood. There are still guns at Vijf Geboden, Emiel Gesquiere's farm, Celeste Planckeel's place, and Oudewal. Nearer to Ypres, though, there are still guns on all the farms. News of the deposing of the King of Greece and the Crown Prince.

In the evening shells fall at the Ouderdom mill.

15 June, Friday. In the night there was quite a lot of shelling. Shells fall around Achiel Vandermarliere's farm, one falling on the barn and killing a soldier. In the morning more shells in the same place. It is really painful to see how the English destroy the crops. There are so many abandoned fields in the parish and yet still they so often set up their camp in a cultivated field and don't touch the uncultivated field next to it. So there are farmers who have had all their meadows taken in one fell swoop. Oscar Ghesquiere had 27 acres of good grass. Now there are 3,000 horses on it. They left him half an acre. He had no choice but to sell all his livestock as quickly as possible. I have known farmers who one day had more than enough food for a whole shed full of beasts and the next day had not enough food for a goat.

We didn't hear much shelling during the night. However, we can't conclude from this that there was no fighting, because I see a lot of motor cars full of wounded soldiers go by.

16 June, Saturday. A great deal of shelling all night around Messines. At 11 o'clock in the morning shelling at Ouderdom mill. 1 falls in the middle of a transport and several soldiers are killed or wounded by it. The weather is stifling.

Above Hilaire Lievens's farm, which is now inhabited by Henri Vermeersch, there was an observation balloon in which the gas was under too much pressure. Because of the heat, it burst into flames and there was a tremendous explosion. The two men immediately jumped out and attempted to descend by parachute. At first, everything went well, but unfortunately when they were 30 metres from the ground their parachutes were set on fire by the falling balloon. One of the men fell onto Lievens's barn, which straight away caught fire and was burnt to the ground. The man was burnt inside it. The other man fell next to the barn and was killed instantly.

In the afternoon I go to Dickebusch with the district commissioner Mr Biebuyck. We go to the boys' school, which has not been shelled but is a real fortress: there are walls around it made of bags filled with earth, the walls are 1 ½ metres thick, and there are 2 or 3 parallel internal walls. There is a roof supported on very strong wooden posts and made of sheets of iron on top of which 4 or 5 layers of sandbags have been placed. Then there is an empty space of half a metre with above it a similar kind of roof on even stronger posts. Their lead marbles won't get through that! The village is full of soldiers now, and there are also far more soldiers around us here in Reninghelst. 2,400 soldiers are billeted on the mayor's farm, and in the evening they play music. We see that the dam of the lake is full of shelters. At the lake we are asked for our papers, which are in order. From the top of the dam we take a quick look at the bombarded area around us. The woods have been horribly mutilated and everything is torn and broken. *Lake House* is the last house still standing; beyond it, all is ruins and wasteland. The scene is the same on all sides of us with here and there an oasis and the odd lone building. The ground has been ploughed up by the shells and along the mayor's grand and beautiful driveway there is hardly a tree left intact. We pay a visit to the mayor, who is still living at his farm by the lake. How those people have managed to hold out there through the entire war at half an hour's walking distance from the enemy is incomprehensible. They are lucky to be alive, although their maidservant was injured in 1916. They have had less luck with regard to their beasts: 2 horses and 12 cows were killed by the shelling. And now they are still living there with 19 cows. The commissioner has asked for information about the possible return of farmers. We are full of hope, but sadly there are still hard times ahead for us.

17 June, Sunday. In the morning, shelling at Ouderdom mill. Possibly their target is the tanks which are based there. In the evening, shelling at Oudewal. 1 shell lands in Florent Dauchy's farmyard.

The communiqué reports a further advance towards Hollebeke: the English are said to be at the edge of the village. A very big dressing station has arrived in the fields between Oudewal and the Comyn and Planckeel farms. The guns have left Oudewal, those on the Planckeel farm remain.

18 June, Monday. In the morning there is a bombardment of the area between Reninghelst and Westoutre, and there is even bombardment 200 metres from Ondank. I have never known there to be bombardments so far over on this side. It appears that the shells came from Warneton, Quesnoy.[41]

Today Father Higgins, who has been lodging here for the last 6 weeks, departs. He is changing division for the 6th time. He will be replaced in the 41st by Father Fortune. Today the young men from Dickebusch, the 2nd half of the class of '18, have to appear before the recruitment board in Watou.

19 June, Tuesday. During the night I hear the whistle of several shells. In the afternoon, the evening and the following night Ouderdom is shelled repeatedly, at least every quarter hour, as is the area around it in a radius of 15 minutes' walking distance, including the unloading quay of Delporte, Cossey

41 This is Quesnoy-sur-Deule, three kilometres from Warneton.

and Verhaege, and the mill. The nearest ones fall 7 minutes from Reninghelst church. At the sawmill in front of the *Lion d'Or* inn several horses are killed. In the afternoon a shell also explodes behind Widow Van Cayseele's barn along the road to Poperinghe. It is the 1st time that there has been shelling in that area, although there is hectic army activity there. In Dickebusch the Red Cross station at Oudewal is heavily shelled. Florent Dauchy's farm gets its share of the damage. Shells around Charles-Louis Charles's place, too.

The Reninghelst Intelligence officer, Van Isacker, is being transferred to Dranoutre. The inspector from Dranoutre is coming here. Van Isacker served the inhabitants here conscientiously and courteously.

20 June, Wednesday. Last night was the most terrible that the inhabitants of Dickebusch have ever experienced. Shells in every corner of the parish. In front of *De Paddebroek* 13 soldiers are killed, and many horses. 1 shell fell on Hector Coene's house. By Saelen's hut 15 horses and 6 men are killed. 1 soldier is killed at Decrock's farm and 1 dies at Henri Lamerant's farm. At the little chapel at Millekapelle several soldiers and 47 horses are killed. Around Cafmeyer's farm, the same story. The same, too, at the Red Cross station and at Vijf Geboden. This night at Dickebusch at least 45 soldiers and no fewer than 150 horses were killed by shells.

In the early morning again 5 shells between Reninghelst and Westoutre as far as Neergraaf. Later in the morning, shelling on Poeper and Busseboom, at its worst on and around Opsomers's farm.

In the afternoon at 3 o'clock, first there are shells at Ouderdom, then suddenly a shell lands at the back door of the farmer, August Verdonck, near Reninghelst church. It falls just below the log pile and the wood is hurled in every direction, some pieces are thrown 80 metres away. A soldier who was washing himself there was thrown 20 metres, over the stream and into the corn. Then another shell lands a few metres from there in a little garden. After this, more shells fall between the square and Ouderdom. They are all the same sort of shells, really fast flyers. One hears very clearly the German gun go off, then there is a brief whoosh, a few seconds, and then a dull explosion, with little smoke. There has never yet been shelling so close to Reninghelst church. It is no wonder that those living around the square are frightened. The Red Cross post at Comyn's farm is bombarded once more, despite their flag and the signs everywhere on the tents.[42]

In the evening there are shells again round Ouderdom and the ammunition dump at Verhaege's farm. Shells also on Poperinghe.

This afternoon 2 English balloons were set on fire by the same German aeroplane at Dranoutre.

At 10 o'clock in the evening there are shells once again around Arthur Cafmeyer's farm. One falls on the room above the cellar, where his brother Theophiel, 48 years old, is sleeping. The unfortunate man is buried under the rubble. His body was found the next day. He leaves 2 orphans, who are staying in the school colonies. In Cafmeyer's house almost all the furniture was smashed to pieces. As if by miracle, Arthur and Madeleine Doom, who were in the house, are unharmed.

21 June, Thursday. At midnight several shells fall not far from Reninghelst village square. One falls a few steps away from the Zevecote signpost on the La Clytte road. At 4 in the morning, shelling at Hallebast. At the same time a German aeroplane drops 3 bombs around *De Hert*. At 6.30, while I was on my way

---

42 In his vocabulary, Van Walleghem makes no distinction between tents and huts. Here the context does not make clear which of these he refers to.

to Dickebusch, there was shelling around Widow Derycke's farm. As good fortune would have it, on this occasion I was walking to Lamerant's farm via Rozenhil, and not by my usual route via Ouderdom, otherwise at that moment I would have been just where the shells fell. Later in the morning, Busseboom and Poperinghe are shelled. At 3.30 in the afternoon a shell in the smith's garden on Reninghelst village square, and an hour later another one behind that spot, in August Verdonck's corn field. At 11 o'clock in the evening, shells in Pieter Cambron's meadow just behind the square. What is the target of this bombardment of and around Reninghelst village square? Is it the railway line? Or transport? Or troops? It is hard for us to guess. The staff of the English headquarters find it advisable to leave Reninghelst and to move to Westoutre. The camp commander follows their example.

When I go to Dickebusch I notice above Kemmel a very peculiar cloud of smoke: a high, broad zigzag shape which hangs in the sky for more than half an hour. What it is I do not know. I notice that in Désiré Lamerant's meadow, next to our war cemetery, there is a big site for tractors; I see at least 50 of the machines there. There is also a very big ammunition dump on Gustaaf Desmarets's farm and in Prolbosch next to it. I see that a lot of negroes are at work there. I see that the Canadian engineers who have been at Widow Derycke's farm for the last 6 months have now left.

22 June, Friday. I carry out the burial in our war cemetery of poor Cafmeyer, the 22nd civilian in our our area killed by enemy fire.

In the night, shells fall on and around Widow Derycke's farm, and at De Canada; 1 lands in Camiel Timperman's garden. In the morning, shells at Busseboom and on Poperinghe. In the afternoon 2 shells fall near Cambron's farm the other side of Reninghelst village square. In the evening, shells fall at Ouderdom and at 10.30 at the further side of Reninghelst square, in Charles Deconinck's meadow, next to the police constable's house and in front of Amand Heugebaert's hut.

We don't hear much gunfire, nevertheless we can tell that there is still a good deal of fighting going on by the large number of wounded who are brought through here.

At Dickebusch this afternoon there was heavy shelling around the lake. The catholic chaplain Major Maloney was just passing there with his orderly when a shell struck. The orderly was hit and was killed outright. Father Maloney was thrown to the ground by the force of the explosion and broke two ribs, one of which unfortunately pierced his lung. Father Maloney was known for his easy relationship with his people and above all for his extraordinary courage. A stalwart, excellent man. Let us hope that his robust constitution will contribute greatly to his complete recovery. A protestant chaplain's orderly was killed this afternoon in the same way.

23 June, Saturday. At 2 o'clock in the afternoon shooting from a German aeroplane sets fire to 3 English observation balloons within 5 minutes, 1 above Oscar Ghesquiere's farm, 1 above Kemmel and 1 above Dranoutre. The Germans have really started to target our balloons lately and are much too successful. It is very clear weather and I count 14 more English balloons and 8 German ones. At 3 o'clock, 2 shells very close to Reninghelst church. 1 shell in August Verdonck's moat, 10 metres from the sacristy, and 1 falls 25 metres from there, behind Grillet's hut. If these last two shells had landed a few metres further on, there could have been 20 dead. Now, thanks be to God, there are no casualties to grieve over. But folk are nonetheless left terrified. In the evening, grenades around the Verhaeghe-Cossey unloading quay.

155

All this week the rear of the front has been very heavily bombarded.

24 June, Sunday. 3rd Patron Saint's day of the war. I sing the mass in honour of our mighty patron saint, beseeching him that we might have a better feast day next year, and that we might celebrate it in our resurrected village, with those who have now fled returned and back together with their loved ones, all together celebrating peace and victory. Saint John the Baptist, pray for your faithful people of Dickebusch! The sweet white Sunday bread is forbidden, but nevertheless I am welcomed by the Lamerant family with sweet white bread, not, it is true, made from traditional fancy-bread flour but made with sieved flour made from their own wheat. I have never tasted such natural Sunday bread, and never any that was more flavoursome.

During my mass 2 shells come whizzing over my barn church, landing 3 minutes' walk further in the fields. They were bowled too long. Nevertheless, the flying pieces hit the wall of the barn. At noon shells around Hector Dalle's farm. At 7 o'clock in the evening shells around Cyriel Onraet's farm, 2 of which land on Henri Lamerant's farm, and then several along the La Clytte road at Vandenbussche's farm. At 10.30 another 5 shells, once again on the la Clytte road, around the brick kiln 5 minutes from Reninghelst church.

Sadly, today a terrible disaster takes place in Neuve-Eglise. Since the destruction of the church, religious services have been held on the farm belonging to Mr Ollivier (*Peluche*). Until a few weeks ago the farm had rarely or never been shelled, but recently the situation had grown much worse. However, it was difficult to move the chapel and it was hoped that things would improve very soon. Today already before the mass shells were exploding in that area. As a result, some people, very reasonably, decided not to attend mass. Nevertheless, a good many were present. They were more than halfway through the mass when a shell exploded a few metres from the barn. People were terrified, of course. So the reverend father said that the people might do as they wished, flee or not. Some fled quickly, others went to stand at the back so that if the danger increased they could get away too, still others remained where they were. 3 minutes later another shell landed, this time right in the barn where the people at the back were standing. The result was dreadful: 8 people were killed outright and more than 20 wounded. Reverend Ollivier, the brother of the tenant farmer, and the director of the boarding school in Avelgem, who was also serving at the mass, and likewise the Reverend Father Vanderheyde, who was at the altar, were unharmed. The wounded were taken to Couthove hospital. The next day 4 more died, and later on 2 more. Unsurprisingly, the whole area has been badly shaken by this painful incident. But malicious gossips have done their work too and a lot of silly nonsense has been talked about it.

25 June, Monday. In our wartime church I say mass in memory of the parishioners who have died in the course of the last year. 47 people are present. Shelling at Busseboom, otherwise nothing special.

26 June, Tuesday. At 6 o'clock in the morning Charles Louis Cannaert's barn burns down. Of course the soldiers had nothing to do with this, as is obvious from their account: none of the soldiers was there when the fire started, therefore, they are all innocent. So the culprit is probably the farmer himself: instead of trying to put out the fire, he got his pigs to safety and wouldn't give the soldiers the ladder that they needed in order to put the fire out. It was lucky that Germain, the police constable's lad, happened to be passing when the fire started and could provide a completely different account. He saw the soldiers come running out of the barn at top speed, then try to put out the fire, then go to save their clothes. For 2 of them it was clearly already too late to do this, because an hour later they were still walking round in their underwear. Germain first helped the farmer to get the pigs away and then immediately, at the request of the soldiers, went to find the ladder, which was attached with a rope in the attic, so that it took a couple of minutes before the ladder was ready to be used. 3 days later, Germain had to appear before the committee of enquiry at the farm. Those gentlemen did nothing but ask the boy one trick question after another, the most stupid, nonsensical questions, which would certainly have bewildered a simple soul. It was fortunate that the boy could stand up for himself.

In the afternoon I have a walk to Mont Rouge. It was exceptionally clear weather and I had a splendid view from the top of the hill. I could see the English guns shooting from Wytschaete and a permanent pall of smoke between Wytschaete, Houthem and Hollebeke. I could also see that the whole line is coming under a good deal of shelling. At that moment Ypres was in fact under heavy bombardment. Oh, if only I could lay my hands on a pair of binoculars, what important things I would be able to see! Luckily I found a kindly customs officer who had a pair and was happy to lend them to me for an hour. What is more, the good fellow, who knew the area very well, stayed with me and gave me detailed explanations. What I saw was wondrous. I saw in the far south the hills of Artois all the way to Lens, the smelting furnaces of Pont-à-Vendin like a monstrous, menacing beast created by the Germans and now the strength of the Germans. I saw Lille, Roubaix and the numerous and populous industrial towns and villages of northern France. At Armentières the chimneys no longer smoked. Comines and Wervicq lay at my feet, though the houses were hidden behind the trees; the church tower of Comines had lost its spire, the spire on Wervicq's church tower was still there. I saw the church towers of Menin, Wevelghem, Courtrai, Becelaere, Dadizeele, Moorsleede and Passchendaele. These last churches were half destroyed by shell-fire. I could see the clock-face of Passchendaele church tower very clearly. I could distinguish very well the various houses by the Moorsleede-Passchendaele station. Then I see the church towers of Roulers and discover that one or two of them have been shelled. They looked like this:

Further to the left I see Hooglede and a little way away from there, just a little further to the left, a big white windmill with its sails turning at full speed. Further still to the left I see another village with a white windmill nearby. This one is not working, but I can see the position of its sails. Beyond, I see the church towers of Lichtervelde, Torhout, Ghistel and Oudenburg. I even see the town of Ostend, which from here appears to me to be composed of great white blocks placed one next to the other. Along the coast I see the dunes, and the towers of Furnes.

In truth I was moved to see that dear region from which we have been shut out for so long, where our loved ones live and sigh and think of us just as we think of them, so near to us and yet so out of reach. It was an especially strange feeling to see signs of life on that side, such as those turning mill sails. I stood there like Moses overlooking the promised land.[43]

27 June, Wednesday. In the morning a mechanical problem forces an English aeroplane to land in Florent Dauchy's cornfield. Unfortunately, as it lands, corn twists around the propeller so that the whole machine turns over and the poor airmen lie seriously injured under the engine. They were taken to the hospital in Poperinghe and died the same day. The German aeroplanes are out hunting English balloons again. At 3 o'clock they shoot one into flames above Hallebast and at 6.30 another at the Galgebossen. I saw the one at Hallebast get shot down and was able to follow the whole operation. I saw 3 German aeroplanes selecting the prey that they would devour. They flew extremely low and it is almost incomprehensible how they were not hit by the English artillery and machine guns which were firing at them the whole time. The men in

---

43 God showed Moses various areas of the promised land from the top of a mountain, but did not allow him to enter (Deuteronomy 34, 1-4).

the balloon saw the danger and jumped out, managing to land without injury. If the numerous personnel who are responsible for the observation balloon had immediately pulled it down to the ground at that moment, the balloon too would have been spared. But no, they didn't lift a finger. While the nearby balloons were pulled down, this one remained hanging in the sky. So Fritz had an easy target and soon kindled a nice little fire. After all, it was only a little rag worth 50,000 francs. The English soldiers in the neighbourhood, who saw the action, were very indignant and on all sides one heard them cry 'Spies.'

In the afternoon I went off to Poperinghe, using the country lanes instead of the main roads. I was between the farms of Ruyssen and De Quecker when suddenly there was a 'poof!' and a 'whoosh' and then another 'poof!,' and it became clear to me that it wasn't safe where I was. There was a 2nd volley, then a 3rd, and this time a rain of bullets. The soldiers around me took to their heels and I did likewise. 4 times I had to throw myself to the ground and 4 times debris fell all around me. In the end, out of breath, I managed to get to safety, finding that such a retreat was harder work than I had thought. Then I went and sat with the Dickebusch refugees, because I was in need of a good brushing down. It was the first time that this spot had been shelled. At Poperinghe there has been little shelling on the town itself in recent days, but a great deal in the countryside, mostly on the parish of St. Jan. There is shelling almost every day around Busseboom now. So far this week there has been no shelling of Reninghelst village square and the fear has subsided somewhat. Even the pastor shows himself now and then. There is a great deal of shelling all afternoon. At 7 o'clock a big ammunition dump explodes at the *Café Français*.

More and more, people are talking about the imminent offensive from the Ypres area to the coast. The French will take over a part of the Belgian sector. They have already arrived in Oost-Vleeteren. Part of the Belgian 4th Division is still in Boesinghe. They are being shelled heavily.

28 June, Thursday. The English chaplain, MacDonald, and a French interpreter-priest from Caen say mass in Lamerant's barn. In the night there was a lot of shelling again and once again we hear a terrifying explosion of ammunition. This is now a frequent occurrence. In the afternoon 5 large shells land on and around Henri Lamerant's farm. 4 soldiers are hurled several metres. One of them is killed, 1 injured, 1 goes mad and 1 is unharmed. Another shell landed on a hut and killed the sergeant major. In the evening, a thunder storm.

29 June, Friday. The night is fairly calm. At noon and in the afternoon shells explode around Henri Lamerant's farm and those of Delporte, Cossey and Vandenbussche. There is heavy shelling all day in the area of Warneton. A lot of motor cars pass with wounded in them. I hear that in the Dickebusch mortuary (Arthur Minne's house, on the corner of Kerkstraat) the bodies are piled on top of one another. Evidence that there's a lot of fighting going on.

Ypres is bombarded almost ceaselessly and many soldiers are killed there.

30 June, Saturday. There is heavy shelling all night and the most intense is from 11 to 1 o'clock. The hamlet called De Poeper is bombarded for 4 hours. There is heavy shelling throughout the day as well. Cafmeyer's farm and the camp behind it are also shelled and several soldiers are killed. The 47th Division is back here again, between La Clytte and Reninghelst, and now the 41st Division is on rest. The 30th Division is here too, having arrived a fortnight ago.

Every day from my room I see Bulteel come to visit the grave of his 3 children that were killed.[44]

Today our young men from the class of '18 (2nd half) leave for the army. They are being sent to Camp d'Auvours. They are: André Van Estlande, Arthur Haezebrouck, Gustaf Dury, Albert Debruyne and Odiel Verschaeve. 3 have a postponement of 3 months: Odiel Lamerant, Maurits Spenninck and Gouwy. Permanently exempt: Camiel Onraet.

For several months now no permits have been issued to go to Dickebusch village, but Jules Noyelle and Cyriel De Haene have now received a permit and are allowed go to work at their house and farm. However, the permit is rescinded after a few days.

The few people who pass through our churchyard comment that the grave of Reverend Dooms is still undamaged and they assert their belief that it will remain undamaged. This priest has the reputation of a saint hereabouts and people still frequently speak of his exceptional virtues. Our verger, Petrus Sinaeve, did not let a single day go by, from the time of the priest's death until he himself fled to safety, without saying a prayer at Reverend Dooms's grave.

1 July, Sunday. Once again, heavy shelling all night and all day. It has been going on now for over 40 hours. In the masses there were as many people as on other Sundays.

Around noon, Ouderdom was shelled. The bakery's outhouse and 2 little houses opposite were hit. In 1 of those houses lived Désiré Van Renterghem from Dickebusch; he had fled his house just half a minute earlier. After that, the area around Micmac camp was heavily bombarded. Shells explode in Cyriel Lamerant's meadow and on Widow Vermeulen's farm and a big shell lands on the gravel road just in front

---

44 Constantin Bulteel had lost three children aged 2, 3 and 10, on 5 December 1916 when a shell had struck his house.

of Gustaaf Forceville's shed. This shell is a new sort, and it is thanks to this that no one was hurt. The shell is called an *obus perforateur*. It bores very deep into the ground and then explodes, throwing everything up high into the air and far outwards. This is the explanation for the fact that the shed, which was only 4 metres away, was barely touched: just a few roof tiles were knocked off by the force of the explosion. Even a motor car which was parked between the shell hole and the shed was only damaged by 2 small pieces of iron. It was worse 30 or 40 metres away, where iron, stone and earth rained down. The same afternoon shells also exploded around the farms of Henri Breyne, Comyn, Jules Spenninck, Achiel Vandermarliere and Oscar Ghesquiere. In the last case, 2 soldiers were killed. It was a terrible afternoon for Dickebusch. In addition, we feel several terrible shocks caused by munitions explosions nearer to the front.

2 July, Monday. There was somewhat less firing during the night, but it was far from calm. Shells around the farms of Widow Delanotte and Arthur Deraedt. In the morning and also in the afternoon shells around Isidoor Kestelyn's farm. In the afternoon there is once again a lot of shelling. For several days now the unloading quay at Dalle's farm has been under heavy bombardment again. The 23rd Division, to which Father MacClement is attached, has come back here. In the afternoon I go to Abeele. I notice that in the big English cemetery at De Leene[45] there continue to be many burials; after the Wytschaete assault, especially, a great many dead were buried. I count 19 English observation balloons.

3 July, Tuesday. Again a lot of firing in the night. Shells at

---

45 This is Lijssenthoek Cemetery.

Comyn's farm. During the day shells around the farms of Cyriel Gontier and Lemahieu.

The Belgian soldier Richard Derycke, killed at Oost-Vleeteren, is buried in Reninghelst. 40 or so of his comrades attend the funeral. The favour of being buried in their own parish is easily granted to the soldiers from the unoccupied area.

I reckon up what the ravages of war have already wrought in our parish and work out that 99 houses have completely disappeared, 50 are beyond repair, 54 can easily be repaired and 64 are as good as untouched. Oh, may this destruction soon come to an end!

4 July, Wednesday. A fair amount of shelling in the night. Shells fall on Lievens's farm and on the fields of Mille-kapelleke. At 3.30 a German aeroplane drops bombs between Arthur Deraedt's farm and that of Charles-Louis Kestelyn. Several horses and men are killed. In the afternoon a big ammunition dump explodes at *Schoonhuys* and an English aeroplane is shot down along the Abeele road.

At 9 o'clock in the morning and again at 4.30 in the afternoon the king of England is driven through the village in a motor car. He went to visit the battlefield of Messines and Wytschaete.

The Dickebusch inhabitants have received more money for billeting the English for the 1st 3 months of their stay in Dickebusch. Another 7% has been paid out.

5 July, Thursday. In the night a lot of shells land round Planckeel's wood and the farms of Marcel Coene and Amand Heugebaert. Several huts are smashed to pieces near Torreel and horses and men are killed.

Early in the morning I see several German observation balloons and not a single English one, although it's normally the contrary.

Later in the morning some very large shrapnel shells explode above Lievens's farm and Kapelleke. Some of the pieces fly as far as Henri Desmarets's farm, which is a good 700 metres away.

At 2 o'clock in the afternoon shells fall on Vandenbussche's farm, then further on, near Jeremie Planckeel's farm, and by Vandevoorde's house at Heet, which is already in Reninghelst. They make the biggest craters that I have ever seen. You could easily bury 5 horses in one. Shells around Busseboom, as well, 1 on Henri Verdonck's farm. It is really a wonder that, notwithstanding the great number of shells that have fallen on Reninghelst from every side and at every hour, we have still had no civilian casualties. Shells on Poperinghe, too. An English balloon is shot down in flames.

Reninghelst people who have been to Rousbrugge relate that the place is swarming with French soldiers.

Chicory now costs 3,40 francs per kilo.

6 July, Friday. 1st Friday of the month: 10 communicants. A lot of shelling throughout the night and at 1 o'clock and 4 o'clock exceptionally heavy. It was worst on the Boesinghe front: St. Hubertus was bombarded 3 times, at 1 o'clock, 2.30 and 4.30. In the last bombardment a shell hits Louis Ghys's house and destroys it completely. Luckily the inhabitants had fled a few moments earlier into the stable, a corner of which was also demolished. Louis and his daughter are unharmed but his wife Eudoxie is hit by a beam which caves in, and her arm is broken. Eudoxie had only been home for 2 days from the hospital in Couthove where she had been treated after the previous shelling, with her earlier wounds not fully healed, when she had to be taken to the hospital once again.

Louis's mule, which was in the stable, lost an eye. But still these good people are happy that everything has worked out so well and consider themselves lucky, even though they have had their share of misfortune. They have twice lost all their furniture, first through fire, then through this bombardment, 2 daughters dead from typhus and the other daughter, Reine, injured in 1915, and now the mother injured twice in 7 weeks.

New troops had arrived near the mill yesterday evening. 3 shells fell in the middle of the camp and yet not a single soldier was hit. One shell even fell 3 metres from a bell tent which was thrown 15 metres by the force of the explosion, and yet the 6 soldiers who were sleeping under it were unharmed. Several shells also in Henri Vermeulen's meadow.

I go through Hallebast and in the direction of Kemmel and I see that a house in Vijf Geboden has been utterly destroyed. Emiel Thuylie's farm has completely disappeared. I visit 7 houses that are still inhabited and of the 7 only one has not been shelled. The people live in them as best they can. Even Henri Depuydt can only use a quarter of his house now. I can see that troops are now quartered all the way to past the Kemmel brook and I see 3 railway lines there.

Words cannot express how everyone is longing for the offensive so that the Germans might be driven back a bit further. For the current situation is intolerable for the civilians here by the front. Nowhere and at no time is one free now, especially in these days of preparation: the fiercer the English attacks grow, the heavier, too, grows the German fire. The soldiers say 'Have patience for one more week.'

For the first time in a long time we hear good news of the Russians. They have begun the offensive towards Lemberg and have already taken 20,000 prisoners of war. Sadly, our joy regarding that front will be short-lived.

7 July, Saturday. Last night German aeroplanes were out and about and we heard the machine guns several times.

In the morning there is shelling on and around the farms of René Verdonck and Widow Nauwynck between Reninghelst square and Busseboom. The communiqué reports a slight advance near Hollebeke. An English balloon is shot down in flames at Dickebusch. This week there were shells at Vogeltje in Poperinghe.

8 July, Sunday. During the night there is once again a lot of shelling near Hollebeke. The day is unusually calm. Lodging at Cyriel Lamerant's farm is the chaplain MacDonald, a Benedictine with the 23rd Division. Today he holds two masses in the barn for the English soldiers. Some of the English Catholics really deserve admiration. For example, we have had staying here since mid-October a sergeant of the 47th Division, a 43-year-old bachelor and a reservist, who fought in the wars in India and Transvaal. This man is alternately in the firing line and the camp around Reninghelst, and whenever he is here he comes to church twice a day without fail. In the morning he is already here at 5.45 and he stays until 7.15, then he goes to his camp to serve at Father Bleasdale's mass. In the evening he comes to the church again for an hour for Adoration. Even this winter in the exceptional cold he was here at his customary hour, and that without an overcoat. Now he comes every day from Winnipeg Camp (at Potente, 45 minutes' walk from here), takes communion each day, prays with great fervour and is extremely happy to be allowed to serve at our mass, which is very welcome given the drastically reduced service the church is currently offering in these parts.

9 July, Monday. The night is fairly calm. During the night 7 tanks from Ouderdom went up to the front along their usual route: the mill, east of Henri Lamerant's farm, and then onwards over the stream between Cyriel Lamerant's place and Paddebroek.

There is more and more talk of the imminent offensive. We see the numerous and large-scale preparations here and we hear of those in nearby sectors: railway tracks are being laid on all sides, artillery guns are being brought up and the ammunition dumps are steadily multiplying. People are predicting an offensive from the river Lys to the sea. It's on everyone's mind. Soldiers and officers are telling the civilians that it will be terrible and relentless. They have to break through whatever the cost, and then within a few weeks Flanders will be free. The newspapers, too, speak almost daily about the importance of the coming attack. Orders are issued from higher levels of government for the instruction of the mayors and police in the villages that will be soon be free. People are full of hope, but those who live next to the front are nevertheless fearful of the bombardment which will precede the battle. Thus a farmer from Vlamertinghe requested permission from the military government to take his animals away to safety, given the danger that was threatened by the imminent offensive. But instead of receiving permission, he received a visit from the local policemen: 'What's this? An imminent offensive? How do you know that? How dare you betray the details of the military preparations?' Isn't that outrageous? However, the spy has not been shot.

In the morning Micmac camp is bombarded. Soldiers are killed on Henri Lamerant's farm and on Widow Delanotte's.

The English communiqué reports a small advance near Wytschaete. Today I hear something that I have never heard before: a group of English musicians playing the Brabançonne.[46] Last summer a Canadian band gave us a concert every evening

---

46 The 'Brabançonne' is the Belgian national anthem.

and they always ended by playing, along with other national anthems, the Brabançonne. English bands never played it. But the musicians that are here now are a happy exception and seem to be of the opinion that Belgium still exists. From this time on for quite some while we were to be granted the pleasure of hearing our national anthem every day.

10 July, Tuesday. A lot of shelling again in the night. I hear a great many shells whizz past but they don't fall nearby. During the day Micmac camp and Busseboom are shelled. A lot of ammunition explodes in Galgebossen between Reninghelst-Poperinghe-Elverdinghe and Vlamertinghe. At Zevecote in Reninghelst, Lermite's inn burns down. It was just 3 minutes from here, it happened in the morning and yet we didn't hear about it until the next day. Such news is too commonplace to cause much of a stir. The reason for the fire is not known.

The 25th and 30th Divisions have arrived here.

11 July, Wednesday. In the morning Poeper and Busseboom are shelled. In the afternoon I see 3 English balloons shot down in flames by a German aeroplane. It was all over in under 5 minutes. Nevertheless, if the men of the 3rd balloon had wanted to, they could have descended in time. The aeroplane was flying very low. One of these balloons was above the Boonemeerschen meadows. The English soldiers told us the next day that as revenge they shot down 4 German balloons the same afternoon, also in this sector. One civilian also claims to have seen this. However, the people of Dickebusch know nothing of it, which is almost incomprehensible. One thing is certain, and that is that the Germans destroy a great many English balloons here and that we very seldom see a German balloon destroyed. It is very rare that an English aeroplane takes on a German aeroplane which is attacking a balloon;

sometimes there isn't even much firing from the anti-aircraft guns. An English chaplain has even told me that the English have decided not to defend their balloons anymore and that the loss of a few balloons here makes little difference. Can you believe that? But the men almost always manage to descend safely. These aerial battles, with the descents by parachute, are curious to see.

A division of Australians passes through La Clytte. My brother Remi is arriving today on leave and will spend a few days with us.

12 July, Thursday. Today in the newspapers we read bad news about the Nieuport front. A few days ago this sector was taken over by the English in preparation for the coming offensive. It was a very important position; the allies were in control of the dunes on both sides of the Yser, and the bridge, too, was in their hands, and this meant that the spot was very suitable for the launch of the offensive in the north. The French (mostly *Fusiliers marins*) had bravely defended themselves there for almost 3 years, fighting to hold off the enemy and to retain control of the area, and they had succeeded. Now the English, together with their fleet, were about to launch an offensive there. Alas, there is a surprise offensive by the Germans and in a few short hours the whole of the right bank of the Yser is snatched from them and both bridge and canal are now in no man's land. It was a bitter disappointment for us when we heard of this defeat. We had heard so often how important these positions were. The English newspapers minimised the blow as much as possible and spoke only about the trivial little bit of ground (1,600 metres wide by 800 deep) that they had lost and the low number of prisoners taken, but they said nothing of the importance of this bit of ground. That is also how the English officers referred to it when I talked to them about this grievous event. Sadly, circumstances have since shown how serious the consequences of this defeat were. It was no longer possible to begin the offensive on that side. Who was to blame for this reverse? History will tell. However, several French newspapers could not hide their discontent and one French colonel asks in the *Echo de Paris*: 'Where were the observation balloons and the monitors at sea?'

Today Bailleul is shelled and civilians are killed. Sadly, another painful event will happen in the evening. From 9.30 p.m. to 10.30 p.m., German aeroplanes fly over and drop bombs at Ouderdom. The English autocannons fire at them ferociously. Unfortunately, an English shell lands on the hut of Arthur Tahon from Hemelrijk, who is now living on Abeelstraat, just outside Reninghelst village. The inhabitants had just sat down at the table. The shell went in turn through the roof, a trunk full of clothes and then the ceiling, went through the child that sat on his mother's lap, blasted off the right thigh of the mother, went through the floor and bored almost 1 metre deep into the ground. Little Albert Tahon, 18 months old, died instantly. His mother (Maria Van Elstlande from Dickebusch, 32 years old) was taken to Couthove and died early in the morning. Never have I seen anything so sweetly cruel as the poor little child. He was laughing with delight when his little body was pierced through, and death was so instantaneous that the lamb never changed his expression. He laughed still on his little deathbed and now he laughs just the same way in heaven. What the Tahon family has suffered through the shelling: in November 1914 Arthur's aunt and cousin were killed, in March 1916 another aunt was killed, in the August of '16 his sister and sister-in-law were injured, in May 1917 his mother-in-law was injured, and now his wife and child have been killed.

13 July, Friday. In the night and the early morning shelling on Ouderdom. At 3 o'clock in the morning a German aeroplane drops 3 bombs at Dickebusch police station. At 3 o'clock in the afternoon, Ouderdom is shelled again. The daughter of Cyriel Jacob, the farmer, tries to flee from the shelling, but while she is crossing the cobbled road in her terror, she is hit by a motor car and seriously injured. However, she recovered after a few weeks.

In the evening Ouderdom is shelled again. The *Casino* inn is shelled; the inhabitants had just fled the house. A few moments later a shell falls on Louis Dewilde's inn. His wife and children were in the cellar and were unharmed. It went worse with Louis, who was upstairs. His arm was severed. The chaplain took him to the dressing station at the boys' school. He was taken to Couthove and died the following day. Seldom have I seen a house so utterly destroyed by a single shell as that of Dewilde, although it was a sizeable house. Impossible to repair a single room sufficiently to be able to live in it.

In Westoutre there are not many troops now. In Reninghelst there are also far fewer. A lot of camps are empty. In Dickebusch, more and more troops are arriving.

14 July, Saturday. The night was fairly calm. In the morning Poperinghe was shelled, 3 civilians killed. The chaplain McCann, who lodged in my house in Dickebusch in June 1915, has arrived here. He is now chaplain to the artillery of the 24th Division. He is a courageous and diligent man. In the afternoon Poperinghe is shelled again. My brother Remi leaves to go back to his regiment.

15 July, Sunday. Last night was stormy, with thunder and lightning and a lot of shelling. There were a lot of shells at Ouderdom and Poeper, and also shells on Cyriel Gontier's farm. Every so often throughout the morning a shell falls here and there in Dickebusch: 4.00 a.m. in front of Dury's hut, 6.30 between Desmarets's farm and Coene's, 7.00 at Decrock's place, 9.00 in Henri Desmarets's garden, 10.30 on Henri Lamerant's farm. A spoonful meted out every hour: this is the most dangerous kind of bombardment. Poperinghe is heavily shelled: several civilians are killed, as are some soldiers who were leaving mass.

In Dickebusch there is much despondency and indignation because of the evacuation plans. There has already been talk of these for several days. 3 days ago, all the inhabitants along the left-hand side of the main road from La Clytte to Dickebusch, including the farmers, were given notice that they must prepare to leave the parish within a few days. Immediate protests to the higher authorities resulted in a few farmers being given permission to stay. And now yesterday evening there comes a new and urgent order. The evacuation region covers the whole area where the 7th English army division is encamped, that is to say it covers everyone who lives in the area north of the farms of Arthur Deraedt, Henri Vermeulen and Arthur Desmarets, but not including these farms themselves. There are exceptions, however. The following may remain: (1) the farmers, but only 5 people per farm, however large the farm may be. The other members of the household and the remainder of the farm workers must leave; (2) anyone who works for the army. This exception applies purely to individuals: the rest of the household must leave.

All the evacuated people must go to Watou. They must all be out of the parish by 12 o'clock this afternoon. They are allowed to take one bundle with them, no more. What a cruel, hateful measure, announced without warning on Saturday evening or Sunday morning. It is the most arbitrary one that I have ever encountered, for I can find absolutely no reason for it. Is it because of the danger? But it has already been amply demonstrated that there is scant concern for the life of the civilians here, and the people who have been told to leave are in no more danger than those who are being allowed to stay, and all are equally needed for the work of the coming harvest. Is it because of spying? You would surely think, though, that after 3 years the English are clever enough to realise that spying is impossible for the civilians. Is it in order to have the place more to themselves and to be more at liberty to use and destroy everything? That is possible. Or is it the whim of a madman and a cruel heart? That is the most probable explanation. And because of this almost all of our families are torn apart and the women and girls are sent out into the wide world while the men are allowed to stay. 120 people are evacuated. Later I was never able to find any reason which could justify this evacuation. What weeping, protesting and cursing there was at Dickebusch that Sunday morning. And they were given just a few hours for all this, which made the case still crueller and more unreasonable. And the Dickebusch police carried out this cruel measure in the cruellest way possible, even laughing at the people. Which means that the grain of respect that I still had left for some policemen disappeared with the evacuees. Above all, Constable Van Assche, from Iseghem, became infamous for his part in this. They said it was just for 14 days, but 3 months later, those 14 days are not over. The police had to use violence with some inhabitants and had to drag them there by force of arms. There were evacuations in several other parishes too: Vlamertinghe, Woesten and Elverdinghe, and things were equally bad in those places. In the French sector they wanted to set about it in an even harsher manner, but they were forced to back down in the face of the strong resistance of the civilian population.

In the 1st mass I had only 40 people, in the high mass 49. It was the feast of St. Donatus and there were 20 communicants. In the evacuated area it is not permitted to run a shop or an inn and civilians must have a special pass with their picture on it. In the non-evacuated area everything remains as it was. There are only 2 inns in the whole parish now: *Le repos des voyageurs* and the one on Jules Spenninck's farm. The civilian population of Dickebusch now counts 215 inhabitants, of whom 35 are refugees. Those who live in the non-evacuated area are not allowed to set foot in the evacuated part, and thus are also not allowed to come to my mass.

On the Yser plain whole villages, including the farmers, were evacuated. The people were loaded onto trains against their will and transported to the south of France. This is how the Germans behave in the occupied part of the country. It is no wonder that our Belgian soldiers join the protests and write and shout: 'Avenge the forced transports!' It is hard to describe the extent to which people carp about and curse our Belgian military command and our Belgian government because these are suspected, rightly or wrongly, of being complicit in this. But one thing is sure, the civilians here have been completely and utterly left to their own resources, with no one to defend them against the whims of our military men, and all we experience of our government is now and then a big speech delivered in the trenches of Sainte-Adresse[47] with resounding sentences about the fatherland and full of beautiful promises, but which are enough to make someone who knows the reality of the front fume with anger. Admittedly, our district commissioners are more on the side of the civilians, but it appears that their

---

47 The Belgian government settled in Sainte-Adresse, near Le Havre in Normandy, France, after the occupation of Belgium, and remained there until the end of the war. This remark is ironic because obviously there were no trenches in Sainte-Adresse.

power is also very limited. Only once in the whole war has a minister been at the front and that was Helleputte, Minister of Agriculture, in 1916. From the very first words of his speech, which he gave at a meeting of mayors and farmers' representatives, he demonstrated that he knew absolutely nothing about the situation faced by the farmers at the front, and he would have done far better to keep quiet. Nor did he ever come back. And some who also receive their share of the embittered criticisms are our priests, and Our Lord himself. To think of it! 'They're all as bad as each other,' they say. Thus some people no longer go to mass, out of bitterness. But we know what their worth was before all this.

16 July, Monday. Quite a lot of shelling in the night. Ouderdom was shelled in the early morning and Poperinghe virtually all day. Today I count 21 English observation balloons. This is the highest number that I've yet counted. One of them is shot down. A German aeroplane is shot down over Devos's farm at Poeper. A few metres from the ground the pilot leapt out of his machine and landed on the back of a horse, which was very startled and ran off with him. Unluckily for him he didn't manage to get far. He was a boy of 18. One of the batteries on Cyriel Lamerant's farm is so badly shelled in the positions they had only been occupying for a day that of the 6 guns only 1 remains.

Today is the funeral in Reninghelst of poor Mrs Tahon and her little child. More than 200 people attend the funeral.

The big political news is the resignation of Bethman-Hollweg, the German Chancellor.

In the Protestant reading rooms of the Y.M.C.A. (Young Men's Christian Association) in Reninghelst one can find *La Vie Parisienne*, one of the filthiest magazines of so-respectable France. This gives one an idea of the moral principles of Protestantism.

17 July, Tuesday. The funeral takes place in Reninghelst of Louis Dewilde, killed last week. Yesterday afternoon the poor man was shelled for the second time when they were transporting his body from Couthove to the Elizabeth hospital in Poperinghe. A shell hit the motor car a few metres from the hospital and the coffin was smashed to pieces. They had to gather up the pieces of the body and put them in a new coffin.

In the morning a lot of Australian artillery passes through here on its way to Dickebusch. Around noon a lot of shells fall in the vicinity of Voormezeele. Every now and then throughout the day a big shrapnel shell is fired at the English observation balloons. Hallebast, St. Hubertus and the farms of Cyril Lamerant, Henri Desmarets and Marcel Coene all receive their share of the shrapnel. At regular intervals, one of these big cigars bursts open. I have never seen big shrapnel shells like these before.

In the afternoon I see a boxing competition in Zevecote. At least 1,000 spectators. The English provide plenty of entertainment for their soldiers. Everywhere now one finds reading rooms and rooms serving as theatres or cinemas. They sometimes hold theatrical performances in the open air, and above all, 'football' competitions. In Reninghelst, especially, there are splendid cinemas and theatres.

The English are jealously protective of their canteens and try to secure their commercial advantage by every possible means. This results in some peculiar measures against the inns and the civilian shops. In general, they are not much cheaper than our shops. On the contrary, in the canteens that serve alcohol everything is much more expensive than in our inns. This is not surprising: the drink in the inns is taxed at a rate that would put the inns out of business, but with sugar and water the innkeeper becomes a brewer and so there are innkeepers who nevertheless manage to make themselves very good profits. The army imports the supplies for the canteen direct from England tax-free, and so the competition is easy. The beer, on the other hand, they buy from the civilian beer-sellers. A good many civilians exercise the profession of beer merchant and some have already earned a pretty fortune this way. Nowadays the innkeepers make the most profit on wine (white wine and Malaga).

18 July, Wednesday. The night was fairly calm. All through the night Australian artillery were passing by, heading up towards Vlamertinghe. Several times during the day there is shelling around Henri Breyne's farm and Henri Saelen's hut. A shell falls on Henri Breyne's barn. Henri Lamerant was nearby and was hit on the arm by a stone.

19 July, Thursday. On three different occasions during the night (9.30, 11.30 and 4.00) Henri Desmarets's farm is shelled. 1 shell explodes in the stable, where 3 soldiers' horses are killed. Robert Bonduelle, who was sleeping in the stable, was unharmed. Other shells fall on Cyriel Lamerant's foal-stable and meadow, and again on Henri Breyne's farm. During my mass another shell lands in Lamerant's meadow and during my breakfast another one, the fragments flying out and hitting the wall of the house, and at 10 o'clock the same again.

In the morning once again a lot of Australian artillery passing through. In the afternoon a lot of shelling around Hollebeke and Boesinghe. The following day we learned that the Germans had attacked there and had taken trenches.

20 July, Friday. Once again there is a lot of shelling around Cyriel Lamerant's farm. In the afternoon, shells at Busseboom and in the evening at 9.30, 8 shells along the railway between

Widow Lagache's farm and Widow Deweerdt's in Reninghelst, on the Poperinghe side.

There are a lot of soldiers in Westoutre again. People are waiting impatiently for the offensive. But they are less hopeful of its succeeding than they were about the Wytschaete offensive.

21 July, Saturday. Our Belgian independence day, last year so solemnly celebrated in our church but this year passing unnoticed since there are no Belgian soldiers here any more.

All night terrible shelling and several ammunition dumps explode at Vlamertinghe. At 2 o'clock in the afternoon 5 large shells land at Kasteelmolen at Reninghelst. Heavy shelling also around Henri Breyne's farm, around Ouderdom and around Drie Goen. Also around the mayor of Dickebusch's farm. I count 23 English observation balloons and 8 German ones.

22 July, Sunday. A great deal of shelling all night. Once again we hear several explosions of ammunition: what a terrifying noise!

All summer, each time I have gone to Dickebusch I have had to first have a good look around to see where there was shelling, and then choose the way that seemed to me to be the least dangerous. But it has reached the stage now that there is considerable danger on all sides and I hardly know any more which way to take. This morning there was shelling on all the roads that I can use. But I am lucky in my choice. When I set off at 5.30 a.m. there is heavy shelling around Ouderdom, especially at Ouderdom mill. So I go by Rozenhil. Then, at 9.15, Delporte's farm is shelled and just before high mass a shell sets the house on fire. The shells come whining dangerously over our makeshift church, to explode fifteen minutes' walk away.

But the people are used to this and are in no way perturbed. Soon it is Rozenhil's turn to be shelled. The frightful cracking sounds of shells landing there goes on for 2 hours. The English chaplain Father Hurley had celebrated the 9.30 mass for Catholic soldiers in the Army Church there and had just left the building 10 minutes before, when a shell exploded and the building was smashed to matchwood. I return to Reninghelst by way of Ouderdom mill, where it is quiet now, and so I am lucky once again. In each of my masses there were 40 civilians present and in the high mass there were about 25 soldiers too. In Dickebusch they are constantly setting up new camps. The dressing station on Comyn's farm is no longer being shelled. Today there was shelling on Poperinghe.

In the afternoon there was shelling first at Celeste Planckeel's place, then on the wood, then at Marcel Coene's place and then Florent Dauchy's. On Marcel Coene's farm an incendiary bomb falls on the barn and all that beautiful and large building is soon in flames. All the best agricultural equipment belonging to his father-in-law, the mayor, worth more than 4,000 francs, is burnt. Around the same time, a German aeroplane drops bombs around *De Hert*.

23 July, Monday. A lot of shelling in the night, although less than during the previous night. Although it is quite dark, German aeroplanes are up and about, mostly above Westoutre and Poperinghe. They drop bombs and they dive to about 100 metres above the soldiers' camps and fire with machine guns. In a camp by the main road from Poperinghe several soldiers were killed and wounded this way. In the early morning German planes were fired at in Poperinghe. A stray anti-aircraft shrapnel shell exploded in the house of Mr Delplace from Ieper. One of the fragments hit his daughter, boring right through her head from the top to below her chin.

Everyone thought that the girl would die the same day, but after 8 days she regained consciousness and after 2 months she was completely recovered.

Last night the 47th English Division made a raid on Hollebeke and took 30 prisoners, who passed through Westoutre in the afternoon. In the early and the later morning there was heavy firing on the whole Ypres front, especially to the north, in the afternoon there was somewhat less. We have good reason to think that the artillery attack in preparation for the offensive has already started and we expect the infantry attack in the middle of next week. The General of the 123rd brigade (41st Division)[48] was killed by a shell today in Voormezeele, along with a major of his staff.[49]

24 July, Tuesday. All night very intense firing around Boesinghe and Steenstrate. It is worst from 1.00 a.m. to 9.00 a.m., then somewhat calmer, but it starts again, as heavy as ever, at 2 o'clock in the afternoon. This evening and yesterday evening, shrapnel shells on Poperinghe station as the trains arrive. Also this evening shells at Busseboom.

Stationed here now are the 8th, 18th, 23rd, 24th, 25th, 30th, 41st and 47th English Divisions and 1 division of Australians.

25 July, Wednesday. Today I have to go to the Intelligence Office in Poperinghe for my special pass for Dickebusch. I had twice been warned that this was urgent. Notwithstanding which I did not receive my pass until 14 days later.

At 12.30 there is shelling round Busseboom, even almost up to Henri Verdonck's farm. A shell exploded in the house of the smith, Louis Vandermarliere. The house was very badly

---

48 Brigadier General Charles William Gordon, buried at Reninghelst New Military Cemetery.
49 Major Kirkland, likewise buried at Reninghelst New Military Cemetery.

damaged. The inhabitants had been in the cellar for half a minute and so no one was wounded. In the evening shells around the farms of Henri Desmarets and Henri Breyne. However, there was considerably less artillery fire today than on the previous days.

Bad news of the Russians again. Tarnopol has fallen. This week our farmers have begun their harvest. It is pretty good, although a large part of the wheat and oats is rather too lush.[50] May and June were exceptionally favourable. July somewhat less so. The crops have done all their growing and ripened in under 3 months.

26 July, Thursday. Besides my mass there were 4 other masses in our barn, celebrated by 2 English chaplains and 2 French interpreter-priests. This is the highest number that we've had so far. New troops have arrived on Cyriel Lamerant's farm and have taken over the last little corner of grass that was left him in all his big farm, even though there was sufficient space for them next to it, where 2 batteries had departed. There are troops in Remi Onraet's meadow too.

After my mass there passes along the railway that runs through the farm an armoured train with a gigantic gun. The whole gun is 25 metres long and it runs on 32 wheels. In all the municipality of Reninghelst there is not an oak whose trunk is as thick as the barrel of this gun. And then there are several wagons behind it with men and ammunition, a whole train, in fact. The men who are sitting in the wagons appear proud of their monster-machine. It travels to Bailleul's mill, sends a few English cigars off to Fritz and a couple of hours later comes back to its stable on a siding between the farms of Cyriel Onraet and Cannaert. Each day it has a couple of such outings

---

50 When these crops grow very lush, they don't make a large quantity of grain.

and when that beast opens its maw, the whole of Dickebusch shakes. I think this fellow has made his presence known as far as Menin. In the afternoon uncommonly fierce shelling around Voormezeele and Wytschaete and fairly heavy in the north of Ypres.

The Germans are again making use of poisonous gas and fluids. A great many injured are constantly being brought into the aid posts. Some of them have had their eyes completely burned by the gas and are totally blind. Others are brought in almost completely naked: the Germans throw a substance onto their clothes which soaks through and burns their skin so that they immediately have to tear off all their clothes.[51] Those people suffer horribly.

Every day the English communiqués report raids in the Ypres area and a number of prisoners. Everything leads us to believe that the offensive will take place soon and we are longing for it. Around 10 o'clock in the morning all civilian traffic is prohibited. Why in the morning? God knows. It is just then that there is the least army traffic.

27 July, Friday. Once more a lot of shelling during the night and this continues the same throughout the day. In the evening Poperinghe is shelled. At 10.45 in the evening several German aeroplanes fly over and drop bombs in Westoutre, on fields and farms not far from New Dickebusch.[52] After that on Achiel Lamerant's farm in Reninghelst where 18 mules are killed, then on the meadow of the Verhaeghe siblings' farm, where 40 horses are killed. On the latter farm there were also

---

51 These are the effects of mustard gas.
52 In his diary entry for 20 June 1916 Van Walleghem explained that some Dickebusch refugees had built huts and sheds on the edge of Westoutre, and that the local inhabitants had given the settlement the nickname *New Dickebusch*.

5 soldiers killed and 13 wounded. Bombs on Dickebusch, too, next to Charles Maes's farm, where 27 horses and 2 soldiers are killed, and 3 soldiers wounded.

I count 26 English observation balloons. This afternoon there was a visit from Father Christ, who was previously a Xaverian Brother and who in 1907 and 1908 worked as a teacher in their institute in Bruges.

28 July, Saturday. Once more a lot of shelling in the night. The Germans fire a lot of shrapnel shells at the English observation balloons. In the evening there are 7 German aeroplanes overhead again, hurling bombs and firing their machine guns on all sides. It is worst around Potente. The firing doesn't stop all day long. Father McCann, the chaplain who has been in Zillebeke, tells us that for every shell that the Germans send over, the English reply with 20.

There are very many troops here in Reninghelst now, and all the inns are full. These are often without beer because the brewers can't keep up an unbroken supply, but a good deal of wine is drunk, which is subjected to the innkeepers' brewing methods. With sugar and water they make a sweet drink that is very much to the liking of the soldiers, and for which they pay good money. Chocolate now costs 6 francs a kilo. Tobacco costs more than 4 francs a kilo. The civilians, too, smoke a lot of cigarettes now. They see the soldiers doing it and it is easy for them to earn enough money to buy them. On the whole, the English tobacco is not much in demand among our people: too strong-smelling and too harsh on the throat. The English, for their part, smoke no Belgian tobacco, and they always have to have their own English brands of everything.

Today the 65 franc pensions for the elderly poor of Dickebusch for 1916 arrive. The same people receive a pension as in 1915, + 2 new ones. ⅓ were refused.

29 July, Sunday. 2 soldiers' masses in Lamerant's barn. During the high mass thunder and artillery fire, both very loud. One young fellow said to me of the thunder: 'It's a pity that I'm not in charge of *that* cannon, sir – the war would already be over!' Torrential rain. The shelling goes on all day. Today is a terrible day for Armentières. This poor front-line town is bombarded simultaneously with large shells and gas bombs. (The latter are like little barrels which break open immediately on landing and which contain a white powder that gradually turns to gas and starts its murderous work.) Because of the large shells, people were forced to shelter in their cellars. And there the choking gas came to attack and suffocate them. Over 1,000 civilians were poisoned and suffered horribly in their lungs and their eyes, and more than 300 died. The most noble of the victims was the Dean, an example of self-sacrifice, who had declared that he would be the last man to leave the town. He lay suffocated in his cellar beside his 2 maidservants.

All afternoon the streets of Reninghelst were swarming with soldiers. From here to the sea there are no fewer than 900,000 soldiers and more new troops and artillery keep arriving. This week Bailleul was shelled several times, in the English hospital 30 soldiers were killed and 40 injured.

30 July, Monday. There was continuous shelling all night and all day, but it was not especially heavy. At Dranoutre, Derckx, the farmer, is killed by a shell.

It is dark, overcast weather. We hear around noon that the English attack is set for tomorrow morning at daybreak. We notice that in the evening there are few soldiers in the streets because everyone is in position for the attack. The soldiers are feeling very optimistic about it and talk of having Flanders completely cleaned up in a few weeks. The civilians are less sanguine about it. They ask themselves 'What will happen to

186

our Flanders? What fate awaits our family and friends on the other side of the front line?' Hope and fear, joy and sorrow exist side by side. Let us trust in God's providence and ask that He deal with us according to His wisdom and goodness! For 14 days already no Belgian on the English and French front has been allowed to go off on leave.

31 July, Tuesday. Today it is 3 years since the Belgian army was mobilised and we thought for the first time about the possibility of war. This anniversary was to be celebrated in a most terrible manner in our region.

Already from the evening onwards there was a great deal of shelling, but at 3.30 in the morning the firing becomes uncommonly fierce and in the semi-darkness hundreds of lightning flashes criss-cross each other. There is no doubt that the attack has begun. At 8.30 we hear the first news that the attack is very successful, and of course there is a lot of exaggeration: people talk about an advance of 5 miles. However, we can soon judge for ourselves that the attack is a success: we can see that the observation balloons have moved forward, we hear that horses have been brought up in order to transport the guns further away, and at 9 o'clock we see the English cavalry approach from Westoutre and go towards the front. They take 2 hours to pass through here and they have with them light artillery. It was a long time since I had seen English cavalry and I admire their beautiful horses and the excellent equipment that they have in abundance.

The shelling dies down around 11 o'clock. In the late morning there are already a lot of motor cars passing with wounded, and they keep coming throughout the afternoon. We have to conclude that the English have not had it as easy as they had in their victory at Wytschaete and have had to pay a higher price for their triumph. The seriously wounded are carried in small Red Cross vehicles, the lightly wounded are transported in lorries. A lot of German wounded are transported too. At 12.30, 130 German prisoners of war pass by and at 2.30 another 30. The men look thin and tired out and some seem really wretched. More prisoners of war in the evening. An officer tells me that the attack was a success in the whole sector of the 5th army and also in the French sector, and the ground over which they have advanced is 24 km long, reaching from Steenstrate to the Lys, and an average of 3 to 4 kilometres deep. This tallies with this evening's communiqué and the communiqué that appears in the newspapers the next day. The French achieved their objective within 3 hours, taking Steenstrate and Bixschoote without much resistance and going on to near Kortekeer. The English took Basseville near Warneton, Verlorenhoek, Frezenberg, St. Julian, Pilkem, Hooge and Westhoek. They already have a total of 3,500 prisoners of war so far. The English came up against more opposition and in some places the fighting was terrible. It was fiercest along the Menin road and around Zillebeke. In particular, in Glencorse Wood and Inverness Copse (the woods which belong to the Vandenpeereboom and Gotschalk chateaux, west of Kantientje) the Germans had established an unimaginably well-fortified stronghold. It was a nest of big guns and machine guns, and the 24th Division and the Irish who stormed the place suffered massive losses and were forced to give up. This was the only objective not attained that day.

The weather was overcast the whole day and the aeroplanes could do little work, but as evening fell it began to rain. At 5 o'clock heavy firing begins again; it lasts for the whole of the 1st part of the night. At 9 o'clock in the evening Micmac camp is shelled: 1 shell falls on the farm and 3 just in front of Cyriel Lamerant's farm. On Hector Coene's farm an officer is killed.

The same evening, 10 big shells on Hazebrouck. In recent weeks this town has suffered a great deal of disquiet because of frequent bombing by German aeroplanes, especially around the munitions factory. But this is the first time that the German guns have been turned on Hazebrouck. The firing comes from the direction of Laventie. The fear in the town is considerable and very many people are fleeing.

1 August, Wednesday. Constant rain all day. Such a heavy blow this is to the offensive of the allied countries! In all my life I've rarely been as sad about the bad weather as I am now. To make things worse, it has also become much colder. Just imagine how much the English soldiers are suffering in their new positions, not having trenches and being forced to shelter in shell holes half full of water and under heavy rain. They went into battle in their summer outfit, in shorts and without their overcoats. Throughout the day we hear very little shelling. Around 10 in the evening, 5 shells on Poperinghe.

This evening's communiqué reports that the Germans have launched a fierce counterattack and managed to take back St. Julian and Westhoek.

2 August, Thursday. Heavy rain all night and well into the morning. I hear very little shelling, but I can see flares all the time, which makes me conclude that the artillery is continually in action. A bitterly disappointed English cavalry returns to Westoutre. Again I admire the patience and tenacity of the English, who in spite of adversity seem neither depressed nor disaffected.

3 August, Friday. 1st Friday of the month, 11 communions. In the night from 11.30 to 2.30, 14 big shells between the farms of Edmond Derycke and Henri Verhaege, at the crossroads between the railway tracks 5 minutes east of the church of Reninghelst and also at the sawmill on the La Clytte road. Again a different sort of German shelling. One cannot hear the shell approaching, there was just a big shock and then a rumbling, from which we concluded that it was an English gun (probably from an armoured train) that fired in our vicinity, and no one worried about it. How astonished we were the next day to see big shell holes close to us. At the beginning of the war we found it much easier to identify the shelling; we knew very well whether it was an English or a German gun that was firing, whether it was a high explosive or a shrapnel shell and how far away from us it fell, whether it was coming towards us or not. But now there are so many kinds of shells that we cannot figure it all out anymore and often mistake one for the other.

Last night, too, shells on Poperinghe. Last night the artillery battle was very fierce. The Catholic chaplain Father McCann of the 24th Division was wounded slightly at Zillebeke, and another Catholic chaplain, Father Knapp, of the Irish Guards, was killed on the same day.[53] Both were well-known for their courage and self-sacrifice. A protestant chaplain likewise lost his life in this battle.

Again rain all day.

4 August, Saturday. 3rd anniversary of the declaration of war against Belgium. Still raining and in the afternoon heavy showers. Such a setback for the offensive! Such a pity also for the harvest. This is really unprecedented. However, it must all be part of God's plan. Let us put our trust in Him. More firing in the afternoon.

---

53 The Rev. Simon Stock Knapp, chaplain 3rd class, died on 1 August 1917, and is buried at Dozinghem Military Cemetery.

5 August, Sunday. The rain has stopped at last, but the weather remains humid and oppressive. The harvest has suffered a lot already. All the crops have been flattened, and all the rye and a part of the oats have started sprouting quite considerably. What will become of them? Especially in Dickebusch, where as a result of the evacuation there's such a shortage of labour. In fact, there aren't enough labourers in any of the towns or villages. The civilians who work for the army aren't allowed to interrupt their labour, and the Belgian soldiers can't get leave of absence to work in the English or French sectors. The military authorities are prepared to make English soldiers available to lend a hand, but the farmers who know what an Englishman is worth as a farm labourer are not very keen to have them.

Throughout the night and the morning there was a lot of gun fire. The communiqué reports that the English have re-taken St. Julian. The French interpreter Rev. Luneau is now lodging at Cyriel Lamerant's farm. He is a brave and wise priest from the bishopric of Nantes, and this week his dedication has been particularly great. Although he was under no obligation to do so, he has spent the last few days in the combat zone of Zillebeke in order to offer assistance to the wounded and the dying, and in doing so was himself wounded slightly in the back by 2 shell fragments. In spite of this he refused all special care and he remains with his regiment. Today he took over my high mass. He recounted horrible details of the fighting. It was his division that experienced the strongest resistance along the Menin Road and in Zillebeke. A large number of German guns, impossible to locate, fired at them from 100 metres. The Irish and in particular the Leinsters[54] fought like lions and thousands of them died. In one case, of an entire battalion only 54 returned. But all of this in vain. The Kantienebossen

---

54 These are the 2nd Leinsters.

191

(Herenthage Wood) remained in the hands of the enemy. Rev. Luneau speaks especially, and with admiration, of the Irish Colonel Murphy[55] of the Leinster regiment, whom his people call 'the invulnerable.' Before the attack and amidst the cruellest bombardments he stood with a sergeant major above the parapet smoking a pipe and calmly writing down his orders (for in that infernal noise talking was impossible). Then he threw himself into the attack and he was the only officer of his battalion to return. On another occasion he took up an observation post in a tree. He was spotted in it by the Germans who aimed at him with their rifles, but without success. Then they fired shrapnel shells at him and hit the tree. The branch on which he sat was torn off and Murphy fell down! But quite unperturbed he wiped the earth off his clothes with his hand and left the spot at a leisurely pace. However, the fights in water and mud were doubly hard and cruel. In some places men sank into the mud up to their loins. Most pitiable of all was the predicament of the poor wounded. Sometimes it took hours to carry injured men 10 minutes' walking distance, and as a result there are lads who had to lie on the battlefield for 2 days before getting to an aid post. Alas a great many died before getting the necessary help, and a great many also drowned in the shell holes. And then to think that all these rescue efforts had to be made under heavy shelling and machine-gun fire. In spite of this, the English stretcher-bearers were admirable, but they were unable to cope. Under these circumstances they always make the German prisoners of war help them, which explains why sometimes 2 days after the battle we still see prisoners pass by here. They are men that have been used for the transport of the wounded. As far as the dead are concerned, it's quite impossible to carry them away.

---

55 This is the brave and popular Alfred Durham Murphy.

They are thrown into a shell hole and buried on the spot. Only some high-ranking officers and special men are buried further away. The artillery has likewise suffered heavy losses in these fights. One battery, of which the headquarters are at Cyriel Lamerant's farm, has lost all its officers.

After high mass, shells at Micmac camp and later at Rozenhil. A particularly large shell exploded right next to Hector Coene's oasthouse a quarter of an hour after I passed there.

In the afternoon the firing is very fierce and from 9 to 11 in the evening it's the heaviest bombardment I've heard in the course of the entire war. We are constantly shaken and thrown about in our beds. It's really worse than at the Messines and Wytschaete attack. The next day we hear that the Germans launched an attack on Hollebeke, got hold of it for a couple of hours, and were then thrown out again. A Belgian Canadian, who was born in Brussels, comes here full of indignation to complain about his English colleagues, who have taken the bell of Voormezeele to Abeele, whence they want to transport it as a souvenir to England. 'No,' says the lad,' that won't happen, even if it costs me 1,000 dollars.'

6 August, Monday. The English communiqué reports a small advance the other side of Kortekeer. Today mist and little sunshine and no aeroplanes. In the afternoon quite a lot of shooting.

In this area we now have a lot of Chinese men whom the English use as labourers. Where these men come from, and how they got here, I don't know. Many of them look very young. They are curious about everything and their behaviour is very childlike, no better than our children of 10 or 11 years. Their favourite pastime is to stand and gape at the shop windows, especially those of the sweet shops and the fruit shops, and when they see something that they like the look of, 10 of them at once go into the shop, ask the price of everything, and if they decide to buy something are then very suspicious that the shopkeeper will cheat them. But a lot of shopkeepers are tired of their ways and make a show of being angry, and then the fellows fly out of the shop like sparrows. Yellow in colour, with a flat nose and slanted eyes, they wear a silly smile nearly all the time and are constantly looking around them, so that it's a wonder that with our crowded roads none of them has yet been run over. They have a blue linen uniform and another one of thick grey fabric and a rain cape and an overcoat, with a straw hat or a brown cap with ear flaps. But they are extremely fond of civilian clothes and if they come by a civilian cap or hat, they will put it on and never take it off. Their gait is rather ungainly and you can see that they're not used to wearing such heavy shoes. It seems to me that they have a lot of guests, for one often sees them busy hunting lice. Their sergeants have stripes, their police a red armband, and you can see how conscious these two groups of men are of their status. With each company there is an Englishman who directs their work. In one of their camps I also saw an interpreter. He looked like a very fine gentleman and was wearing the long Chinese robe.

They are quartered in camps surrounded by barbed wire and they live in bell tents. They go to their work in groups. They are principally occupied in mending roads and digging ditches, and mainly along the unloading quays. They're not lazy and work at least as well as our civilians and the English soldiers. But what a noise they make as a group of them pass you. They all shout at once and all of them as loudly as they can. I prefer to hear them singing, their singing isn't at all bad. They all know a few odd words of English but none of them can actually speak the language. So when I passed them just before noon, I heard over and over 'Watch? Watch?': What time is it? I think their stomachs were rumbling, for when I showed them that it was just five minutes before noon, they nodded with pleasure because they would shortly be able to fill their bellies with their beloved rice. With them it's rice, rice and more rice. Morning, noon and night, always rice that they gobble up with their little sticks. Recently I came across a Chinese who was wearing a watch on each wrist. How proud he was when he saw that I was looking at his watches!

Several thousands of these men are working in Reninghelst and more of them in Poperinghe. They are like big children and they have to be handled like children. Therefore, to keep order among them the argument of the cane has to be used, and so their sergeants carry a thin iron rod which comes down now and then on the men's skin. The men don't resent this, they laugh and then are well-behaved again. They have other punishments too, and recently on passing by their camp I saw one with a yoke on his neck (like a lavatory seat), and another with a block and chain on his neck and thus collared, these men had to dig a ditch. They are not allowed to go into the inns. They certainly have little understanding of the war. When they hear a shell coming they stand and gape at it and when it bursts open, they clap their hands and laugh. However, in Poperinghe some of them were killed and then the rest were doubly shocked. In Reninghelst they have 2 big camps, 1 on the farm of the Verhaeghe siblings and 1 next to Henri Verdonck's farm.

As regards religion, I have discovered that there are some Catholics among them. While almost all of them stare at me in astonishment and don't know what to make of my cassock, I have met some who point to me and then to heaven. In the hut at Hector Dalle's farm there was one who showed me the crucifix and then pointed to me (the man of God), then to himself, and then pointed one finger up to heaven (God). The priest who is the director of the secondary school in Poperinghe has heard the confession of several of them by means of 2 prints bearing the ten commandments, one in Chinese and one in French. When he asked them to make an act of contrition, the lads began to cry. I did encounter a Chinese priest in Proven, with a floppy black hat and an overcoat, but which religion he belongs to I have no idea.

In the French sector there are no Chinese[56] but a lot of Annamites.[57] They wear a khaki uniform, are less yellow and also smaller than the Chinese, but they nevertheless bear a strong resemblance to them. They look very young.

Today I read in the *Vingtième Siècle* that I and the mayor of Dickebusch are awarded the Civilian Cross 1st class for proven service under the bombardment. Some other priests and others who have distinguished themselves at the front are in the same case. A few days later I was informed of this by the minister and the governor, and one day, a month later, I received a little box with a white cross in it, with on it: '1914-1915.'

Today I receive my yellow pass for Dickebusch and am amazed to find that it only gives me permission to enter Cyriel Lamerant's farm[58] from the roads to the west of the farm and there is no mention of the rest of the parish, where my services might equally be required. Those men imagine that our work consists only in saying the mass. However, I shall not keep asking for a less restricted pass, I shall just go wherever I like over the whole parish and I'd be perfectly happy to be charged by the police, because I know that they are in the wrong.

7 August, Tuesday. No rain, but misty. Still no balloons and not many aeroplanes. In the morning Ouderdom and Busseboom

---

56 The French did employ Chinese labourers, but not at the front.
57 Annam was at this time the name of a French protectorate covering part of present-day Vietnam.
58 Thus giving access to the makeshift church in Lamerant's barn.

are shelled. The *Het Wieltjen* inn in Busseboom is hit by a shell. No casualties. Although we still hear very little gunfire, the great number of wounded brought into the dressing stations leads us to conclude that there is fierce fighting going on. The news from the Russians is getting worse and worse.

8 August, Wednesday. A lot of changing of artillery. In the evening, heavy thunder and torrential rain. A fair amount of shelling. I go to Locre Hospice[59] and see, not far from there, laid out in a field, a relief model of the whole of the German front south-east of Oosttaverne. Along the gravel road in front of the hospice I meet Portuguese soldiers working on the railway line. They are dressed in blue like the French, but they wear a different cap.

9 August, Thursday. In the night 3 German aeroplanes drop numerous bombs on Hazebrouck and in the morning the same town is shelled by the guns. Aeroplanes come to Dickebusch, too, during the night, and drop bombs on the fields between Kapelstraat and Kemmelstraat, killing a lot of horses and also several men. In the evening bombs on Poperinghe. The 47th Division goes on rest to somewhere near St. Omer. The weather has become clearer. Observation balloons have appeared in the sky again and we can see that several of them have moved forward.

10 August, Friday. Clear skies and strong wind. I count 24 observation balloons. In the night we hear German aeroplanes. They drop bombs on Poperinghe. In the afternoon 4 German prisoners of war pass through here. The chaplains tell us that the German soldiers are content to be taken prisoner, but not

---

59 Locre Hospice was a convent where orphan girls were trained in domestic work.

197

the officers, or at least they act as though they're not. It is really scandalous how much damage the English troops are now needlessly doing to the cultivated fields of Dickebusch. Jerome Decroos had a good acreage of corn ready to be harvested and all at once the English descend on it with their horses and make it into one big stable yard so that within a couple of days everything was destroyed. And to think that there are uncultivated fields all around there, but no, they would rather go where they can do most harm. At Celeste Planckeel's farm the soldiers go and take the sheaves of grain out of the stooks to sleep on or to give to their horses. If the farmer complains he is laughed at and told that he should just leave his farm if he doesn't like it. Often it is simply impossible to get compensation. The first question that is asked in any investigation into a compensation claim is which army unit it was exactly that caused the damage. If the farmer cannot identify the unit, they say that he has no evidence. If he tries to find out which unit it is, then he's a spy, because he has no right to be sticking his nose into such matters. And so if the farmer doesn't want to end up with all sorts of mud sticking to him, he does better to keep quiet and put up with whatever happens. All the farmers want is to be able to harvest their crops as quickly as possible and get them under shelter, but alas, where can they find the people to help them?

The agricultural committee has at last received permission from the English army to allow Belgian soldiers into the English sector for harvest work and immediately the requests were sent to the army commanders. But 14 days later not a single Belgian soldier is to be seen. It's senseless, but that's army sense. And so it is that the farmers who accepted English soldiers have come off best. It's true the work is only half done, but at least it is half done.

11 August, Saturday. There is a lot of shelling in the evening and 3 times during the night German aeroplanes come. How chilling their drone is in the quiet night! They drop bombs on various camps. On Isidoor Desmedt's farm near *Boerenhol* 9 soldiers are killed and at least 30 horses. Next to Jules Spenninck's farm at Millekruisse 20 soldiers killed, 38 wounded and more than 40 horses killed. And 4 soldiers killed on Arthur Deraedt's farm.

The weather has turned bad again and in the evening there is a tremendous thunderstorm. 64 prisoners of war pass through Reninghelst. The communiqué talks of a small advance around Langemarck. The 56th Division arrives here. I hear that the 30th Division are rather weak fighters. Father McCann shows me his metal vial of holy oil that has been flattened by a bullet from a shrapnel shell. The Red Cross train goes daily to the dressing station at Comyn's farm to collect wounded.

12 August, Sunday. Good weather, but another thunderstorm in the evening. Only 75 civilians in the two masses. The communiqué says that the English have taken Westhoek and part of Glencorse Wood (at Vandenpeereboom's chateau, on the Menin road), along with 250 prisoners. I see a great many Scottish troops go up towards the firing line. At Vlamertinghe an English captive balloon above Dambre's farm is shot down in flames. By Dickebusch the English balloons have noticeably moved forwards. There is one at the mayor's farm, one at Spillebeen's, one at the big railway crossing, and one at the Hendrickx chateau.

The interpreter-priest Monsieur Luneau, who has spent another few days in Zillebeke this week, tells me of the cruel events there. It is one great lake of mud, but worse still is the horrific shelling. Sometimes, in an area 500 metres square, 3 to 5 shells land every second, and this for hours on end. The English are losing a lot of men, too. But what must the losses of the Germans be when you consider that the English are firing at least 10 times as many shells as the Germans.

13 August, Monday. There was a lot of rain again last night, and a lot of shelling too. Monsignor De Brouwer orders the *oratio imperata*[60] for good weather. The air is suffocating and the sky is overcast, but nevertheless we see several observation balloons, at which the Germans fire shrapnel shells. The communiqué reports that the English lost Glencorse Wood the day before yesterday (at the Vandenpeereboom chateau, at Kantientje, Veldhoek), but that they have advanced in the area of the railway from Ypres to Zonnebeke. During the day the firing is not very heavy. At 7 o'clock in the evening several shells fall on and around the town cemetery in Poperinghe. That is the most dangerous part of the whole town: from the secondary school to the Elisabeth hospital. There are two crossroads within that area over which all transport for the front has to pass, and those are the Germans' targets.

14 August, Tuesday. In the early morning there is a German counter-attack which is successfully repulsed. At midday and in the evening more thunderstorms, and heavy rain all night again. Between the thunderstorms, however, there is sunshine. There are several English observation balloons out. In the afternoon a German aeroplane suddenly shoots out from behind the clouds and fires at a few of the balloons, but none of them is hit. Nevertheless, to be on the safe side, the men immediately jump out of their baskets and descend by parachute. The men in the balloon over the lake jump too, and

---

60 An *oratio imperata* is an invocative prayer imposed by Roman Catholic authorities in circumstances of serious collective need or disasters.

sadly they land in the water and drown. Just two days ago we were talking about the danger of this happening and now look, it already has.

15 August, Wednesday. Assumption Day, 40 communicants. In the night there are constant flashes of light, hundreds per minute, which suggests to us that there is a terrible amount of shelling going on, even if we hear little noise, with the wind in the wrong direction. Rain and thunder almost all day. Even in the winter I hardly saw so much water and mud as there is now. No one has ever known such weather in August. The harvest is rotting in the fields. The bad weather is a calamity for the harvest and also for the fighting. Now, God has his purpose in everything and all that He does is for the best. Many people are hopeful that Our Lady's assumption day will bring an improvement in the weather.

In the moments of sunshine there are a lot of balloons and aeroplanes. Before the high mass I count 33 aeroplanes at the same time. At Reninghelst a lot of camps are deserted, but from St. Hubertus to Ypres it is swarming with soldiers. In the late afternoon shells at Ouderdom mill.

16 August, Thursday. In the evening and at night a lot of shelling, especially the large calibre guns, but from 1 a.m. till 8.30 in the morning all the guns are firing with all their might. It is a frenzy of shelling. It is worst north of Ypres. I hear that the English are attacking with 5 divisions. The firing remains quite fierce for the whole day. Our Lady has brought an improvement in the weather and today is very windy and sunny.

17 August, Friday. We hear little news about the outcome of yesterday's fighting. If one speaks to the officers about it, they know nothing, or they say flatly that it was fine, from which we suppose that it is not fine.

Today we read in the newspapers the Pope's Peace Note addressed to the warring countries. To be frank, the first reading of it hit us like a bucket of cold water. 'No indemnities for Belgium' seemed incomprehensible to us. However, a 2nd and 3rd reading showed us that indemnities for Belgium were not excluded and were to some extent implied. Further information from papal clarifications strengthened us in that belief. Moreover, consideration of the uncertainty of total victory and the terrible sacrifices which that would require in terms both of human lives and of money soon made us change our minds. We were of this opinion: if one could completely defeat the enemy and make it impossible for him to start a new war and recommence the slaughtering, good, then it is best to press on with the war until total victory is attained, and no sacrifice seems too great to us. On the other hand, if one cannot achieve that outcome – and there are many reasons for suspecting that one will not be able to: the lethargy of revolutionary Russia, now so far gone that the country cannot offer serious resistance any more; treachery and corruption in France (Almeida, Bolo, Caillaux, the friends of Minister Malvy)[61]; the heavy losses of shipping to the German submarines; the long wait before America will be ready – then it will be best to negotiate and if possible make peace, and not sacrifice millions more lives and billions more in money to the destruction of war. That was the view

----

61 Almeida was the Portuguese head of government who led his country to war in 1917 against the will of the president; Bolo Pasha was a Frenchman who became a German agent; Joseph Caillaux was a former French prime minister who lobbied for a compromise peace with Germany; and Louis-Jean Malvy was French minister of the interior and rumoured to be the lover of Mata Hari and the instigator of the mutinies in the French Army in the Spring of 1917.

of the priests in this region in mid-August. That was even more strongly our view later on, and subsequent events only strengthened this thinking.

What a lot of drivel has been spouted by the English Protestant newspapers and the French newspapers, both secular and Catholic, in their criticism of the note. A lot of foul comment has come out of the 'pure' *Vingtième Siècle* as well. *De Stem uit België, Vrij België* (*La Libre Belgique*), and *De Belgische Standaard* offered a more sensible view, but had to leave a lot unsaid because Anastasia's scissors are unpredictable.[62] We hoped that all countries would reply and at least put a toe in the water of discussion, but it was a bitter disappointment to us that France and England remained silent. God grant that they do not have cause to regret it! Will they obtain better peace terms than now after more months of fighting and more misery?

Today the weather was very sunny again, but the heat was stifling. I count 35 English observation balloons, from the sea to La Bassée. The Germans fire a lot of shrapnel shells at them.

In the evening at 9.30, 5 German aeroplanes come to Reninghelst and remain for more than half an hour over the square and its surrounding area. Anti-aircraft guns and machine guns shoot furiously at these birds of death, but they don't seem to pay them much attention. There are 5 terrible cracking noises one after the other nearby and we guess that the birds have laid their eggs here. It was Zevecote that received this treat. They fell in the gardens of the right-hand 3-house terrace, just 3 or 4 metres from the houses. One of the craters, where 3 bombs exploded in the same place, was enormous. The rear side of the houses was horribly damaged but no civilian was hurt. It was worse in a soldiers' hut in Pieter Cambron's meadow. 2 soldiers

---

62 In French, the expression 'Dame Anastasie' refers to censorship.

were killed there and 3 wounded. A Protestant minister from the Y.M.C.A. next to the meadow was injured too. 20 metres from where the bombs exploded are the soldiers' cinema, theatre and canteens, always brightly lit. There is no doubt that the aeroplanes had seen all that light and were aiming for it. The police are always very strict with civilians in the matter of lights, but very lax with the soldiers. One hour after these events I saw that in Durein's house all the upstairs windows, where the officers' rooms are, were lit up.

There was an amusing little incident once in La Clytte parish. One evening the pastor was sitting in his dining room with the shutters closed. Suddenly there was a knock at the door. It's a Belgian policeman, who asks the pastor to stop showing a light. 'Well, sir,' says the pastor, 'you can see that my shutters here are closed. Perhaps things are otherwise in my sitting room, you can have a look.' The pastor knocks on the sitting room door and pushes the policeman inside, and the man finds himself face to face with the General and his chief of staff. The poor fool stands there dumbfounded, not knowing what to say, and he makes his excuses and leaves. An hour later the sitting room shutters were still not closed.

The aeroplanes also bombed Mont Rouge, Poperinghe and the big hospital in De Leene (Lijssenthoek). One bomb fell on the Australian hospital where there were injured German soldiers, and 18 Germans and 2 nurses were killed.

18 August, Saturday. Little shooting during the night, although I hear a few shrapnel shells whistling past. At 2 o'clock in the morning the aeroplanes come again. I hear several bombs fall, but some way off. The communiqué speaks about the offensive of the day before yesterday and says that the English and the French attacked on a front of 18 kilometres. The French advanced as far as Martjevaart and are in control of both banks at Drie Grachten. The English took Langemarck and have already advanced 800 metres beyond there, but suffered a grievous reverse at Zonnebeke. At first everything went well, they had passed Polygon Wood and had almost reached Zonnebeke. But suddenly the Germans, who had amassed a great number of troops at Zonnebeke, mounted a ferocious counter-attack. The English, who had already lost a number of people in our offensive, could not withstand it and had to give up the ground that they had won. In the inns, and in talking with the laundry-women, the soldiers relate terrible things about the fighting at Zonnebeke: how unexpected the counter-attack was, how they were taken by surprise, how they lost communication with their artillery and how the artillery more than once shot into the ranks of their own men. They lost more than 6,000 men there and were forced to leave their wounded behind in enemy hands. The allies took 400 prisoners of war in this attack.

The communiqué also reports that the Canadians have carried out an attack east of Loos and took 1,800 prisoners of war.

Rev. Van Houver, of Westoutre, has received permission from the Pope to celebrate mass in his house. For this I lend him the altar stone, a complete set of mass vestments and a stole of each colour. The other vestments and stoles remain with Madame Brigou.

Today is fairly quiet, though at 10 o'clock in the evening we hear aeroplanes again. In the distance we hear bombs exploding.

19 August, Sunday. When I go to Dickebusch I see that the tanks have set off again along their usual route. I see one tank standing by Cyriel Lamerant's stream. It's covered with branches. I can see around it very well, but from the outside there is little to see. It's all wheels and cladding. There are various little openings and I would like to see the inside of it, but I don't dare risk it because if I were caught I would certainly get into trouble. Civilians who have seen the intestines of that monster declare that the mechanics of it are marvellous. A French interpreter-priest conducts the high mass, so after my mass I take a walk to the village. Dickebusch is now one uninterrupted army camp throughout its entire extent. In front of the presbytery, in Thevelin's meadow, there is also a big new camp, 'Lakeside Camp.' I see that the train track has been extended from Dalle's farm to *Paradijs*, where there is now a big unloading quay. I see that Jules Goethals's barn in Kerkstraat and the wall of the presbytery garden have been demolished. All the fruit from the gardens has already found its way into the soldiers' stomachs. In the church I find that a shell has exploded in the wall behind Saint Sebastian's altar ½ metre above the ground and has made a big hole 2 metres high and 1½ metres wide. The strongbox which was built into the wall is lying ripped apart as though it were made of paper. The choir has been cleaned up and there are planks across the altar and the altar table, from which I conclude that mass is sometimes being said here, and indeed while I am there Father McCann comes in, with about 125 Australian soldiers, to celebrate mass. I go to the convent school, which is still standing, and there, too, I find a chaplain saying his mass for the English soldiers.

I see that the triangle of land that Jules Philippe uses is already full of graves of English soldiers and I hear that they have already established a new cemetery on Comyn's land, next to the big dressing station. At Razelput I read a signpost: 'To Vierstraat, Brasserie, Kruisstraat, Confusion Corner.'

The 47th Division, which was on its way to 14 days' rest in France, is called back after 3 days. Father Bickford is quartered near the Vandenpeereboom chateau and tomorrow they have to go to the Menin road. We expect a new English attack in the next few days.

A German aeroplane is shot down today in Dickebusch.

At 9.30 in the evening a whole squadron of German aeroplanes flies over. What a hideous roar, low and threatening: one can hear that the birds of death are heavily loaded with bombs and that the motors are longing to be rid of them. They fly over the whole area and for more than an hour they circle over Reninghelst village square. What terrifying moments for us. Artillery and machine guns fire as hard as they can at these instruments of death but the birds don't wait long to unburden themselves and they fling bombs in all directions. What monstrous blows! Soon through my window I see the whole square lit up, and I hear that 2 lorries behind the start of Abeelestraat were set on fire by the bombing.

The following day we heard what death and destruction the aeroplanes brought about. 3 bombs had fallen on Charles Deconinck's farm at Reninghelst square, killing and injuring several soldiers and horses, and also injuring Charles's horse. More bombs had fallen on Elie Planckeel's farm. Still others on a camp at Rozenhil. There, too, horses and men had been killed. At Dickebusch, camps had been bombed next to Henri Breyne, Charles-Louis Charles and Henri Vermeulen, and many horses and men had been killed. At Speelhof, between Ouderdom and Potente, a bomb had hit an ammunition dump. The ammunition caught fire and exploded and the explosion was so powerful that all the windows in a radius of 10 minutes' walking distance were blown out.

20 August, Monday. From 2.30 a.m. until 7.00 a.m. very heavy artillery fire north of Ypres. At 5.45 I say mass at Cyriel Lamerant's farm and then take the sacrament to 5 sick parishioners. I notice that during the night tanks have once again set off for the front. Some of them started off close to the centre of the village, heading towards Ypres, the others went via Hallebast towards Hollebeke. At 9.30 I see an aerial fight between English and German aeroplanes. A German machine drops like a stone and smashes into pieces next to Amand Heugebaert's farm. In the evening, from 9.15 to 10.45, there are German aeroplanes above the centre of the village again. We hear several bombs fall, but at some distance from here. We also see English flying machines which have lights (they look like comets). The next day we hear that an aerodrome was heavily shelled next to Vogeltje.

21 August, Tuesday. During the day the Germans fire a lot of shrapnel shells at the English observation balloons. There are very few troops in Reninghelst, almost all have gone to the firing line. We are expecting an attack tomorrow. No aeroplanes this evening.

22 August, Wednesday. At 4.30 in the morning several German aeroplanes bombard the Dickebusch camps. At Razelput they kill 27 horses and 3 men, at Jules Spenninck's farm 18 horses and 4 men. On Marcel Coene's farm, in the wood, 33 horses dead and injured horses and men everywhere. At 5 o'clock the English begin their attack, and for 5 hours the artillery fire is extremely heavy. It is fiercest around Zonnebeke and the Menin road. Around midday a few prisoners of war pass through Reninghelst. The following day's communiqué reports that the English have attacked on the front between the Menin road and Langemarck and have advanced 500 metres. The Germans retain control of the woods at Vandenpeerenboom chateau, the woods belonging to Godschalk chateau are partly in English hands.

Today shells explode by Hector Dalle's farm and at the lake. At the lake 2 men and 16 horses are killed.

The communiqués say that the Italians have attacked and have taken 6,700 prisoners of war, and the French have carried out an attack around Verdun and report 5,000 prisoners of war.

In the evening, a great deal of shelling. We see shrapnel shells bursting open above Elverdinghe. At 9.30 we receive another visit from the nocturnal birds of death. They remain above us for half an hour and drop several bombs around the farms of Cyriel Steen, Dehouck and Lagache, and also a few minutes' walk north of Reninghelst church, where they kill 4 horses. On Theophiel Dauchy's farm at Rozenhil they kill 6 men and 24 horses. The English sweep beams of light around the sky all the time, seeking out the aeroplanes.

23 August, Thursday. At 4.30 in the morning a German aeroplane drops 2 bombs by Hector Dalle's farm, and after my mass, at 8 o'clock, a shell explodes next to Benoit De Crock's barn. Today 13 prisoners of war pass through Reninghelst.

The weather has been good for 8 days now and yet still there remains a great deal of harvesting to be done. Due to a lack of labour. Still no Belgian soldiers have come to help. And meanwhile the destruction caused by the soldiers grows steadily greater. The Australians are the worst. Some farmers are bringing in their harvest while it is still only half dry, in an attempt to save at least some of it. Those compensation requests that the authorities are prepared to accept are accounted losses of war, even when they are due to theft. They will be evaluated and paid after the war. How can that be right? And meanwhile the farmers can just keep paying out more and more money. If they think that anyone will protect them they are mistaken. I am absolutely at a loss to understand what the purpose is in having a Belgian representative here.

In the evening we hear aeroplanes again, but they don't come to the village square.

24 August, Friday. Strong winds. In the whole day I saw just one aeroplane. The Germans make a counter-attack along the Menin road and gain some ground. The English re-take it immediately.

25 August, Saturday. The wind has dropped somewhat. The Germans fire a lot of shrapnel shells at the observation balloons. At 4 o'clock in the afternoon 5 German aeroplanes drop bombs on the camps at Hemelrijk and the Vandenpeerenboom chateau, killing horses and men. At 9.30 in the evening more aeroplanes, which drop bombs around Monsieur Hendrickx's chateau with the same results.

26 August, Sunday. In the night the English make another attack along the Menin road, on Glencorse Wood and Inverness Copse (which is what they call the woods at the Vandenpeerenboom and Godschalk chateaux). They reach their goal but are unable to hold out there because they come under such intense fire and they are forced to retreat to their previous positions. The English say that they have never come up against the kind of fortifications that exist in the Kantienebossen (Herenthage Wood). There are several uncommonly strong shelters there, made of reinforced concrete, and in them there are not only many machine guns but also small artillery which sometimes fires at very close range. Up to now the heavy English artillery has not been able to destroy those 'pillboxes' (as they are called). The best English divisions have stormed them, but to no avail, and in the process they have lost a great many men. Now they are trying to come up with a new tactic to conquer these fortifications.

The morale of the English troops on this front is considerably lower due to the fierce resistance of the enemy. The best soldiers here are the Leinsters from Ireland and they are also the best Catholics. Father Hurley says that his brigade lost 300 men last week just in the trenches, without any attack.

In the morning at 8.30 shells come whistling above our chapel and explode five minutes to the east of Reninghelst church. Between my masses I visit the new English cemetery along Windeweg next to Emiel Comyn's farm. The first burials were carried out on the 1st of August and now there are already 240 soldiers buried there. They are all men who died in the dressing station next to the cemetery (the 'Corps Main Ambulance').[63]

It is already 3 weeks since Poperinghe was last shelled by the guns. The aeroplanes, though, continue to bombard it.

A record in church services! In Reninghelst today, vespers, the stations of the cross and the prayers were all completed in just 30 minutes. Assuredly, the Protestants who now and then stick their heads into our church must have a high opinion of Catholic services and the Catholic religion. If any Protestant here gets the idea into his head to convert it will certainly not be the fault of his reverence the pastor of Reninghelst. The Catholic church services here are rarely if ever conducted with even the slightest regard for the proper order of things.

27 August, Monday. Torrential rain all night and very strong winds. In the afternoon a lot of shelling.

28 August, Tuesday. Exceptionally strong wind. Along the main roads a lot of trees are blown over. At 10 o'clock in the morning shells by Delporte's farm and at 3 o'clock

---

63 This is now The Huts Cemetery.

in the afternoon shells by the Goethals-Verraest farm. The communiqué reports that the Italians have already taken 23,600 prisoners of war.

29 August, Wednesday. At midnight shells close to the Goethals-Verraest farm.

30 August, Thursday. The English communiqué reports a small advance towards Poelcapelle.

The harvest is more or less in now, where it is worth being gathered in, which is far from being the case everywhere. Over ⅓ of the mayor's crops couldn't be picked and he couldn't bring in another third. Arthur Cafmeyer had 5 acres of corn but couldn't bring in a single sheaf. Jules Goethals had used 3,000 francs' worth of fertiliser on his crops and couldn't cut a single sheaf of corn. Camiel Derycke managed to harvest just two cartloads from his whole farm. Now that almost all the harvest work is done, the military authorities judge that the moment has come to allow the Belgian soldiers work leave. And so the police are sent around to the farmers who requested workers, to find out what still needs to be done. And thus, after a few days, we see the occasional soldier turn up here and there, coming to work. Some farmers get them, others don't.

31 August, Friday. In the afternoon the weather was better than in the preceding days and once again we see balloons and aeroplanes. 6 German birds circle above Dickebusch for a long time and drop several bombs at the lake and at Hallebast. At the lake several horses and men are killed. At Hallebast a big bomb falls at the crossroads just in front of Arthur Desmarets's front door and kills the English sentry who was standing on duty next to the Belgian policeman. Another bomb just next to the spot killed 40 horses.

In the evening several motor cars pass through here with English sailors who have come to visit the front line. Smartly dressed men in blue suits with white caps and broad white shirt collars over their lapels, all of them cheerful and polite.

1 September, Saturday. Full moon. In the night we hear aeroplanes several times and we hear bombs explode, but the aeroplanes don't come to the village. Some bombs are dropped on Proven.

People are no longer very hopeful that the offensive in Flanders will be successful. What we think now is that they will advance a few kilometres further and then come to a halt.

In the afternoon I go to Abeele and come back by way of Poperinghe. Rarely have I seen so many soldiers, with divisions coming to the front and divisions leaving. Along the road from Abeele to Poperinghe I saw at least 500 motorcars.

I notice that in Poperinghe a lot of hop fields have been flattened by the strong wind of last week. In several of those fields people are already picking the hops. In general, this has been a very bad year for hops, the yield has been low and the quality poor. Recently the hop fields have been blighted by sooty mould and near the roads the dust prevented the blossoms from opening. The buyers are offering 150 francs for 1st quality, 140 francs for medium quality and 120 francs for the lowest quality. These would be high prices in normal circumstances, but in the current conditions farmers can't survive on them. Daily pay for workers is 3 times as high as in peacetime, coke and sulphur are phenomenally expensive,[64] and some farmers haven't even been able to lay their hands on them. As a consequence, many farmers, finding that all their work and costs are unrewarded, abandon the harvest and leave their hops to rot in the field. By

---

64 Sulphur is a treatment against mould or mildew, coke was needed to provide heat in the oast houses to dry the hops.

my estimate there remain about 10 hop fields in the Reninghelst municipality, and I only know of 3 that have been picked.

I go to visit a refugee farmer from Dickebusch who now does jobs as a carter. He tells me that he drove from Poperinghe to Dunkirk to collect 4,000 kilos of malt. For those 4,000 kilos, the brewer pays 7,600 francs. For the transport he pays just 125 francs. To earn this, the refugee has to borrow his neighbour's horse, at a cost of 40 francs, and pay for its feed for the two days of the journey.

It is horrific how the soldiers have ravaged the potato fields. Camile Derycke of Dickebusch has 900 rods put down to potatoes and every potato has already been stolen. On the farm of Cyriel Verpoort, his neighbour, the same story. Arthur Desmarets caught a soldier digging up his potatoes. The soldier tells him that he was sent by an officer. He goes to the officer, who admits it and simply replies 'To pay after the war.'[65] All the Dickebusch farmers who have sown or planted crops this year regret it bitterly.

2 September, Sunday. At noon, shells near Celeste Planckeel's farm and in the afternoon between Benoit Decrock's farm and Cyriel Lamerant's. At 10.30 in the evening the German birds of death fly over to us once more. Their bellies heavy with their wares of death, for an hour and a half they strain and moan above the terrified inhabitants of our village square. Machine guns and artillery fire and shells exploding, all at once and almost continuously. What dreadful hours. Several shells fall on and around the square. In Mr Six's meadow, behind the curate's house, 20 men were wounded and 6 horses killed and 18 wounded. 300 metres east of Reninghelst church a fire bomb falls on an ammunitions train, killing

---

65 This quote is in English in the original diary.

several soldiers outright. Within moments several wagons catch fire. At risk of their lives the soldiers uncouple the 3 wagons that are burning the most and drive the rest of the train, with two wagons on fire, in the direction of Westoutre. When they reach the stream they start throwing water on the fires and succeed in putting them out. Meanwhile, the fire in the 3 abandoned wagons had got a still stronger hold and 10 minutes later all 3 of them flew into the air. What a colossal explosion! Not a house in the square was left with all its windows intact. The curate's house suddenly had 15 new ventilation holes. In the church, too, panes were blown out on all sides and sadly even the stained glass windows suffered badly. A refugee from Dickebusch, Henri Vieren, is living in a house just 30 metres from the site of the disaster and the house was shaken so violently that there were almost no tiles left on the roof and there were great cracks and holes everywhere. Luckily, on either side of the place where the wagons exploded there was a big bank of earth left from the digging of the bed for the railway track, which meant that the force of the explosion was somewhat broken, otherwise the whole house would have collapsed.

In Locre a bomb falls on a house about 40 metres from the hospice. The whole building collapsed and one daughter of the house was killed. Another daughter and the father were injured. A lot of bombs on Bailleul as well, and many civilians and soldiers are killed. A German aeroplane is shot down.

3 September, Monday. In the morning, shelling near *Boerenhol* in Reninghelst. In the afternoon I go to Mont Rouge and from the hill take a look at how things now stand on the front line. I see that there is already grass growing on the shelled ground of Wytschaete, but two tracks towards the ruined village are clearly visible. I also see 2 or 3 places where the monotony of the light green carpet is broken; these are doubtless the enormous craters caused by the exploding mines. Apart from that, everywhere I look along the front line there is nothing but bare, churned-up earth.

A Dickebusch cavalry soldier who is currently quartered in France, near Bourbourg, says that the French are very strict with regard to the behaviour of the Belgian soldiers. They are not even allowed to knock a nail into a wall and any damage that they cause is docked from their pay. It's a pity that the French soldiers don't bear that in mind when they come to Belgium. The Belgian soldiers who are over there complain that everything is terribly expensive there, more than double what it is in Belgium. And they get insulted by the local people, and fights have broken out more than once.

In the evening and virtually the whole night German aeroplanes. They drop bombs at Charles-Louis Kestelyn's farm at La Clytte, where horses and men are killed, also bombs at *De Ondank* in Westoutre. Also a bomb just in front of Cyriel Lamerant's farm. And in between the guns spew shells at Delporte's farm in Ouderdom.

4 September, Tuesday. German aeroplanes above us almost all morning. At 10.00 I was in the English cemetery when a stray anti-aircraft shell lands and explodes 10 metres from me. The 58th and the 33rd Divisions have arrived here. We have a visit in the curate's house from Father Claeys, chaplain to the 33rd Division artillery. Father Claeys comes from Courtrai and in 1895 he spent a year in the Bruges seminary. Now he is a professor in the Glasgow seminary. 4 months ago all his English and Scottish seminarists, who had mostly not been called up, were mobilised. This meant that the seminary had to close. Father Claeys and another professor, keen to prove their patriotism, volunteered as chaplains. 2 months ago they arrived in La Panne, in the Nieuport sector. His colleague was killed in the hospital and now Father Claeys has arrived in Reninghelst with his division. There were also a lot of Irish seminarists in the seminary, but few of them joined up. Because of this they will no longer be respected in England.

Today several friends came to visit in the curate's house and we had 2 card tables. It's a long time since anything like this has happened.

In the last few days Dickebusch has been heavily shelled, especially around the mayor's farm.

5 September, Wednesday. Another horrible night. All through the night the birds of death were circling above. 2 bombardments were especially dreadful. Several bombs fall close to Kasteelmolen, others along the gravel road from Hemelstraat to Neergraaf. Some also fall on Quebec camp, along the La Clytte road. The hut that Father McCann slept in is blown to pieces and his clothes are full of holes. 4 shells fall on Cyriel Lamerant's farm, too, and it's a wonder that no one was hurt. The bombs that hit it were of the smallest, but also the nastiest, kind. They explode as soon as they touch the ground and burst into a thousand and more pieces. As a consequence, they only make a small pit in the ground (sometimes scooping out just 3 buckets full of earth) but the thousand pieces fly along the ground, tearing it up and spraying out for 30-40 metres all around. A wall can withstand them, but the bits of metal go straight through the side of any hut, whether it's made of iron sheets or of wood, and then they still have enough force to go through horses and men. If you are hiding behind a wall, then you have little to fear from these, but if you're not, they're the most dangerous of all. 1 fell a foot from the horses' stable, in front of the horses' noses, and luckily the pieces didn't get through the wall. A 2nd one

217

fell on a soldiers' hut which was entirely destroyed, a 3rd on the railway line and a 4th on the road barrier in front. On all sides, pieces of metal bored through soldiers' huts. Luckily the soldiers who had been billeted there had left just that same morning and the huts were empty. The previous night there were a colonel and several officers sleeping in the hut that was destroyed. A cruel bombardment, and everything worked out well! May God continue to protect the good Lamerant family who so willingly give up their barn to serve as His temple in these sad times.

As well as this sort of bomb the aeroplanes drop another sort: these are very big, sometimes more than 1 metre long and 30 cm in diameter. They, too, have a fairly thin outer casing but they are filled entirely with powder. This means that they are light relative to their size: 80 to 90 kilos. The way they work, however, is completely different. They cause a huge explosion. If they fall on a house, they will certainly demolish the whole building, and if they fall on open ground, they make an enormous crater. And yet it can happen that one falls 5 or 6 metres from you but nevertheless you remain unharmed, while at the same distance the small ones would leave you full of puncture holes. The aeroplanes use the big bombs mostly for bombarding buildings, railway lines and ammunition, and they use their small bombs mostly to bombard the camps.

A lot of people in the parish didn't sleep last night and spent the whole night in fear in the safest corner of their house or cellar, waiting for the skies to clear. Others make up a bed for themselves in the kitchen or the cellar and try to snatch a little sleep here and there. We, too, here in the curate's house, are uneasy, but we decide that there is nowhere in the house that is particularly safe, so we don't think that the difference in safety is worth the trouble of moving to a different sleeping place, and we stay in our beds upstairs in our bedrooms, placing ourselves in the good hands of our guardian angels.

Sad news that Riga has been taken by the Germans.

6 September, Thursday. At 10 in the evening and at midnight several shells explode between Ouderdom and the village, around the Verhaeghe, Steen and Cossey farms. After that, bombardment by aeroplanes and guns at *Boerenhol* and at Drie Goen, where 30 mules were killed. At 4 in the morning thunder and rain and at the same time heavy gunfire, the worst of it to the north of Ypres. Thunder from the skies and thunder from the guns, both at once and both at their most violent. I sit by my window and marvel at the lightning. At 6 o'clock the thundering of the guns calms down somewhat but at 7 it starts up again even more fiercely and lasts right through the morning. In the afternoon things are quieter, but at 7 in the evening, alongside a fresh thunderstorm another frenzy of shooting. It really seems as though men and nature are crashing out their thunder and lightning in competition with each other.

I notice that there are far fewer soldiers than usual at the north-west side of Dickebusch.

7 September, Friday. A dark night. No aeroplanes and also little shooting. A lot of people haven't slept so well for a long time.

In the morning a few prisoners of war pass through Reninghelst. In the afternoon a lot of German aeroplanes, which drop several bombs. At 1.30, 3 civilians who were working mending roads were killed near Mr Behaegel's chateau at Locre. 2 of them were refugees from Wytschaete and 1 was a refugee from Messines. Several soldiers were killed as well at Jules Desmytere's farm in Vlamertinghe. In the afternoon 16 tanks went past Cyriel Lamerant's farm, on their way from the front, going back to their hangars in Ouderdom. In the evening a lot of shooting.

The soldiers say little about yesterday's fighting, although it was very fierce. The communiqué mentions a small advance north of Frezenberg.

8 September, Saturday. Feast of the Nativity of Mary. At 11 o'clock at night we hear aeroplanes but they don't fly over Reninghelst. We hear that they dropped bombs round the Torreel woods at Dickebusch.

More tanks returning to their hangars. Soldiers from the Intelligence Office in Poperinghe come round the village asking civilians for any photographic postcards of 30 or so villages, mainly in the Roulers, Thielt and Courtrai areas. I am able to give them a few of Pitthem. In the same way, a lot of people from those parishes have already been called to the Intelligence Office to provide information about the villages in question.

In Russia the situation goes from bad to worse.

A great deal of shooting in the evening.

9 September, Sunday. Calm night, but a lot of shelling at 4 a.m. Around noon German aeroplanes fly over Dickebusch and drop a great many bombs. At least 80 mules are killed at *Het Zweerd*, the fields looked like a slaughter yard. Horses and men killed at Celeste Planckeel's farm, too. More men killed at the big dressing station by Comyn's farm. I estimate that in Dickebusch this summer there have already been between 800 and 1,000 horses and mules killed.

The tank soldiers, who are quartered on the fields next to Benjamin Haelewijn's house, are packing up and are off to France with their machines.

I baptise Oscar Gesquiere's child in La Clytte chapel.

In *De Belgische Standaard* I read that Pitthem station was bombed in the last few days.

10 September, Monday. A calm night and not much shooting during the day. Shelling at Ouderdom. A lot of Australian artillery arrive.

Father Gill, S.J., who was at Dickebusch with the 3rd Division in the summer of 1915, is here once again. He is now a major in the 25th Division. Today he celebrates mass for a large number of soldiers in Lamerant's barn. He recalled how he had celebrated mass in the same place two years ago.

At 9.30 in the evening German aeroplanes over Reninghelst. We hear bombs explode, but not close to the village square.

11 September, Tuesday. All night fierce gunfire. In the morning, shelling at Hallebast and Razelput. German aeroplanes above virtually all day.

In the garden of Locre Hospice is the grave of Major Redmond, who died in the battle of Wytschaete. A lot of important people come to visit his grave, and sign the visitors' book[66] that the sisters have made in his honour. Next to the grave of Major Redmond another burial place is prepared for the chaplain Father Doyle,[67] an exemplary priest and a courageous man who died 14 days ago between Frezenberg and Zonnebeke and whose body lies unburied in the front enemy line.

From 9 to 11 in the evening there are aeroplanes above us almost continually, though most of them are English ones, with lights, on their way to the enemy heavily laden with the wares of destruction.

Every day the English communiqués talk of the numerous enemy positions, stations, airfields, camps and towns that their aeroplanes have bombed. To our sorrow we also hear

---

66 This has been preserved and is now kept at the In Flanders Fields Museum, Ypres. One can also find Van Walleghem's signature in it.
67 Father Willie Doyle's body was never recovered.

how those bombardments kill many of our civilians.

12 September, Wednesday. A lot of shooting all night, extremely fierce from 2 to 7 o'clock. We feel several strong shocks. The last few days we have been able to hear the guns much better than usual and it seems to us as though the enemy has got closer. Australians continue to arrive almost all day long. Australian artillery are on Cyriel Lamerant's farm now and they are also in the curate's house in Reninghelst. A lot of big guns go off to the front, too. We hear that the English have given up on their offensive at Nieuport and that this allows them greatly to increase their strength here. And so we expect even fiercer fighting within a few days.

We have a visit from Adiel Algoet, a soldier from Pitthem, who has been granted work leave in La Clytte at the farm of Victor Verelst, who is also from Pitthem. Quite a few Belgian soldiers are coming on work leave now.

Almost all the working folk are now working for the Englishman, on train tracks and roads, sawmills and unloading quays. And it is scandalous how bone idle they are. They are paid 4 to 5 francs per day and many of them don't deserve half a franc. I can't help wondering what the future holds: will these people still be capable of work after the war, or willing to work for a much lower wage? The youngsters, especially, below the age of military service, who haven't known any work other than war work, will be completely spoilt. You come across fellows of 13 or 14. You do also find the occasional sensible father who won't allow his sons to work for the army.

At 9 in the evening German aeroplanes again. We hear them in the distance dropping bombs. English aeroplanes, with their lights on, take off in pursuit of the enemy.

13 September, Thursday. A great many more Australian

artillery leave. The 24th Division with Father Clinton and the interpreter-priest Monsieur Luneau leave. Father Clinton acknowledges that the English destroy so many crops needlessly, and he says that it doesn't happen in France. There remain here the 39th, 33rd and 21st English Divisions.

Many tanks are loaded onto the train and leave the area.

14 September, Friday. Night and day fairly calm.

A lot more Australians arrive and also Chinese workers. Behind the sheep barn there is a model of the Zonnebeke area, which the English have yet to take. In Russia, quarrel between Chairman Kerensky and Commander-in-Chief Kornilov. More and more we deplore that the Pope's peace note has been ignored.

15 September, Saturday. Calm night. At noon a squadron of 15 German aeroplanes comes to reconnoitre over Dickebusch. We hear that on the Belgian part of the front, camps and stations were also heavily bombarded. In the evening the Australians make their presence clearly felt. The streets are a great deal more boisterous and noisy. 'They're a good lot,' say the innkeepers.

On every street corner in the municipality there are notices on the walls about the requisitions. They say what crops the farmers can keep and what they have to hand over. As *foodstuff* they may keep: 200 kilos of wheat per person and 1/4 kilo of potatoes per person per day. For *sowing and planting* they may keep:

wheat	175 kilos per hectare
haricot beans	200 kilos per hectare
barley	180 kilos per hectare
potatoes	1,600 kilos per hectare
peas	200 kilos per hectare

Everything else will be requisitioned by the committee or by the army:

wheat at	45 francs per 100 kg
rye	40 francs per 100 kg
oats	40 francs per 100 kg
barley	42 francs per 100 kg
chicory	8,50 francs per 100 kg
French beans	75 francs per 100 kg
peas	70 francs per 100 kg

The farmers are also given notice for next year's harvest: 3/8 of the cultivated land must be used for wheat, 1/8 for potatoes, 3/8 for fodder crops and 1/8 for industrial crops. The farmers are not allowed to take more than 100 kilos of grain at a time to be ground, and they have to have a special permit every time they take grain to the mill.

There is a lot of criticism of many of the arrangements. For example: 'The brewers are to pay 200 francs for malt and the farmer will get 40 francs for his barley. What happens to the difference?'

The traders are currently paying 3.30 francs per kilo for chicory and for the new crop the farmer is promised 8.50 francs per 100 kilos. There was a strange business concerning last winter's requisitioned chicory. Around New Year the beans were going for 115 francs per 100 kilos (because a lot were being smuggled into France). All at once the price was cut to 35 francs for the beans that remained. The sellers appealed over this price and meanwhile the beans sat untouched in Watou while foreign chicory had to be imported all the time at very high prices.

Another notice about payments is on the walls. This one says that goods bought from the supply committees can be paid for with Belgian money. On their side, the committee reserves the right also to pay suppliers with Belgian money. This is a good measure, because a lot of bakers, councillors etc.

have been only accepting French money and then exchanging the French money for Belgian, sometimes at a profit of 5 or 6%, while making their own payments in Belgian money.

Every civilian must indicate which baker he gets his bread from. Since there is no longer a baker in Dickebusch, the Reninghelst baker Patou has been appointed to deliver bread, and he receives a commensurate amount of flour.

Horses are extraordinarily expensive nowadays. An ordinary three-year-old horse costs 2,000 francs.

Despite all the regulations, when civilians do business with one another they often go much higher than the regulation price. For example, oats are sold for 60 or 65 francs. But the farmer has to make sure that he can deliver the quantity of grain that he's required to hand over, otherwise he'll be tried and fined. In France the regulation price is higher than in Belgium, and there, there is even more cheating.

16 September, Sunday. At 5 in the morning for an hour, and again at 9.30 for an hour, extremely heavy firing in the Wytschaete area. After high mass a squadron of 17 German aeroplanes arrives above Reninghelst. They are only reconnoitring and don't drop any bombs. They don't fly high and I notice that 3 of them are exceptionally big. I'm told that these are 'Gothas' and that they are mostly used for bombardments because they can carry great quantities of murder-wares.

Several English and Australian soldiers come to my chapel for confession and for communion. Between my masses I visit the village. I notice that there is a double railway line from Oudewal to the centre. Another line leads from Dalle's farm to Thevelin's warehouse, and this line is full of wagons. I see that what remained of the convent has gone, and also Theophiel Debaene's house has disappeared. English soldiers are repairing the roofs of the houses that are in the best condition, using the roof-tiles from the more badly damaged ones. Thus my house will once more be dry. In the church I find the Catholic chaplain MacClement, and Agius from Malta. One of them will begin the mass for the English soldiers at 9 o'clock while the other hears confessions.

Yesterday and today shelling a few minutes north-east of Poperinghe.

Today the 47th English Division leaves the Ypres front for good, having been here almost without a break for 11 months. The English chaplains are divided into two groups: C. of E. (Church of England) and non C. of E. In each group there is a major, the others being captains. In the Non C of E group are the Catholics, the Presbyterians, the Evangelicals, etc. and one of them is the major. Sometimes it's a Catholic, sometimes it's another one.

17 September, Monday. Calm night. Early in the morning tremendous firing in the distance. We go to Locre to the funeral of Rev. Plaetevoet, the priest at Locre Hospice, who died there last Wednesday. Monsignor De Brouwer and 17 priests were present. Rev. Plettinck, curate at Kemmel, is appointed in his place and becomes director. He will fulfil these duties for as long as they can be combined with his duties as curate of Kemmel. He will live in Mr Plaetevoet's house and on Sundays he will do one mass in the hospice and one at a farm in Kemmel. There are fewer than 70 people left at the hospice.

On the way home we go up the Scherpenberg. We see a lot of artillery firing and can make out very clearly the church tower at Wervicq.

Our expectation of an imminent English attack grows ever stronger.

18 September, Tuesday. Nothing of note. The 5th Australian Division arrives. A lot of men go off to the trenches. In the evening we see incessant lightning flashes, from which we conclude that a lot of shooting is going on. We hear little, however. The wind is in the wrong direction.

19 September, Wednesday. Again, despite the fact that there is a great deal of shelling, little noise reaches us. In the evening, however, the continuous lightning flashes leave us in no doubt. This afternoon we hear that the English attack will take place at 5 o'clock tomorrow morning.[68]

20 September, Thursday. Heavy downpour during the night. At 5 in the morning I hear no more firing than usual and conclude that no attack is happening at all. But when I arrive in Dickebusch I hear a lot more shelling and I am told that the attack did indeed begin at 5 o'clock. At 8 o'clock the artillery fire increases. I go with a French interpreter-priest to Hemelrijk. At Lemahieu's farm I meet an entire train full of lightly wounded troops which is on its way to the dressing station. The armoured train at Bailleul's mill is thundering out its fire. A big gun behind *Lake House* and another one on Petrus Storme's farm are also firing almost continuously. Suddenly I see big jets of smoke shooting up over Zillebeke. It looks like a giant fountain of smoke. The interpreter tells me that it's the English, who are using gas on a position that continues to put up resistance, as a means of gaining control of it.

In Hemelrijk there is not a house left standing. Close by, there is still *Lake House*, the Peirsegaele brewery and the *De Hovenier* inn, and a couple of houses left in the hamlet of Krommenelst. I pay a visit to our mayor. The poor man is

---

68 The Battle of Menin Road, 20-25 September 2017.

in a very bad way. He is only allowed one man to help him with all the work of the farm and he and his wife are half dead with drudging and slaving. On top of this he's being robbed left and right. There are Belgian policemen in his house and they criticise him if he sells a few kilos of potatoes to the soldiers, but when the soldiers steal the potatoes from his field instead of buying them, the policemen turn a blind eye and just let them carry on. Along either side of the mayor's drive smart huts have been built, and 5 generals are quartered in them. I also see that Alfons Heugebaert's house, Henri Van Damme's house and *De Lelie* have all been demolished. Out of Coene the baker's row of houses only Frederik Baeke's house is still standing.

In the village centre I encounter 60 prisoners of war. I see 40 more in a camp in the low-lying meadows called Boonemeerschen (between Hallebast and Razelput). I come across another 40 near Hallebast and I notice that a good ¼ of them are wearing a Red Cross armband. I find this odd and wonder if it's perhaps a German trick to get better treatment? In the afternoon 200 prisoners of war pass through Reninghelst on their way from Vlamertinghe. I hear that by the evening 200 prisoners from the camp in the Boonemeerschen and the one by La Clytte have left. So there are certainly prisoners, but unfortunately we also see a great many English wounded and we have to admit that the English have paid a high price to capture them.

I notice that the dirigible balloons have moved forward. I see one above Pannestraat, one above Chateau Segard and one above Spanbroekmolen.

Poperinghe shelled today.

21 September, Friday. In the evening I notice several English aeroplanes, each with 2 lights, a big one on its head and a little one on its tail. The English change their lights frequently to prevent the Germans from passing their aeroplanes off as English ones, as has already happened. Recently in Poperinghe an aeroplane lit in the English manner arrived over the Vogeltje airfield. The English suspected nothing untoward, but then suddenly instead of landing it dropped bombs.

In the night I also hear several German aeroplanes, without lights. But they didn't cause trouble. The artillery, however, was worse, bombarding various places between Dickebusch and Reninghelst almost all night. It was worst at Hoge Dreve and near Jules Ooghe's house, then further along at De Canada and at Micmac camp, also at the Delporte station, then at the Rozenhil sawmill, and beyond, up to Stukje, 4 minutes from Reninghelst church. In several places horses and men were killed. Sadly, Father MacDonald's orderly was among the victims at Micmac, a good-natured fellow in his mid-forties. At the Lamerant farm they sometimes had a bit of fun at his expense because of his simplicity He declared that he had never had any desire to wed: 'I never kissed a woman.'[69] I was talking with him just yesterday morning when he came to the barn to serve at the French interpreter-priest's mass. The poor fellow was torn to shreds.

In the afternoon I set out on a walk, passing Torreel, *Zorgvliet*, Petrus Storme's farm and so forth. I see a tank at Ouderdom and 2 on Cyriel Claeys's farm. From *Zorgvliet* for as far as the eye can see along Ypres it is one army camp. Really, if the Germans drop shells they can't miss. It is beautiful weather and I see a lot of balloons and aeroplanes. I observe a group of German aeroplanes heading for an English balloon. They try to attack it but fail because they come under too much fire from the anti-aircraft guns. At

---

69 This is quoted in English in the original text.

Petrus Storme's farm I find 4 farmers at table (Storme, Lietaert, Camiel Derycke and Verpoort). They are the only local inhabitants left in the area, and all 4 men stay on only to keep their right to exemption on the basis of being farmers. Other than that, they can gain nothing at all by remaining, since everything they had has either been destroyed or stolen. Just one of the four, Petrus Storme, had any potatoes left to harvest (about 800 kilos). Camiel Derycke planted 2 acres and not a single plant remains. For his 2 acres, Lietaert received 500 francs compensation. Because they cannot get any workers, they are obliged to help each other. At the moment they are threshing together at Storme's farm. The war affects everything. They were eating their last slice of bread. From then on it was going to be the same mix of potatoes and pork[70] for every meal until they could get a loaf of bread again. However, they were undaunted and they were having a merry time together. They are no longer being shelled, except now and then for a large shrapnel shell aimed at the balloon.

I meet a great number of Australian troops going off to the trenches. It is amazing how calm they appear, you would think that they were going off to a perfectly ordinary, peaceful job, and yet many of them will not return.

The closest guns are now on Ypres-Kruisstraat, apart from the occasional very big one which is positioned a little further back. On my way I can see that a lot of tanks have passed by. At 7 in the evening very heavy firing. A while later I see a shelled balloon burst into flames above Pannestraat. In the evening 3 German aeroplanes arrive and drop bombs at Millekruisse. One falls on a passing lorry full of shells,

---

70 This may look like a rich meal compared with what others at the front had to eat, but in fact, this was probably the typical meal of potatoes with scraps of pork added to flavour them.

which catches fire and is straightaway blown sky high. The occupants of the lorry are blown up with it and Oreel from Kemmel, a refugee who lives opposite, is injured in his house. He is taken to Couthove hospital. Several houses are severely damaged.

22 September, Saturday. The English communiqué talks about Thursday's attack. It began at 5.40 and took place on a front 14 kilometres long, from Hollebeke to Langemarck. It reports that the English took the Kantienebossen (Herenthage Wood), and also the west side of Polygon Wood to a depth of 600 metres. Further north they made advances of between 1,200 and 1,500 metres. They now occupy the hamlet of Zevecote,[71] a short distance from Zonnebeke.

They are laying a wooden roadway straight from Zevecote to Abeelestraat through Cambron's meadow. This is very necessary to ease the burden on the cobbled road, which really no longer has sufficient capacity for the amount of traffic and the number of troops passing through.

Calm day.

23 September, Sunday. At 4 o'clock in the morning a German aeroplane drops bombs around Micmac camp and at 6.30 around Millekruisse. From 5 a.m. to 6.30 intense artillery fire. People say that the Germans are mounting a counter-attack and are succeeding in taking back several positions. After high mass German aeroplanes come overhead and 3 stray shrapnel shells fall on Cyriel Lamerant's farm.

The 23rd Division is leaving. I hear from eyewitnesses of Thursday's fighting that the bodies lay very thick on the battlefield.

---

71 Not to be confused with the same place name in the next sentence, which is a location in Reninghelst.

In the newspapers we read Germany's reply to the Pope's peace note. It stinks of falsehood and duplicitous language. I prefer to read the letters of my soldier brothers. Remi says that he left for Lourdes yesterday, on leave, and Joseph goes off on Wednesday.

24 September, Monday. All night, and especially towards the morning, there was a very great deal of shelling. People say it's a German counter-attack. From 8 till 2 shelling on Poperinghe, more or less one every fifteen minutes. In the afternoon I am in Poperinghe and I hear that a mother and 2 children were killed and another child injured.

25 September, Tuesday. Again a lot of shelling all night. In the last few days there is almost constant fierce artillery fighting, and the artillery are suffering heavy losses.

26 September, Wednesday. All night, but especially in the early morning, very heavy shelling. The English carry out an attack near the village of Zonnebeke, advance 1,100 metres and succeed in taking the village. In the evening a good many prisoners of war pass through Dickebusch. For the whole summer there have been a great many lorries passing through here loaded with ammunition, but today is extraordinary. It's my belief that no fewer than 1,000 went past the curate's house. The traffic is unbelievably heavy and is constantly increasing. It really seems as though the more railways and side roads they construct the more the ordinary roads are overburdened.

The 41st Division suffered very heavy losses last week in the attack south of the Menin road and has to be reformed. The men are not happy because they have had to fight so long here on the Ypres front. It has been almost a year.

232

Camiel Derycke of Hemelrijk's barn burns down through the carelessness of the soldiers.

27 September, Thursday. A lot aeroplanes during the night, English and German. At midnight bombs were dropped on Millekruisse and several horses were killed or injured. After my mass I baptise in her father's barn the little Jeanne Lamerant, born here yesterday. We eat a good sweet Sunday bread sandwich and drink a delicious cup of chocolate to the health of the mother and child. May God preserve child and family.

We read a statement from Cardinal Gasparri in the newspaper about the Pope's peace note as it concerns Belgium. He tells us that the Pope accepts the idea of compensation for Belgium. We lament more each day that the allies have not heeded him. Especially now that things go increasingly badly with Russia.

The Germans say in their newspapers that St. Peter's church in Ostend was shelled by the English last week during the early mass and that 17 civilians inside were killed. The English newspapers deny this and claim that their aeroplanes have not observed the slightest trace of any bombardment. After the war I shall try to find out where the truth lies.[72]

28 September, Friday. In the evening a lot of English aeroplanes in the air, with lights. At 11 o'clock German ones too. We hear several bombs fall. A big bomb falls just in front of the door of the *St. Hubrecht* inn, several more round about

---

72 On Saturday 22 September 1917 Ostend was heavily shelled by British navy ships. The St. Peter and Paul Church, where 150 to 200 people had gathered for mass, received several direct hits. There were many wounded and seven people were killed (six locals and one German sailor), of whom three in the church and one just outside it.

it and also several in the area of *Het Zweerd*. Fierce shelling in the second half of the night, and especially towards morning.

The English communiqué says that in their attack the day before yesterday the English took Polygon Wood, as well as the first houses of Zonnebeke and its station. They came up against fierce resistance along the Menin road.

A great many prisoners of war march through Westoutre.

During the first part of the night we have several German aeroplanes above us. There is one machine that the English hold in their searchlights while they fire heavily at it. It is a wonder to see: it looks just like a golden oriole.[73] We hear several shells explode. 6 soldiers are killed on Petrus De Knudt's farm.

29 September, Saturday. A great deal of shelling in the 2nd half of the night, especially towards morning. At 4 a.m. aeroplanes above again. They drop bombs on Reninghelst near Hilaire Deconinck's farm. 1 officer and 30 soldiers are killed and 11 officers and many soldiers are wounded. All day there are a lot of German aeroplanes above us.

30 September, Saturday. A terrible night again due to the German aeroplanes. From 8 to 1 they are constantly circling over Reninghelst and, we understand, over the whole region. There isn't a single neighbourhood where we don't hear bombs dropping. Also very heavy artillery fire all night, but especially towards morning. Bombs on all sides. One falls on the house of the farmer Raymond Rouseré in Reninghelst, but luckily does not explode. Another one falls in the kitchen of August Hennin, from Dickebusch, who is living in Poperinghe. That one also doesn't explode. At Zevecote several soldiers

---

73 A golden oriole is a bright yellow bird which could be seen in Flanders during the summer months.

are killed. Along the Locre road the daughter of the Delva family from Roulers is hit in their little hut by the casing of an anti-aircraft shrapnel shell and seriously wounded in the leg. It was really a dreadful night, all the more so because we could hear the firing better than usual because the wind was coming from the east.

(This also happened on the Saturday evening.) It is not 8 o'clock in the evening when the German birds of death, again in great numbers, fly over, and this time they intend to give Poperinghe a proper German treat. We soon heard the grim sounds of explosions in every quarter of the town. One of the first victims was the deanery. 2 or 3 large shells fell simultaneously on the right-hand side of the building. The whole of that side collapsed and fell into the vaulted cellar. The other side remained standing but was twisted out of its frame. The house next to it likewise partially collapses, and the façades of the 2 houses opposite are blown in, so great was the force of the blast. The dean had a lucky escape. Just a few moments earlier he had taken shelter on the cellar stairs with the two nuns who lived in the same house, and that's where he was standing when the house collapsed right in front of his feet. Just one more step in the wrong direction, and he would have been a corpse. Nevertheless, he was unable to get out of the rubble himself, and soldiers from the neighbourhood freed him. Whiter than a miller he fled along with the nuns to the house of the curate, Mr Hellijn, in whose half-bombed house they will now all have to live together. A shell falls at the house of Lecomte, the builder. It rips off the leg of an officer but doesn't explode. It was a monstrous contraption, 1 metre long and 0.25 metres in diameter. It was the most gruesome night Poperinghe had experienced so far. No fewer than 180 bombs were dropped on the town.

Between my masses I pay a visit to the village centre.

I see that the English are demolishing the old house of the municipal council. On the unloading quay from *Paradijs* to Dalle's farm, a very large quantity of supplies is being unloaded. The Cannaert sisters' barn has been turned into a cinema. Today the Catholic mass takes place there, too. A good deal of shelling almost all day.

At 8 o'clock in the evening aeroplanes arrive again and they remain above us almost all night. They drop 15 bombs at Ouderdom.

1 October, Monday. A lot of shelling in the second part of the night, exceptionally heavy from 5 to 7. After that somewhat quieter and then from 9 to 2 very heavy again. We hear that it's a German counter-attack and that the enemy has reached the first defence line of the English. Yesterday and today a great many Australians were transported to the front by lorry. Sometimes 80 lorries in a row went past. The English say that they are going to carry out a major attack this week.

We hear that the best French airman, Guynemer, was shot down in Poelcapelle this week.

2 October, Tuesday. A lot of aeroplanes again in the first part of the night. 2 civilians were killed in Poperinghe. In Westoutre 6 bombs fall near New Dickebusch. Several more around Rozenhil. In the morning the Australians recapture the lost ground and even achieve a small advance. They now have control of the station and the church in Zonnebeke. In Dickebusch shells fall around Razelput and Lemahieu's farm.

3 October, Wednesday. At 10.30 p.m. we were woken up again by explosions and artillery fire and presently we hear the spine-chilling drone of the birds of death above our heads, with artillery and machine guns firing at them with all their might.

Suddenly, and almost simultaneously, 3 terrific crumps and a loud tinkling of broken window panes (5 in my bedroom and 17 throughout the house). What can have happened? I wait 3 or 4 minutes until the machine has gone some distance away and then I go and see. I find that 3 shells have fallen almost in the same spot, on the railway line next to the oast house on the Verdonck farm, and have created a deep pit. The smell of powder was still overwhelming, and there was no one around. I heard aeroplanes coming again and I hastened inside. This time the shells fell 60 metres from the curate's house and 30 metres from the church. The following day we heard that an officer from the laundry, sleeping in a hut 30 metres from there, was sliced into little pieces by the flying fragments of the shells. Shells also fell in Six's meadow behind the curate's house, but didn't cause any injuries. Also in Dickebusch, around the farms of Benoit Decrock, Cyriel Lamerant and Henri Breyne.

Today I go by motor car to visit some refugees from Dickebusch in and around Crombeke, Rousbrugge and Proven. For Crombeke I need a special pass because it's in the French sector. Along the main Poperinghe-Crombeke road I notice a big airfield with large hangars. It has been there for 3 months and in that time there have already been 14 aircraft lost. I see that the whole area is criss-crossed by railway lines. In Rousbrugge and Crombeke I notice all sorts of different French soldiers, mostly northerners, of whom many are Flemish-speakers, but also *chasseurs alpins*[74] and *Turcos*.[75] Also Annamites, who are used as labourers. They look very similar to the Chinese but are more smartly dressed.

It is impossible to describe how dearly the Dickebusch people who were recently evacuated long to return home.

---

74 Light infantry specialised in mountain combat.
75 Van Walleghem means Zouaves (regular French troops originally based in North Africa), who, like French colonial troops, wore an oriental uniform.

Many of them have come back, but keep themselves hidden in their own homes. For the moment the local police pretend not to know that they are there.

4 October, Thursday. No aeroplanes during the night, but shells on Poperinghe. In the morning the English mount a big attack. However, we hear little shelling, the wind being in the opposite direction. We soon hear that they are pleased with the outcome and round noon we see 150 prisoners of war pass by. They struck me as the strongest and quickest Germans that I had ever seen, all men in their 20s. They were from different regiments, including Prussians. It looks as though the Germans have placed their best men here.

Bad weather in the afternoon.

The Belgian policemen who used to live in *De Hert*, and who moved from there to Henri Vandecasteele's farm because of the great danger that they were in, have now gone back to *De Hert*. A new police post has been established in Lucie Cordonnier's house. The first post has moved from Charles Van Eecke's house to the *De Canada* inn. Add to these yet another police post, at the mayor's farm, and that comes to 4 police units. Soon there will be as many policemen in Dickebusch as ordinary civilians. And why on earth all those men are necessary, God knows. The men are well paid and get plenty of gifts from the civilians who have good reason to keep on the right side of them.

There was an English officer in Hallebast recently who said that two months ago he was still in a village in East Flanders, and that he had been there for 9 months.

5 October, Friday. 1st Friday of the month. In the night we are shaken by 2 exceptionally strong shocks. We assume that it's the armoured train firing its shells somewhere at Ouderdom and, untroubled, go back to sleep. So we were amazed to find out half way through the morning that it had been shells, and that one had even fallen just 60 metres from us, in Six's meadow, behind the curate's house. It blew 3 soldiers' huts to pieces and made a hole easily big enough to bury 5 horses in. Luckily the soldiers had vacated those huts 2 days before and so there were no casualties to grieve over. Poperinghe was also shelled last night. Bad weather all day.

The English communiqué tells us the result of yesterday's attack. It took place on the part of the front between Tower Hamlets (5 minutes' walk south-east of Kantientje) and the railway line from Langemarck to Staden. The English captured a part of Poelcapelle, 's Graventafel, Broodseinde, Molenaarelsthoek, Reutel and Polderhoek. The Germans were just on the point of launching a major attack themselves and had filled their trenches with fresh men. So they had no inkling of the forthcoming attack. They were completely stunned and gave themselves up without much of a fight. The communiqué reports 3,000 prisoners. The English claim that they had few losses, and this time I am willing to believe them. Today another 900 prisoners of war pass through Westoutre. Our windows were shaking all day and we inferred from this that heavy fighting was still going on.

6 October, Saturday. In the night there are English and German aeroplanes in the skies above and we hear shells fall. In the morning Poperinghe is shelled. A few more prisoners of war march past. In the afternoon there is fierce shelling, worst in the French sector. The weather continues bad. The 14th Division, which was here 2 years ago, has returned. Father Booker is still with them. Although there are already troops in camps all the way to the other side of Ypres, there are still a lot all the time in Westoutre and Reninghelst. The 33rd Divisional

Artillery has already lost more than half its men. In a lot of divisions, the artillery has suffered worse than the infantry, which is not surprising given that the artillery has no means of hiding its guns in that razed, bare landscape. They stretch a net with bits of green stuff woven through it over their gun, but inevitably, the aeroplanes spot them soon enough. An English chaplain tells me that the guns on the English part of the front are so thickly ranged that if they were placed side by side along the whole line they would not all fit in. The Australian chaplains are always at the front with their men and so we seldom see them in Reninghelst.

We are increasingly convinced that the English are not very bright as a people. Up until now we have found little or nothing to learn from them. On the contrary, we still see new examples of stupidity every day. Along the Abeele road and as far as Dickebusch the Chinese are busy filling in the ditches. What will they do with all the water in the coming winter when soon all the drainage pipes and culverts will be blocked? And the best of all, while they are busy filling in the ditches along the Ouderdom road, 300 metres further on they are cleaning out the ditches, knowing that tomorrow or the next day they may be filling those in, too. Such squandering of money. Another instance. A farmer made a compensation claim because the cavalry had turned his chicory field into a stable yard and had destroyed the chicory plants. And the officer's response was: 'Well, you shouldn't have put those things in the ground.'

7 October, Sunday. During the night German aeroplanes were at work again. We hear bombs fall. For the whole night, and in the morning as well, we can hear big shells falling on Poperinghe. The shells on Poperinghe are probably being fired from Houthulst Forest. Very bad weather again. The English communiqué now reports 4,500 prisoners.

At midnight the clock is stopped for one hour and we go back to the old time.

We receive a visit from Father MacGeannes, a brave and good-humoured man, who celebrated Saint Patrick's day with us and Father O'Connor last year. Notwithstanding the long years of war and the wretchedness of life he remains as cheerful as ever. He is now with the 49th Division. Father Bull, who was quartered here last winter, is also in his division. He is staying at Wieltje and says that there are soldiers and horses camped as far as beyond St. Jean.

8 October, Monday. During the night once again there are several heavy strikes. Despite the strong westerly wind, we hear a lot of shelling and even in the blustery wind we see aeroplanes setting out. Skills in flying must have made great advances to be able to set out in such weather. The shelling is very fierce in the morning along the French part of the front.

In the morning 15 shells fall on and around the dressing station on the Vandermarliere farm, 20 minutes' walk from Poperinghe along the Reninghelst road. Several soldiers are killed or wounded. Those shells were fired from a distance of at least 20 kilometres. In the afternoon a lot of rain.

9 October, Tuesday. Really atrocious weather all night, and the soldiers are out there in it, because the guns are flashing constantly for all they're worth. And despite the weather I see aeroplanes again in the morning.

Today saw the marriage here in Reninghelst of an English soldier and a girl from this parish. A good many onlookers, civilians and soldiers. The soldiers appeared to be having a lot of fun at their pal's expense, while he looked embarrassed and made haste to get into the motor car. The soldiers had written on it 'We are married to day in Reninghelst.' [76] And so the couple set off for Poperinghe. A few days later the newly wed young woman embarked for England to comply with the English army's regulations which require that soldiers' wives remain in England.

10 October, Wednesday. Once again several terrible crumps during the night. Rain again. I have rarely experienced so much rain as we've had in recent days. The communiqués talk of yesterday's French-English attack. The French advanced to the south-west of Houthulst Forest whereas the English went to the south-east, and also beyond Poelcapelle and Broodseinde in the direction of Passchendaele. The English took 1,000 prisoners of war and the French 300. Today 100 prisoners of war pass through Reninghelst. The English say that the Germans' barrage is much less to be feared than last year and that they are no longer frightened of it.

Lodging with us in the curate's house is the interpreter Herman, a French artillery lieutenant. He has been with the English for 3 years now and he tells us his experience of them. He says that the English army has made a lot of progress in every respect but that unfortunately there are still a few things that need to be improved. An Englishman will not learn from another's experience and will only learn through his own. This has led to the needless waste of many thousands of lives and of vast sums of money, and, alas, to the loss of much precious time. At the beginning of the war it was a matter of each man to his own job. An infantryman wouldn't dream of picking up a spade to make a trench a bit better, an artilleryman wouldn't build a hut himself: that was what the sappers were for. And as well as that, the army had ridiculous quantities of support staff.

---

76 This is how Van Walleghem renders the English message in his manuscript.

A simple lieutenant was given 2 orderlies. A 10-man mess had at least as many cooks. The supply services and signals were brimming over with staff. (I must admit that this was true. In 1915 I had the 11 cooks of the army headquarters in my kitchen and I was providing lodging for the general's 7 orderlies.) All of this meant that they didn't have many troops available actually to fight. Now it's completely different and there are very few superfluous support staff and the men can do different sorts of work, just as they do in the other armies.

In the beginning of the war the English had not the slightest understanding of the art of war, and in fact they held it in contempt. For them, the best soldier was the one who put his life at risk in the bravest manner. Hiding in the trenches seemed to them to be ridiculous and cowardly, so they felt they had to show their head now and then to the Germans, who were thereby enabled to send many of them to their eternal rest. When they attacked they advanced straight as ramrods: taking cover and crawling along the ground was not noble, not manly enough, and so most of them were mown down before they reached the enemy. But now they have learned and they are beginning to understand that the art of war doesn't consist in the useless sacrifice of one's life but in inflicting as many losses as possible on the enemy without being hit oneself.

The whole of the first year of the war the artillery was extraordinarily bad. Most of the officers were completely ignorant, many hadn't had the slightest training, and so it wasn't surprising that they often shot their own men and fired their shells at the enemy entirely haphazardly. Although it is still by no means perfect, this too has improved greatly. They have learned by experience and when one considers the enormous quantities of guns and ammunition that they have at their disposal, one has to admit that their shellfire must be terrifying, even though very many of their shells are wasted. I heard this too from a Belgian officer who recently visited both the French and the English fronts. On the French front, in the places where the soldiers had captured ground, the trenches and the defences were utterly destroyed, while between the trenches there were few shell craters. On the English front, by contrast, the ground was completely covered in shell craters, just as many of them between the trenches as on the trenches, which goes to show that the English wasted a lot of their powder on misaimed shells.

The interpreter assures us that there are still few English artillery officers who know as much as an ordinary French gunner. He knows 4 colonels in the artillery who are only 21 years old, and one who is just 20. The English general commanding the artillery was an ordinary chauffeur before the war. He knew him in Marseille. He went into the army at the start of the war as a gunner, became commanding officer in March 1915 and a year later general. In the English army the officers are always promoted within their unit, and this means that if a lot of them are killed in action, a *sous-lieutenant* can very quickly become a colonel. When they have been temporarily assigned a higher rank for 30 days, they acquire the rank permanently. Things are very different in the French army.

11 October, Thursday. Very heavy shelling all the second part of the night, especially from 4 to 7 o'clock. In the English sector 200 new interpreters have arrived. Of what use all these people can be only the good Lord knows. There were already too many of them floating around, the French ones especially are completely and utterly useless here. It is claimed that they are here to act as intermediaries between the army and the inhabitants in the newly captured villages. In any case, there are now enough of them to supply all the parishes of West Flanders. The interpreters are usually the most demanding in the houses in which they are quartered, probably because they earn the most. We experience this in the curate's house too, where 2 of these new customers are lodging. In a house which for 3 years of war now has constantly had lodgers, and not one of them, whether an ordinary officer or a general, has made the slightest complaint, a boy of 20 starts to make a fuss, complaining that this and that are all wrong and that things have to change, adding as conclusive argument: 'Vous savez, je suis le baron de Woelmont,'[77] to which we reply 'très bien, monsieur l'interprête.'[78] Already the next day, however, he managed to be polite. He also told us then that he knew a bit of Flemish, but only enough to speak to the servants. He was in fact a Limburger.[79]

We have had the Australians living among us now for several weeks and we are getting to know their good points and their faults. They are a good-looking and lively people, sturdier and more coarsely built than the English. Not a single dullard among them. They are no dirtier than the English, but they don't spend the whole day washing and shaving. They are courageous fighters and know no fear. That's one of the reasons why they are usually put in the worst sector, which they are also proud of. Although when they've had a bit to drink and are quarrelling with the English, they often bring up against them that they always have to risk their necks while the English choose the best spots. But they are rather

---

77 'You know, I'm the Baron of Woelmont.'

78 'Very well, monsieur interpreter.' The expected way of addressing a baron would be 'monsieur le baron.' This was clearly intended to put the baron in his place.

79 Limburg is a Flemish-speaking province of Belgium. However, the baron, in common with many others, may have considered Flemish to be suitable only for the working classes, French being considered the language of the bourgeoisie and the upper classes. Van Walleghem probably believes that this is why the baron was initially unwilling to admit to a knowledge of Flemish.

wild. Their biggest [fault?] is drunkenness, and the main cause of that is that they are paid so much. An Australian earns 6 shillings a day, a New Zealander 5, a Canadian 4 and an Englishman 1. So when they are on rest and they come into the village, sometimes after a couple of weeks in an area where there is neither inn nor house, and thus with their pockets full of money, they are eager to go out drinking. And so beer and wine and champagne do their worst. Innkeepers and wine-merchants make a lot of money, but they also have to suffer the consequences. It is not unusual for the soldiers in their drunkenness to smash an inn to pieces. And when the official closing time arrives it is often impossible to get the drunken men out; they just keep asking for more drink. It has to be only the womenfolk of the inn who attempt to deal with them, and by coaxing and cajoling they are usually successful. The menfolk of the inn mustn't intervene, otherwise they quickly end up in a fight. Above all, the Belgian constabulary mustn't show their faces at this time, a restriction which they are very ready to accept. They are also reasonable enough now not to impose a fine on the innkeepers if they haven't managed to get all their customers out by 8 o'clock. After 8 o'clock all the streets are full of the wild caterwauling of drunken men. In that respect they are no better than our drunken Flemings, more's the pity! However, not all the drunkards are wild or raving: a hundred times I've heard one call out to me, 'Father, me Catholic, rosary,' as he shows me his rosary beads. In general, the Australians do even more damage than the English, and our farmers complain bitterly about them. Just as in the Canadian army, one finds a lot of thieves among the Australians and already a lot of inhabitants have discovered that their chickens or their fruit have been 'borrowed.' In this respect they are worse than the English.

12 October, Friday. In the morning the English attack on a 10 km front between Reutel and Houthulst Forest. Once again their progress is halted by the rain, but they manage to take several positions, as well as 500 prisoners of war. The soldiers say that you can't imagine how strong some of the German shelters are. Some of the walls are made of reinforced concrete 1 ½ metres thick, which not even the biggest shells can destroy.

I am summoned, along with some others, to the mayor of Dickebusch's farm where, according to the message that I received, the English paymaster will pay me for the objects belonging to the church which were burned in Henri Lamerant's barn. He will be there from 10 to 11.30. We stay there until after noon and we see neither hide nor hair of a paymaster. It's as if they want to make fools of people, to make them trudge 7 kilometres through the mud and then keep them twiddling their thumbs for a morning, with no word of information. Well, we're only Belgian civilians, after all. The charming gentleman never deigned to explain himself.

There are now 9 generals at the mayor's farm, 1 in the house and 8 in huts. We see that the observation balloons have moved forward again, there is now one at Bartiers's brewery (Elzenwalle Brasserie), 1 at Kalfvaart on the northern outskirts of Ypres, and 1 at the Boesinghe canal.

13 October, Saturday. Bad weather all day and all night. We hear the sad news of the death of Father Bergin, Irish Jesuit and chaplain of the 13th Australian brigade. He studied in Jerusalem but when the war began he was forced to flee to Egypt. There he made the acquaintance of a Catholic Australian Major-General who held him in great esteem and asked him to accompany the army. In the Australian army it is necessary to work one's way up from the lowest rank before becoming an officer, and thus he signed up as a medical auxiliary. As a chaplain, he soon attained the rank of captain and was now a major. We got to know him in September 1916 and admired him as a very industrious, intelligent and modest priest. And from what we have heard, his courage was as admirable as his other virtues. A few weeks ago he returned here to the Ypres front and yesterday evening he fell, sacrificing himself in the name of duty, killed by a shell a few minutes' walk from the village square of Zonnebeke. His body is being brought here this afternoon for the funeral tomorrow. This week Bailleul has been bombarded several times.

14 October, Sunday. Nice weather. Also a lot of balloons and a lot of aeroplanes. Around noon we see 6 German prisoners of war. After the English 11 o'clock mass the funeral of Father Bergin takes place. We carry it out with as much ceremony as possible, with 8 priests (3 chaplains and the 5 priests staying in Reninghelst), and also a lot of soldiers accompany the body and provide military honours. His mortal remains now lie outside the churchyard hedge, just in front of the brewery.[80]

Father Claeys is leaving to work as chaplain in a hospital near Villers. His successor is Father Mimi, who is not exactly the finest of chaplains. He is also lodging at Cyriel Lamerant's farm.

In Father MacDonald's brigade, the 23rd Division, there are only 1,000 men left. It's not that the number of dead is so great, but there are many wounded and many who are sick due to the gas.

In Dickebusch, where a lot of evacuated women have already returned home, there is again an order that everyone must leave immediately, and again the sad exodus begins. In the whole area controlled by the 2nd army no one is allowed

---

80 The Rev. M. Bergin MC, Chaplain 3rd Class, Australian Army Chaplains Department, died on 12 October 1917. He is buried in Reninghelst Churchyard Extension, grave 1.

to return. Hateful, and as incomprehensible as ever!

At 10 o'clock in the evening, aeroplanes again. I hear a lot of shelling but no bombs fall here.

15 October, Monday. Around noon a German aeroplane flies over Reninghelst and drops 2 bombs on Kasteelmolen. A 12-year-old boy, Crombez by name, a refugee from Roulers who was coming from school, was hit and killed instantly. A soldier who was next to him was wounded.

Today Jan Plak's wife, who had returned without permission, was arrested on Florent Dauchy's potato field by 2 constables who brought her triumphantly to Reninghelst.

Odiel Lamerant and Gouwy from the class of 18, who had 3 months' temporary exemption due to ill-health, are judged fit for service and go off to the army. Maurits Spenninck is granted another 3 months' exemption on the same grounds.

In the evening a lot of German aeroplanes are on their rounds. They drop bombs between Millekruisse and Kemmel. Several civilians have been fined for showing a light in the evening in their houses. In the officers' rooms, however, the lights are as bright as ever.

16 October, Tuesday. It seems that on the front line it is horribly wet and it is almost impossible to do anything. We hear that the English suffered heavy losses at Broodseinde and Poelcapelle, where there was terrible fighting at Monsieur Nevejan's brewery.

17 October, Wednesday. Overcast night. No aeroplanes. In the morning a German aeroplane has a wing shot off above Cyriel Lamerant's farm and comes down a couple of kilometres away, near Omer Verraest's farm. It takes almost a quarter of an hour before the wing is on the ground. The German machine was one with 3 engines, a Gotha, one of the biggest that we've yet seen here. There were 3 men in it. 1 jumped out and tried to descend by parachute, but failed. The other 2 were crushed under their machine. Immediately, the English aeroplanes which had thrashed that fellow also landed, to inspect their vanquished prey.

18 October, Thursday. The English communiqué reports that the Germans south of Passchendaele have retreated 1,000 metres. In the evening aeroplanes over Reninghelst. They drop 7 bombs on Stukje.

19 October, Friday. A lot of heavy artillery is on its way to the front. We are expecting a new English attack soon. In the afternoon very fierce artillery fire which lasts for 20 hours, going on until Saturday morning.

20 October, Saturday. Good weather, though misty. In the morning a German aeroplane flies very low over Reninghelst. It is fired on from all sides with machine guns, but still manages to escape.

The Germans capture the Russian Island of Ösel.[81]

German aeroplanes in the evening, but they don't drop any bombs.

21 October, Sunday. Good weather. At 5 o'clock in the morning German aeroplanes over Reninghelst. They drop a lot of bombs around *Boerenhol* and Drie Goen. At Drie Goen horses are killed. A corner of Leon Blanckaert's house is blown off, too. There are also bombs in the morning on Poperinghe, on the station side.

In Dickebusch there are now 3 dressing stations, one in the

---

81 Now Saaremaa in Estonia.

boys' school, one in the dairy and the big one near Comyn's farm. In the cemetery next to this last, 860 soldiers have been buried since 1 August.

At 5.30 in the evening German aeroplanes arrive again. They drop bombs around the big station half-way along the Poperinghe road, and drop 2 bombs along the same road 5 minutes from Reninghelst church.

22 October, Monday. In the morning a lot of firing north of Ypres. In the evening, the beginning of the first quarter of the moon.[82] Everyone is very frightened and people are anxiously asking themselves what new disasters the new moonlight will bring us.[83] At 8.30 the German birds of death are already above our heads and the big guns and the smaller popguns[84] are firing for all they are worth. Several terrible crumps, some very close, announce that Fritz is already unloading his cargo. We hear, too, the shards of glass and the roof tiles falling to the ground. We also hear several bombs fall which

---

82 Literally, 'the first moonshine.' 22 October was the last day of the new moon, and the first quarter began in the afternoon of 23 October.

83 This appears to be a reference to a belief current in these parts at this time (and still held by some) that (a), it was possible to predict the weather for the rest of the lunar month on the basis of what natural phenomena had been seen in the new moon (the first phase of the lunar cycle), and (b), by extension, it was possible to make other kinds of predictions for the rest of the month at this point. These predictions would indeed have taken place on or around the 22nd October, the last day of the new moon, or the 23rd October, the first day of the first quarter.

84 The word Van Walleghem uses is 'klakbossen,' which refers to a toy that is rather more primitive than a popgun. The word comes from the dialect of Van Walleghem's native area, Pitthem. A 'klakbosse' consists of a short hollowed-out stick of elder and a narrower rod which fits into the hole and has a handle attached to it. A ball of chewed paper, flax etc. is inserted at each end of the wooden tube in order to 'load' it. By pushing up the rod, the air between the balls is put under pressure and one of them is released with a bang.

don't explode. These shake the ground terrifyingly. It's precisely as if a 100-kilo sack of salt had fallen from a height of several metres just 3 steps away from us. The next day we find several bits of stone in the attic of the curate's house. These had arrived courtesy of a bomb which had fallen on a stone-paved road in Charles Deconinck's meadow, a good 250 metres from here.

23 October, Tuesday. Very bad weather all day. Also few aeroplanes. It appears that a big English attack was to take place this morning but was partly prevented by the bad weather. The English Cardinal Bourne visits the Catholic soldiers of the front. Today he is at Locre, where all the English chaplains from the region, if they can by any means get away, come to greet him.

24 October, Wednesday. A great deal of firing in the afternoon. In the last few days, 2 Catholic chaplains of the 5th Division have been seriously wounded.

25 October, Thursday. The communiqué says that the French have carried out an attack in the Aisne, and have taken Malmaison and 3 other villages and taken prisoner 160 officers, including 3 colonels, and 7,500 soldiers, and captured 25 guns. The communiqué also says that the day before yesterday the French and the English attacked and made a small advance in Houthulst Forest.

I go to Westoutre to the English paymaster and receive 400 francs for the font and the vestments which were burned on Henri Lamerant's farm. I had claimed 480 francs.

For a few days there have not been many soldiers on the square in Reninghelst. Today there are once again a lot of Australians, men who come from the fighting and have come here on rest for a few days. They are in a very bad way, sick from the gas, hoarse, and coughing dreadfully.

The English laundry here at Reninghelst village square is much reduced in size. More than half the staff have been transferred to the sawmill at Rozenhil, where the women are employed cutting to size the little planks for duckboards. The people are transported morning and evening in lorries which go around the neighbouring villages. Menfolk and womenfolk are all jumbled up together and their behaviour is far from responsible. It is mainly the steadiest women and their daughters who have remained at the laundry.

It is still only evening and the winged murderers are already plying their trade. In the first part of the night they come at least 10 times, and each time stay for a good while. We hear bombs fall on all sides. Along the gravel road at Kasteelmolen a bomb falls in front of a civilian hut in which the Dequirez family, from Kemmel, were living. The little home is smashed to matchwood, and an English soldier is killed and boy and a girl are injured. What that family has suffered in the course of the war. A soldier son was killed in the fighting around Antwerp. Four months later a daughter was killed in her bed by a German bullet in the little house in which they lived in Kemmel, at Hooge Basseye, a distance of 20 minutes' walk from the enemy. Then last September another soldier son, in a train full of soldiers on leave, was killed by a German bomb on Rosendael station. And now 2 more children injured and their hut and furniture in pieces.

The aeroplanes also dropped 3 bombs at the crossing next to Henri Lamerant's farm.

26 October, Friday. Very bad weather all day. Flooding in Westoutre marshes. In the morning a lot of shelling. We also see a lot of red flares go up.

27 October, Saturday. At 1 o'clock in the morning, aeroplanes up above. At 6 in the morning an anti-aircraft shrapnel shell explodes just in front of the door of the curate's house. There is a lot of firing in the morning and we hear that an attack is underway. At midday 187 prisoners pass through Reninghelst. The weather is good today. Shells fall around Potente and Torreel.

28 October, Sunday. Clear night. A lot of English aeroplanes circle around above us. The German ones don't come to Reninghelst. At 4 o'clock in the morning intense heavy artillery shelling begins and it continues all day and through to 2 a.m. without pausing or diminishing. This is truly one of the most savage days of the war. We don't know what may be going on, but as far as we can see the soldiers seem no more agitated than normal.

The communiqué reports that the English and the French attacked on Friday and advanced to Draaibank and to the edge of Passchendaele.

News comes that the Austrians have attacked on the Italian front and the Italians had to flee into the Julian Alps.

29 October, Monday. Full moon.[85] Twice, a German aeroplane flies overhead, but drops no bombs.

The French communiqué reports that on Saturday the French made an attack and captured Merckem, De Kippe and Verbrande Smisse.

The Austrians announce that they took 60,000 Italian prisoners of war.

30 October, Tuesday. In the night the German aeroplanes come

---

85 Van Walleghem is one day ahead of the official schedule again.

several times, dropping bombs on Reninghelst at Rozenhil, and also on the farms of Dehouck and Steen, by the village square. At Steen's farm several soldiers' horses were killed. At Dickebusch there were shells around Kapelleke. Also a lot of bombs on Poperinghe, mostly torpedoes.

The communiqué says that the Belgians carried out an attack yesterday, crossing the Ypres canal and the flooded meadows in boats, capturing several German positions and continuing to Blankaart Lake, and then, with the French, taking Luighem. (Little wonder, then, that there was so much gunfire.)

The Austrian communiqué reports worse news: 100,000 Italians captured and 700 guns.

Bailleul comes under shellfire throughout the day.

31 October, Wednesday. The weather was bad all day yesterday and we hope that it will continue so during the night so that we can sleep undisturbed. But it is just the contrary. The winged murderers can take their outing at their ease. All night they disturb our sleep with their spine-chilling drone and their savage blows. We hear bombs falling far and near. From 3.30 to 5 a.m. especially, the ferocity of the bombing was terrible. But the guns wanted to play their part in the bombardment too, and all night we heard shells go shrieking over our heads to wreak further destruction on poor Poperinghe. Bombs fell on Poperinghe and on Reninghelst, close to Dehouck's farm, also on Delforche's farm (on the La Clytte road) where the daughter of Pyck, from Dickebusch, was injured. On Charles-Louis Kestelyn's farm a lot of horses are killed.

In the afternoon more shelling on Poperinghe. My sister has been to Bailleul and says that the town has been horribly shelled, especially around the station and the market square.

1 November, All Saints' Day. 40 communicants. Last night was very clear. A good many birds of death on the wing. From 9 to 10 p.m. we hear them constantly above our heads, and again at 3 a.m. We also hear a lot of bombs falling. In the morning we hear that there were bombs dropped on Edward Huys's farm at Schaapstal. 1 soldier was killed there and 16 were wounded, and a lot of horses were killed too. In Poperinghe, bombs everywhere. The bombardment in Dickebusch was extremely bad: the aeroplanes were overhead for the whole night and dropped a lot of bombs on the camps near Van Eecke's mill and on Widow Adriaen's meadow and round the lake. In the course of the night many men and more than 100 horses were killed.

During vespers 100 German prisoners of war pass through Reninghelst. The communiqué reports that the Belgians have carried out several raids and took 67 prisoners of war at Merckem. The English communiqué says that on Tuesday the English carried out an attack between Passchendaele and Houthulst Forest and advanced a little. By contrast, the news from Italy grows steadily worse. Nevertheless, the English officers confidently reported yesterday that telegrams had come in which said that the Italians had regained all the ground that they had lost and had taken 40,000 prisoners of war. Sadly, it all too soon became clear that they had let themselves be fooled into believing a lot of nonsense.

There are 237 civilians left in Dickebusch, although a few evacuated women are also in their homes, keeping themselves hidden.

For 3 Sundays now I have seen a policeman at high mass. He is the head of the *De Hert* post, a pleasant man from Wevelghem. Until now I had never seen any Belgian policemen at my masses at Lamerant's farm. It appears, however, that some do go to the mass at La Clytte from time to time. But it's a rare policeman who attends mass, even though their duties in no way prevent them from doing so. A lot of shelling in the afternoon.

2 November, Friday. All Souls' Day. 18 communicants. A quiet day, rather misty.

3 November, Saturday. Misty, no aeroplanes. From 3.30 to 8 in the morning a lot of shelling. The Austrian communiqué reports the capture of 60,000 new Italian prisoners of war and 700 guns last Wednesday. All together that makes 200,000 prisoners and 1,700 guns now. The soldiers here are very much affected by this setback and are saying that the enemy is impossible to beat. People long more and more for peace.

Dispute between the two newspapers, *Le Vingtième Siècle* and *De Stem uit België*. *Le Vingtième* accuses Father Callewaert of boloism[86] on account of his defence of the Pope's peace note. This week *De Stem uit België* is not permitted at the front. *Le Vingtième* increasingly seems to us to be a hateful paper because of its sly propaganda against the Flemish cause[87] and against anything that doesn't accord with the newspaper's militaristic thinking. However, we are obliged to read this grubby rag because it is always our source of the most recent news, thanks to the special privilege accorded it by the government, which ensures that it reaches the front more quickly than all the other newspapers.

France is in turmoil at present because of Daudet's

---

86 Bolo Pasha was a French Levantine financier and a German agent. Hence *boloism* was used to refer to defeatist propaganda which was likely to benefit the enemy.

87 During the Great war, the awareness among Flemings of their own identity was enhanced due to the perceived subordination of all things Flemish, particularly within the Belgian Army.

accusations of Minister Malvy, the suspected traitor. Today's *Echo de Paris* must have printed some unpalatable truths, because the Belgian constabulary has received orders to confiscate all the copies of that paper that have arrived here.

4 November, Sunday. Misty night and no aeroplanes. From 3 o'clock until 7 o'clock very fierce shelling. People are saying that the Germans are using gas, and indeed, the wind is in a favourable direction for that.

Father Mimi, chaplain with the 33rd Division, who lodged for a considerable time at Cyriel Lamerant's farm, leaves this morning without so much as a thank you or a goodbye. *Bibax et pigerrimus.*[88]

News reaches us that Arsène Coene from Dickebusch, the son of Henri the baker, was wounded along with 5 of his pals at 2.30 in the morning on 3 November in Oostkerke. His life is in danger. He is being cared for in L'Océan hospital in Vinckem. These are men of the battery that at one time stayed on Cyriel Lamerant's farm.

5 November, Monday. An order has been issued for the Chinese forbidding them henceforth to go into the shops. The civilians are no longer allowed to sell them anything. No one knows the reason for this. Some people say that the Australians have been getting the Chinese drunk in the inns by putting rum in their coffee. Others say that they were giving too much away to the women and children. However, after a certain time this restriction on them is relaxed. The Chinese are childlike, but they are not stupid. They understand very well the value of things and they won't easily let themselves be cheated. They always look for the best and the most beautiful goods and

---

88 Latin for, roughly, 'Drink-friendly, work-shy.'

won't readily buy rubbish. They pay well, but like to haggle. They are most attracted by the smartest shops, and it's also in those shops that they make most of their purchases. I don't know what they earn, but some of them have a lot of money on them. They buy a lot of pocket watches and rings. Some shopkeepers have learned a bit of Chinese expressly to entice them into their shops, and they have found that this works.

Every farmer in Dickebusch has received a notice listing what he must deliver to the supply committee. The calculation is based on the maximum harvest possible from everything that was sown or planted, just as if nothing had been destroyed and all the crops had grown perfectly. Alas, what a difference between this picture and the reality. More than half the harvest was trampled and the rest was largely destroyed or left untended. They reckon on 1,500 kilos per acre, while the best fields yielded only 500 kilos per acre. Cyriel Lamerant alone is obliged to deliver 4,500 kilos of corn, which is as much as all the farms in the Reninghelst municipality together. Naturally, the council protests immediately. The committee promises to investigate their complaints sympathetically.

A lot of goods come to us through the committee. People are allowed to collect a certain quantity of petrol at 75 cents per can. Also 1 kilo of chicory at 1.85 francs. Each person has the right to 125 kilos of potatoes for the whole year. Coal is delivered to the council and is shared out among the different households: 150, 200, 250 or 300 kilos per household each month. A lot of people find it strange that chicory is sold at 1.85 francs a kilo while the farmers are only paid 8.5 francs per 100 kilos for their chicory roots. A chicory-drier reckons that the committee should be able to supply the ground chicory at 85 cents, that is, 1 franc less per kilo. We hear that the quarrel about last year's requisitioned chicory beans has been settled, and that the drier has been paid 0.75 to 1 franc.

259

In Reninghelst the price of baker's bread is now 1 franc per 1 ½ kilos. Corn costs 45 cents a kilo. The army buys potatoes at 12 francs per 100 kilos, but the price will go up by half a franc every month. The supply committee is bitterly criticised by a lot of people.

The *Ster* inn at Heet, where an English soldier was stabbed to death, is closed for the duration of the war. Today I go to Locre and notice a lot of new camps.

6 November, Tuesday. In my wartime church I say mass in memory of the priests and the benefactors from our diocese who have died during the last year. At 6 o'clock, when I was just near Ouderdom, I see the sky light up above Ypres and a few seconds later an immense firework explodes, with hundreds and hundreds of flashes criss-crossing each other and between the flashes the constant bursting of shrapnel shells and numerous red and white rockets. From where I was I had an uninterrupted view of the whole of the Ypres front and that firework display in the half-light over the whole front from Wytschaete to Houthulst Forest was really magnificent. Several thousand guns spat their murderous metal into that clashing multitude. And yet there was little noise because the wind was blowing the sound away from me and if I had not been able to see that hellfire I would have found it difficult to believe that an attack was underway. It was several months since I had had such a clear view of an artillery attack. I had seen some at much closer range with the guns thundering at full force, but I had never seen one on such a broad front by so many fire monsters.

Who could it be that was carrying out the attack? I must admit that this time I had not heard about any imminent attack. It was only after half an hour that I saw the first aeroplanes. After an hour the shelling began to diminish.

Today there is no mist. Bailleul is shelled again. Despite the darkness, several English aeroplanes in the evening and in the night.

7 November, Wednesday. No more mist and numerous observation balloons once more.

The English communiqué says that the Canadians made the attack on Passchendaele yesterday and captured that important position as well as Mosselmarkt and Goudberg. They took 471 prisoners.

The German communiqué says that the English also made an attack, on Gheluvelt, but suffered heavy losses and were repulsed.

Around 4 o'clock 256 prisoners of war pass through. I must say, they were the strongest-looking Germans that I've seen, and all of them in their 20s. Evidence that the Germans have put their best troops in here. A Catholic chaplain is killed at 's Graventafel.

8 November, Thursday. From 3 to 5 o'clock in the morning German aeroplanes overhead. They drop several bombs around Achiel Lamerant's farm and the Verhaeghe siblings' farm, near the Chinese camp and also near the anti-aircraft guns on Maeyaert's land. 1 big shell in front of the *Wandeling* inn. In Westoutre, shells on the Rouseré farm near the home for old men. In Dickebusch, 4 big bombs on Jules Spenninck's farm.

At 11 o'clock in the morning a German aeroplane is shot down.

In the Belgian sector near Nieuwe Herberg a shell explodes in a soldiers' hut and 36 men from the *3ᵉ de Ligne* are killed. In Poperinghe the Capuchin Father Decoster is run over by a motor car.

9 November, Friday. Several shrapnel shells explode around the balloons. In the evening a lot of English aeroplanes, it being a clear starlit night.

Several English divisions from the Ypres area go off to Italy. They are happy to go. People are saying that the attacks will be stopped here now.

The French set Vladslo church on fire with their shelling. In Russia anarchy is everywhere. Kerensky has been ousted. Lenin is taking control.

The Austrians report 250,000 Italian prisoners of war and 2,300 guns. Things have become much worse for the allies.

10 November, Saturday. Bad weather all day, and yet a lot of shelling with exceptionally heavy ammunition. This morning the Canadians make another attack on Passchendaele, and advance a bit further along the West-Roosebeke road.

In Reninghelst the schools are closed due to measles.

11 November, Sunday. Very heavy rain all night and even heavier shelling on the whole front, but worst around Gheluvelt. The shelling continues just as heavy all day and carries on until midnight. That is 30 hours without a pause. And despite the bad weather there are aeroplanes constantly above, both German and English. We don't know what's going on. A chaplain tells us that it is only artillery fire, extremely heavy on both sides, although in the soggy ground a lot of shells don't burst open. We are amazed that the following day's communiqué doesn't say a word about this shelling.

Due to the torrential rain many of the roads are flooded and since the drainage pipes have been blocked and the roadside ditches filled in, the water can't drain away and around the village square almost all the cellars are under water.

12 November, Monday. In the night we hear several German aeroplanes, but not above us. We also hear bombs explode. Good weather.

In the morning the shelling begins again and lasts all day. During the morning shells fall around Marcel Coene's farm. An Australian division leaves and in its place comes the 66th English Division with chaplain Major Stuart. It comes here from Locre.

13 November, Tuesday. The shelling continues all night and is extremely heavy in the morning. Then it slackens off and there is not much during the day, but it becomes furious again in the evening. At 11.30, 70 prisoners of war pass by, completely covered in mud. Really, we don't understand this terrible shelling. Neither in the streets nor among the officers is there anything unusual to be seen. But I can't believe that anyone would launch an attack of any importance. The ground is so bad that it would be impossible to make any progress on it. We think that this shelling is quite possibly connected with the fighting in Italy and that they are each trying to stop the other one from going to offer support.

Since last week the 4th Belgian Division, including my brother Remi, has been back at the front, to relieve the French in the Merckem sector. In the Nieuport sector the English are again replaced by the French. The English have lost a great many people there and have gained nothing by it.

Lloyd George says: 'We have been fighting this war for 3 years and for 3 years we have been making stupid mistakes because of a lack of unity in action.' This is precisely what the farmers of Dickebusch have been saying from the beginning, and now they are adding: 'Next year, people will be saying: 4 years of stupid mistakes.'

14 November, Wednesday. The terrific shelling continues until midnight, starts up again at daybreak, slackens off somewhat and at noon is furious once more. During the night shelling on Celeste Planckeel's farm. The bombing lasts all day. The communiqué reports a German attack on Passchendaele, successfully repelled by the Canadians.

In the morning an English soldier is shot against the convent wall here for refusing to go into the trenches.[89] It was his own comrades who were appointed to the firing squad. Many of the soldiers have already spoken of how painful this is to them. Some of them weep with remorse.

The funeral takes place in Westoutre today of the soldier Arsène Coene from Dickebusch, who died on Saturday in the war hospital at Vinckem.

The Belgian men aged 30-35 who were mobilised in February arrived at the front a few days ago.

15 November, Thursday. During the night a fair bit of shelling. At De Poeper a Chinese camp is shelled and several yellow men are killed. In the afternoon a lot of firing again and in the evening even worse. We hear a lot of shells whistling past.

There is now a brigade of New Zealanders camped on Reninghelst village square. Their hats are rounder that those of the Australians with a red or black or blue ribbon round them.

The recently evacuated inhabitants of Dickebusch can put in a request to return home. Several have already been granted permission and are allowed to show their faces in Dickebusch once more.

We are forced to acknowledge that some English officers are far from being 'gentlemen,' and there are even some who

---

89   The executed man was 20-year-old Private William Smith from Manchester, who served in the 3rd/5th Lancashire Fusiliers. He is buried at Reninghelst New Military Cemetery, grave ref. IV.B. 28.

think that their bedroom is the right place not only for the lesser call of nature but also for the greater, not just at night but also during the day. This sort of cleanliness was shown by a Protestant Chaplain-Major at the Westoutre curate's house.

The Chinese are once more allowed in the shops, but may not ask for coffee.

16 November, Friday. Heavy shelling all night, but from 3 a.m. onwards uncommonly ferocious, and remains so the whole day. A little calmer in the evening. In the course of the day shells fall between the farms of Henri Desmarets and Celeste Planckeel. In the evening the bombardment starts again. The first shells fall around Cafmeyer's farm, then around Baes's and then for the whole night until 10 o'clock the following morning a shell approximately every 5 minutes between Ouderdom, Micmac camp and Rozenhil. It's the longest bombardment that I have ever known. 18 hours long. Several shells fall on the railway line and the sawmill and a number of men and horses are killed. At Lemahieu's farm an armoured train is firing again.

17 November, Saturday. Thick fog. I hear that the English intended to carry out an attack here today but have been prevented by the fog.

The Belgian Intelligence officer for Dickebusch and Reninghelst is transferred and is replaced by the one from Ploegsteert. A lot of these officers are none too well thought of.

In France, Clemenceau's government is appointed.

We hear through Sister Marie Vromman from Holland that all continues to be well with our family in Pitthem.[90]

Today the shelling was lighter than on the previous days.

---

90 As his hometown Pitthem was in occupied Belgium, all correspondence had to go via the Netherlands, which was neutral.

A lot of people here have said that the shelling from the guns over the last week was the worst that we've experienced in the whole war. And yet the communiqués mention nothing special at all.

18 November, Sunday. A fairly calm night. Despite the mist, a lot of aeroplanes. An English balloon is shot down in flames over Chateau Segard. 2 soldiers' masses in the barn and at least 200 New Zealanders present.

The communiqué says that the Germans made an attack against the 4th Belgian Division at Merckem. They threw gas shells. First a kind which gave off a gas that didn't smell much but that caused nausea and made the men vomit, which prevented them from being able to put their gas masks on. And then they threw poison gas which did serious harm to the eyes and lungs. In this way they succeeded in taking 3 Belgian positions, but in a counter-attack the Belgians recaptured 2, with 10 prisoners. Many Belgians died or were taken prisoner, and many were taken to hospital blind. It was the 8th and the 19th *régiments de ligne* which suffered worst.

The German communiqué says that yesterday the Germans took 63 English prisoners at Passchendaele.

The Catholic chaplain Father Looby of the 50th Division died this week at Passchendaele. It has not yet been possible to retrieve his body.

Along the main Ypres road beyond the *America* inn there is only one house left standing, and that is the Peirsegaele brewery with the farm next to it. The farmer Alouis Van Cayseele, from Vierstraat, has recently been allowed to go and have a look at his farm, and he found his binoculars and his roller still there.

In the afternoon a lot of shelling.

266

19 November, Monday. Misty and quiet night. The English communiqué reports a small advance north of Passchendaele.

We hear that a boy from Dickebusch, Marcel Timperman, has been run over and killed by a wagon in Bourboujon, in the Cher et Loire, France.

20 November, Tuesday. Several periods of heavy shelling, especially in the afternoon. Bailleul shelled again: this is the case almost every market day. Several of the recently evacuated Dickebusch inhabitants receive permission to return. The tobacco farmers now sell their goods at 5 francs a kilo. The tobacco sellers charge 7 francs for cut tobacco.

In Poperinghe August Hennin from Dickebusch, aged 74, was run over by an English motor car. Death has really been after the good old soul for some time: in July, while he was still in Dickebusch, several soldiers were killed by a shell in front of his door and the metal shards flew into his house, but the family was unharmed. In September, when he had fled to Poperinghe, another shell right in front of his door. 14 days ago an anti-aircraft shell fell in his kitchen where the family was at table, but didn't explode. The very same week, he was preparing to move house in Poperinghe, but a few days before the move the new house that he had rented was hit by a bomb. Alas, death has finally got his prey. A peculiarity of that family was that they always wanted to flee to the neighbours, where it was sometimes more dangerous than in their own house.

21 November, Wednesday. Quite a lot of shelling during the night. Bad weather. The Belgians continue to be terribly pounded by shelling at Merckem. In Italy, fierce fighting at the Piave river.

In Poperinghe there is an uprising in the Chinese camp. An

English officer was set upon by the Chinese, the English shot into the melee, and 3 Chinese were killed. That's the story that we hear.

In the sawmill at La Clytte a boy is caught in the belt and completely crushed.

22 November, Thursday. Quiet day.

23 November, Friday. Clear weather again and a lot of aeroplanes and balloons. A clear moonlit night, too, and people are anxious again.

There has been a constant stream of troops changing over and we notice that the number of troops in these parts has been greatly reduced. Almost all the Australians have gone, although there is still a brigade of New Zealanders camped by the square.

We hear that the English have achieved a big victory at Cambrai. They took 8,000 prisoners of war. This time the attack took place without a preceding bombardment, and the tanks and the cavalry played the most important roles. Now we understand why the tanks left here a couple of weeks ago. However, the news of the victory is not enough to repair the morale of the troops.

24 November, Saturday. A fair amount of shelling. During the night we hear a lot of English aeroplanes. In Russia things are in a worse and worse mess. The result is that the largest country, which in the beginning was our greatest hope, must now be left out of the reckoning. Lenin, with the Maximalists in the vanguard, is proposing an armistice.

25 November, Sunday. Strong wind. Soldiers' mass in the barn for 200 New Zealanders. In the civilians' mass I notice 20 more people already.

A lot of shelling in the afternoon.

The communiqué reports a slight advance towards Zantvoorde.

26 November, Monday. Quite a lot of shelling in the night, but fairly calm during the day.

27 November, Tuesday. A lot of rain overnight. A fair amount of shelling. In the evening very heavy shelling, mostly north of Ypres, and a lot of aeroplanes.

A fortnight ago, 15 or so Belgian soldiers arrived for the requisitioning of potatoes and straw. It seems that this year things will be done in a more intelligent manner than last year, when straw was required to be delivered during a period of torrential rain and the potatoes to be delivered in the midst of a deep frost.

For some time now the price of horses has been dropping because of the very high cost of oats. Civilians sell them amongst themselves at 90 francs per 100 kilos.

28 November, Wednesday. Full moon. During the night we hear a lot of aeroplanes but we don't hear any bombs fall. In the morning a lot of shelling.

The communiqué reports that the Germans are shelling the Passchendaele area very heavily. Perhaps they are going to chance an attack around there.

We receive a visit from Father Delancy S.J. of the 50th Division, who was here 2 years ago. Father Evans is still with them. Wolferston is ill and has been away for several days.

29 November, Thursday. A great many English aeroplanes during the night and at 4 o'clock in the morning very heavy shellfire. At 4 o'clock in the afternoon shelling begins around the Delporte farm and all evening we hear shells whistling and exploding between Micmac camp, Ouderdom and Rozenhil, and at the same time we can hear shells landing on Poperinghe.

Along the railway line between the ammunition dump at the Verhaeghe farm and Schaapstal there is a camp of negroes (West Indians). A great many of them are Catholics and some of them are also serving in the artillery. We notice that they smoke a lot of cigars, while the other soldiers smoke more cigarettes. In Reninghelst the soldier Leon Roelens from Ten Brielen is buried. He was 20 years old, killed on patrol.

In Reninghelst I bless the marriage of Maurits Cuvelier and Madeleine Vercruysse, both living in Dickebusch at the moment.

30 November, Friday. The shelling of Poperinghe continues throughout the night, and round the Delporte farm (between Ouderdom, Micmac camp and Rozenhil) it goes on into the morning. 20 horses were killed in Widow Beirnaert's meadow. On a train in Ouderdom 5 soldiers were killed and 8 wounded. On Hector Coene's farm and the adjacent meadow there are no fewer than 25 large shell craters. Also in Dickebusch 3 big shells fell and exploded a few metres from the house of Benoit Decrock.

We hear that also last night the French hospital in Rousbrugge was shelled by the German aeroplanes. 6 doctors and 15 soldiers were killed.

Elverdinghe and Woesten were heavily shelled this week too.

In the evening beyond Ypres there is one flickering mass of hundreds of gun-flashes, and we hear the guns thundering a lot.

1 December, Saturday. Calm night, full moon but misty. In the evening I see a lot of gun-flashes but I can't hear the guns.

2 December, Sunday. As I walked to Dickebusch I could see that the wild criss-cross flickering of the gun-flashes beyond Ypres was exceptionally furious. An attack, surely. And indeed, the next day's communiqué reported that the English attacked north of Passchendaele and took several farms and fortified positions.

3 December, Monday. At night we hear aeroplanes but no bombs. A lot of shelling all day. Every day the Belgian communiqué reports German shelling and raids on Merckem, where my brother Remi is now. The Germans counter-attack near Cambrai and take several villages back.

In some of the Chinese camps there are angry protests which have begun to turn ugly. Yesterday they stabbed an English captain. Today there were 30 of them at Busseboom who refused to work and lay down on the ground to be beaten. They would sooner have a beating than stop their stubbornness. I passed the camp at Verhaeghe's place and saw three of them with their arms outstretched and tied to the wire, and one with his leg tied to it. That can't be pleasant in this weather, because it's well below freezing today.

Sister Gabrielle from La Clytte returns from France.

4 December, Tuesday. Around 1 o'clock in the morning German aeroplanes. We hear shelling and bombs exploding. Today again a lot of shelling.

The Russians publish various articles of the treaty between the allies. Among them is one article that causes the Catholics great pain and the revelation of which is a trump card in the Germans' hand. It is an agreement between Italy, France, Russia and England not to heed the Pope if he should try to intercede for peace or to mediate in any way. Now we know why there was no reply to the Pope's peace note. Thanks to this sort of thing our government is increasingly losing the trust of the people. And we ask ourselves, 'Where are they leading us?' God preserve us. Now, too, because Russia is no longer a friend, the dark side of its past conduct is made known, and notably how the Russians persecuted the Catholics of occupied Galicia. Crimes about which our newspapers remained completely silent except for *De Stem uit België*, for which that newspaper had its knuckles rapped by the *Vingtième Siècle*.

5 December, Wednesday. At 1 o'clock in the afternoon 4 shells by the main road from Poperinghe to Abeele. The *Rood Kruis* inn is hit and soldiers and a daughter of the house are killed and civilians wounded.

In the afternoon I go to Abeele, returning in the evening. In the evening there were German aeroplanes overhead. From at least 10 different places at once searchlights sweep round the sky looking for the birds, but in vain. I can hear them, but I can't see them. One of those death-dealers reached Poperinghe unseen. In the house of the curate, Mr Hellyn, where the Dean was now also living, both priests were sitting reading their office when a bomb fell on the corner of the house, next to the sacristy of St. Bertinus's church. The explosion was terrible. In the curate's house windows and doors were blown out and a portion of the walls were destroyed. Mr Helleyn and the two nuns were unharmed. The Dean was hit by a door that landed on top of him, and also received a slight shoulder wound from a sliver of flying metal. The splinter of metal was removed in the Couthove hospital. The sacristy and the choir of St. Bertinus church were likewise badly damaged. Since then the church and the curate's house are no longer used. His reverence the Dean and Mr Hellyn are now living in the civilian hospital and perform the parish services in the chapel there. The Dean sleeps in Vogeltje.

I read a German newspaper which has been dropped by the aeroplanes. It is the *Gazette des Ardennes*. There I read the names of the victims of the English bombing of Ostend on the 5th of September, 6 civilians dead and 36 injured.

Many farmers are abandoning their farms and leaving for France. Their farms are easily sold, and usually at a high price, to other farmers who are themselves refugees to this area or to the newly rich. However, the farmers who still wish to leave have to get a special permit, and the authorities are reluctant to grant these now. Our national government prefers to keep the farmers in Belgium. That's all well and good, but then the farmers at the front ought to be treated in a reasonable fashion.

6 December, Thursday. The frost continues. At 2 in the morning very heavy shelling. At 7 a.m. shells on Abeele station. It is the first time that Abeele has been shelled by the guns. At 5.30 p.m. aeroplanes bomb Vlamertinghe. One machine is hit and goes up in flames.

7 December, Friday. I go to the centre of Dickebusch. There are not many troops there. In the cemetery next to Comyn's farm there are already 1,030 soldiers buried. Calm day. A visit from Father Bull, who lodged here last winter. Then he was with the 47th Division, now he's with the 49th.

8 December, Saturday. Calm night and day. At Cambrai the English are driven yet further back and the Germans report 9,000 prisoners and a haul of 148 guns. It appears that several English generals were at fault because they did not take sufficient precautions against a counter-attack.

Nowadays we are not very hopeful about the war and if we dared to speak our thoughts openly, we would have to admit we live in fear of having to move out of here in the end.

News of the armistice between Russia and Germany.

9 December, Sunday. Armistice between Russia and Rumania as well. Calm day.

10 December, Monday. At midday German aeroplanes drop newspapers. It is the *Gazette des Ardennes* again, from 8 December. I notice 2 articles in particular: the first is called 'Who against Hindenburg,' and in it the Germans criticize the allies for having no unified command of the armies, with each of them pulling in a different direction, while the Germans have one man who commands all and place all their trust in him. The other article is a lamentation over the evacuation of Comines which was so well carried out by the kindly Germans after the English tyrants had killed more than 100 citizens and injured 300 more!

Big explosion in Halifax in Canada.

A chaplain tells us here that his horse sank in Zillebeke and they had to kill it there and then. He also says that Gheluvelt has been taken twice already but that each time the English had to let it go because of counter-attacks.

At midday shells around Planckeel's and Pol Nollet's farms. In the afternoon and evening German aeroplanes drop bombs on Dickebusch and Vlamertinghe.

11 December, Tuesday. Again a lot of shelling in the afternoon and it lasts all the following night. Mostly south of Ypres.

12 December, Wednesday. A lot of shelling again in the night. Also several German birds which come under heavy fire. In the afternoon the shelling is very fierce.

We hear the joyous news of the taking of Jerusalem by the English.

We also hear that the Germans made a raid on Messines yesterday.

13 December, Thursday. Again a lot of shelling, in the night and in the day. Today the town of Hazebrouck is shelled by the guns. This time the bombardment is terrible and no fewer than 70 civilians are killed and 250 injured. Among the victims are the Dean, the parish priest of Caestre and a curate from Armentières who were all killed in a cellar next to the deanery. You'd really think that the Germans have something against deans. The communiqué doesn't mention the shelling of Hazebrouck.

14 December, Friday. Night and day calm. A chaplain, Father Woodlock of the 30th Division, is lodging in the curate's house. He is a Jesuit who doesn't know any French, which is rare indeed, since almost all of them have studied in Louvain.

Kemmel church is the only church in the deanery of Ypres which can still be repaired.

My brother Remi comes on leave. What a dreadful time he's had of it in his sector of Merckem where he has been on the prowl observing the enemy between De Kippe and Aschoop. Nowhere any trenches, just shell holes more than half-full of water. They set off on Saint Eloy's day for 6 days' duty, staying the first 3 days in a cramped and flimsy shelter where the men were almost on top of one another and where there was no way of getting the slightest rest. Then they were each loaded up with 6 kilos of grenades, 100 bullets, 2 loaves, 2 tins of meat, 2 canteens of coffee, weapons and backpack, and they moved forward to within a few metres of the enemy. No duckboards anywhere, but take your chances walking in the dark through water and mud. They went in groups of 8 or 10, all holding on to the same length of rope so as not to sink or drown. With good reason! The ground is nothing but shell holes one on top of the other, some a good 5 or 6 metres deep, and there is so much mud that the heavily-laden soldiers repeatedly sink into it to above their knees. And they needed that rope. They had to use all their strength to pull one of their pals out of the mud. It took them hours to cover a half hour's walking distance and they arrived at their post soaked in sweat, only to be shivering with cold a few hours later. And yet no one fell ill. Three days they stayed there in that shell hole, a few metres from the enemy, changing position now and then to keep from sinking. After a few hours it started to freeze, so they had hard ground to stand on, but now the cold in their feet was unbearable. At night they went up and lay down on the ground. Their coffee was frozen, their food tasteless. And eventually after 3 days they were told they might leave their post and after toiling through the mud for half a night under their heavy loads they arrived at Oost-Vleeteren. They hadn't slept for 6 days and had had nothing hot to drink for 3 days. Never in all their life had they been so exhausted. How good the hot coffee tasted, and how welcome the sack of straw was! From their post they had been able to hear the Germans and had also seen them sometimes. But not a bullet was fired from rifle or machine gun. They must in their turn have been heard and seen by the Germans. There was a silent agreement, so to speak, that in that situation they would not use their rifles or machine guns. If they had had to shoot, the losses on both sides would have been so terrible that scarcely anyone would have escaped the bullets. Nevertheless, on both sides the bigger guns were being fired and therein lay the most danger. Around them they saw several bodies of Belgian and French soldiers, but each night some of these were removed and buried.

15 December, Saturday. Calm day. The ground has dried out a bit. A general permission is issued which allows all Dickebusch inhabitants who were evacuated this summer to return.

One welcome change is that the passes no longer have to be signed by the Belgian Intelligence officer.

16 December, Sunday. The communiqué reports that the Germans have regained some ground at Polderhoek Chateau at Gheluvelt.

A collection in my wartime church for a Christmas gift for the Belgian soldiers raised 112.75 francs. I give 50 francs to the work of the Reverend Delbare and the S.K.V.H.,[91] and 90 francs to the work of the *Belgische Standaard*.[92] Baptism in the barn of Florent Dauchy's child.

17 December, Monday. During the night a lot of big shells. In the evening aeroplanes.

18 December, Tuesday. I take Holy Communion to 6 sick people and then go with my brother Remi to the village. The ground is frozen and easy to walk on. My house there has been fixed up as a warehouse and accommodation. The windows are covered with boards and canvas and the attic has been covered with sheets of metal. In my garden there is a Y.M.C.A. hut which is used for meetings and church services. The front of Justin Thevelin's house has been repaired too. Henri Brutsaert has returned to his farm this week.

---

91 The Secretariaat der Katholieke Vlaamse Hoogstudenten was an organisation set up in 1916 whose aim was to safeguard the moral welfare of young men serving in the Belgian army.
92 The *Belgische Standaard* was a Flemish newspaper set up by a member of the order of the Capuchins in 1915 and distributed to Belgian soldiers. It promoted the establishment of reading rooms for soldiers.

19 December, Wednesday. I sing the Golden Mass,[93] at which 20 people are present. My brother Remi leaves for his regiment.

20 December, Thursday. The freeze continues, it is very cold. We go to visit the priest at Kemmel in his hospice-director's house at Locre. The good man has bettered himself considerably.

There are not many troops anywhere around. And yet the newspapers say that the Germans are going to fill the whole of Flanders with their soldiers. Food is growing dearer and dearer, as is fodder for the beasts. A pig was recently sold here for 925 francs. A farmer was offered 1,200 francs for 1,000 kilos of horse beans for horse-feed to be delivered at his convenience, and 130 francs for 100 kilos to be delivered immediately.

21 December, Friday. Nothing special.

22 December, Saturday. In the afternoon a lot of shelling.

23 December, Sunday. In the night and in the morning a lot of shelling. Another new decree: (1) the coffee houses, too, may only be open to soldiers from 12 to 2 and from 6 to 8, just like the inns; (2) the inns are closed to civilians as well outside the soldiers' hours. Once again the opposite of what is reasonable. They are against civilians talking much with soldiers and then they only allow civilians to go to the pub when the soldiers are there.

The English are buying a lot of pigs for Christmas. They pay the farmers 3 francs a kilo live weight.

---

93 The *Missa Aurea*, sung in the Roman Catholic church on the Wednesday of Ember Week in advent.

24 December, Monday. The English communiqué reports that the Germans have taken an English forward line along the Langemarck-Staden railway line over a stretch of the front 700 metres long. This explains the shelling of yesterday morning.

Today little shelling. Thaw.

In the evening a lot of singing from soldiers already celebrating Christmas.

25 December, Tuesday, Christmas Day. In our barn we have a beautiful celebration of Christmas Day. Christmas mass at 6.30, 53 civilians take communion and the Christmas song is sung beautifully by the young girls. Second mass at 8 o'clock, and at 9.30 the high mass at which at least 80 New Zeelanders are present. I hear 20 soldiers' confessions before the mass and I give general absolution for the rest. 40 of the soldiers take communion.

It was pitch dark going to Dickebusch, but the soldiers had the happy thought of setting fire to one of their huts along my road and so they lit me on my way. In the morning a heavy snow shower which sent the superstitious English into paroxysms of delight, a white Christmas being a sign of good luck. There's a lot of this sort of superstition among the English soldiers. They are really furious if they see a pair of shoes on the table, which is bad luck. And the orderlies here are astonished if they see us play a game of cards on a Sunday evening: for those Pharisees this counts as some sort of sacrilege.

This year it really is a noisy Christmas. The New Zealanders, especially, swig and swill and reel and rant and pick quarrels with the Chinese. The Chinese become resentful and band together and in the afternoon and evening, fights break out in several places. Such wild fellows, those New Zealanders! We hear that during the night they did some thieving in various places. 15 hens were stolen from Henri Lamerant and at Jules

Delanotte's widow's place the thieves were caught in the act of stealing hens. At Jules Maerten's in Kapelleke a New Zealand sergeant is caught at 9.30 at night in a pig shed where he was killing the pigs with a heavy stick. They shut the door and he tried to escape through the roof, but fell down. They drink a lot and they thieve a lot.

26 December, Wednesday. Snow again. At night a lot more shelling. It picks up again in the afternoon and lasts all evening. We hear that a German attack at Passchendaele has been repelled. All night we hear many drunkards. At Zevecote they steal Charles Delanghe's goat and cut her ears off. The next day she is found like that in an abandoned camp. A lot of soldiers are very thirsty after all their drinking yesterday. This morning I enter a house where 2 soldiers have come for some bottles of beer which they are taking back to their camp. They pay 9 francs in small coins. They explained that they had all emptied their pockets and had scraped together the 9 francs.

We hear that several Chinese who had been in fights with the New Zealanders yesterday were shot this morning on Mont Noir. Can this be true? It seems so, yes.

27 December, Thursday. Snow and frost and quite a lot of shelling.

28 December, Friday. I put in a claim for 4 school benches from the boys' school which were burnt at Henri Lamerant's farm by the soldiers. 2 at 40 francs and 2 at 25 francs = 130.

29 December, Saturday. Misty, frost and little shelling. Today we read Germany's peace proposal and conditions. Difficult. My brother Joseph comes on work leave, apparently at Cyriel Maeyaert's farm. He's going to sweat.

30 December, Sunday. Thaw. This morning at the home of secretary Achille Camerlynck 2 soldiers were found dead and 3 others very ill, poisoned by a stove which they had put in their room.

Today I see a Chinese furiously angry with a schoolboy. I understand that the boy had stuck his little finger up at him, which makes them boil with rage. If instead one sticks one's thumb up at them they are delighted.

31 December, Monday. Quiet during the day. At 5 in the evening German aeroplanes arrive above Busseboom and Rozenhil. At 9.30 German aeroplanes again. We feel the spine-chilling thud of a large shell that falls not far from us and doesn't explode. At Elverdinghe a shell falls on the hut of the acting mayor, Doctor Louf. His housemaid is seriously hurt and dies a little while later from her injuries. The doctor is lightly wounded. Nevertheless, the courageous man refuses to leave his village and goes to live with the curate.

Today Kemmel chateau burns down through the carelessness of the soldiers.

And thus the war year of 1917 comes to an end. In the course of this year I baptised 7 children. 11 civilians died in Dickebusch, 2 of whom were refugees and 3 of whom were children. 16 Dickebusch inhabitants died elsewhere: 4 in Reninghelst, 2 in Poperinghe, 2 in Watou, 2 in the La Panne hospital, 3 in the Montreuil hospital, 2 in the Couthove hospital and 1 in the soldiers' hospital in Vinckem. Currently living in Dickebusch are 87 families, together consisting of 298 people. After the evacuation of July there were only 67 families left, comprising 237 people.